TRUMPONOMICS

Also by Stephen Moore and Arthur B. Laffer

*An Inquiry into the Nature and
Causes of the Wealth of States*

*Wealth of States: More Ways to Enhance
Freedom, Opportunity and Growth*

Return to Prosperity

The End of Prosperity

ALSO BY STEPHEN MOORE

Fueling Freedom

Who's the Fairest of Them All?

It's Getting Better All the Time

ALSO BY ARTHUR B. LAFFER

Eureka!

The Private Equity Edge

TRUMPONOMICS

Inside the America First
Plan to Revive
Our Economy

STEPHEN MOORE
and
ARTHUR B. LAFFER

ALL
POINTS
BOOKS

TRUMPONOMICS. Copyright © 2018 by Stephen Moore and Arthur B. Laffer.
Foreword copyright © 2018 by Lawrence Kudlow. All rights reserved.
Printed in the United States of America. For information, address
St. Martin's Press, 175 Fifth Avenue, New York, NY 10010.

All Points Books is an imprint of St. Martin's Press.

www.allpointsbooks.com

Design by Meryl Sussman Levavi

Graphs by Paneverde Design

Library of Congress Cataloging-in-Publication Data
is available from the Library of Congress.

ISBN 978-1-250-19371-1 (hardcover)
ISBN 978-1-250-19372-8 (ebook)

Our books may be purchased in bulk for promotional, educational, or
business use. Please contact your local bookseller or the Macmillan
Corporate and Premium Sales Department at 1-800-221-7945, extension
5442, or by email at MacmillanSpecialMarkets@macmillan.com.

First Edition: October 2018

10   9   8   7   6   5   4   3   2   1

Contents

Foreword

by Lawrence Kudlow

"America is open for business, and we are competitive once again."

—Donald Trump at Davos, 2018

When Donald Trump asked me to serve as the chairman of his National Economic Council in March 2018, it was truly the honor of a lifetime. I joked with the president that I had worked for Ronald Reagan in the early 1980s on his economic revolution, and my mission in life is to serve the president roughly every 35 years.

I don't agree with President Trump on every issue—and he knows that—but on the big picture of unleashing a new era of broad-based prosperity for America, we are in 100 percent agreement. Trump says we can get to 3, 4, or even 5 percent growth through tax reduction, deregulation, American energy production, and fairer trade deals, and he is exactly right. We are devoting nearly every working hour at the White House to achieving a sustained higher growth path that will create higher take-home pay for all Americans. And by the way, I can tell you after a few months on the job, this man is indefatigable. Donald Trump doesn't stop. He barely sleeps. It's almost impossible to keep up with him. He is truly obsessed with restoring American greatness.

Now, step back a minute. When Donald Trump first announced his run for the presidency three years ago, I, like Arthur and Steve and most people, was filled with skepticism. I wondered whether this was a publicity stunt, not a real bid to sit in the Oval Office. On some of his calls for trade tariffs, I was openly critical.

But when Arthur Laffer, Steve Moore, and I sat down with this billionaire businessman turned politician in Trump Tower in the spring of 2016, the three of us saw Trump in a whole new light. Here was a pro-growth, pro-business candidate who understood the vast underperformance of the U.S. economy and, even more importantly, the potential for dramatically faster growth. He wanted tax cuts. He wanted to deregulate, he wanted to get the government out of the way.

Most of all, we loved his Reaganesque optimism. It was infectious.

What a contrast with the left—which was full of negativity. We can't grow faster than 2 percent. We can't get wages up. We have to live with secular stagnation. We can't rebuild our coal industry. Climate change is going to bring the end of civilization. The inner cities cannot be hopeful and prosperous places again. And, of course, Trump can't possibly win. Well, he proved them all wrong! And he's still doing that.

Arthur, Steve, and I spent much of the next six months on the campaign trail perfecting and then selling the Trump tax plan. Then when he was elected, we worked with the White House and Congress on the strategy to get it passed and signed into law. Arthur was the intellectual godfather of this amazing tax plan. Steve and I worked together doing the blocking and tackling to help the president get this over the goal line. It was a rocky road for sure. You will learn in this book, however, that Trump was an easy sell. He has an amazingly instinctive appreciation of which policy dials in Washington need to be twisted in another direction so that the economy can flourish. He always told us that the tax plan had to help the middle class—and that was always the mission. Our goal was to pass a tax cut that would help American businesses expand and invest and thereby hire more workers and boost their wages and salaries. It had been 17 years since the middle class had seen a rise in their incomes, and it was about time they got a raise.

I agree wholeheartedly with Arthur and Steve that the tax plan—along with other Trump initiatives—has supercharged the economy. As we used to tell Trump: it worked for Reagan, it worked for JFK, it will work for you. The tax plan, mixed with other pro-growth policies, has worked better and faster than we ever expected. As Trump has often said of the current American economic expansion: "The world is witnessing the resurgence of a strong and prosperous America. There has never been a better time to hire, to build, to invest, and to grow in the United States."

He's right. And what a salesman.

Trump's policies, in just one and a half years, have begun to restructure the American economy. We've moved from "secular stagnation" (i.e., high taxes, massive regulation, huge government spending, and a disdain for business and investors) to a new private-sector incentive system that *rewards* success.

By slashing individual and corporate tax rates, providing 100 percent immediate expensing for plants and technology, and making it easy for big companies that fled our high-tax system to bring the money back home, he has ended the war against business and investment.

And it has happened faster than anyone imagined possible.

More than 250 American companies have announced gigantic investment projects, paid sizable bonuses to their workforces, increased 401(k) contributions, and raised corporate minimum wages and other benefits. As of May 2018, the stock market gains had increased Americans' net wealth by an astounding $7 trillion. This is the only realistic chance of bailing out excessive government-union pensions and benefits—even though these very unions totally opposed Trump's corporate tax reform.

Ankle-biting Democrats say, "Rising business profits will go to shareholder buybacks." It isn't bad for the 100 million Americans who own stock in companies like Apple and FedEx. Meanwhile, new money is circulating throughout the economy to start new companies and reoxygenate the system.

Walmart—which had bitterly fought attempts to raise the federal minimum wage—raised its internal minimum wage for virtually all its wage earners, gave bonuses of up to $1,000, expanded maternity and parental leave, and committed $5,000 to every employee who adopts a child. Costco quickly followed suit with its own policy.

And don't forget the president's argument about the importance of regulatory reduction. "Regulation is stealth taxation," Trump has often said. "We are freeing our businesses and workers so they can thrive and flourish as never before."

Hold that thought, Mr. President. Oh, and don't forget that the Trump tax bill ended the Obamacare individual mandate and opened the door to energy drilling in the Arctic National Wildlife Refuge (ANWR).

Even on trade and globalization, Trump has told his international counterparts: "As president of the United States, I will always put America first, just like the leaders of other countries should put their countries first also. *But America first does not mean America alone.*"

This book offers the first real, day-by-day tale of how Trumponomics came to be—how it all happened. What a journey. I know that because I worked right alongside Steve and Arthur every step of the way in 2016 and 2017. It was a mighty struggle, and we each have the lashes on our backs for joining with Trump to help him make America great again. We were for Trump before it was cool.

They are my brothers; and we are still brothers in arms. I pridefully and eagerly took the job working for Donald Trump because, as we all agree, there is still so much to do to make America great again. This book shows how.

TRUMPONOMICS

Introduction

Donald Trump won the biggest upset in American presidential history by promising the American people a transformative change in U.S. economic policy after eight years of an economic rut under Barack Obama and eight years before that of George W. Bush. Trump won by focusing on jobs and the economy, but he didn't adopt a conventional left or right economic agenda.

He brought to Washington, D.C., a new economic populism that mixed some conventional Republican ideas—tax cuts, deregulation, energy development, and returning more power to the states—with more traditional Democratic issues—trade protectionism and infrastructure spending. Trump embraced the populist issues of immigration reform and requiring Europeans to pay for more of their own defense.

We wrote this book to try to define the man and the ideas behind this new economic theory—Trumponomics—that has the whole world in suspense and discombobulated. Can it work? Will it work?

Trump's election was a political "black swan" event. We have never seen anything remotely like this president in any of our lifetimes. His outside-the-box political strategy worked like a charm, bursting through the blue wall of industrial states like Michigan, Ohio, Pennsylvania, Wisconsin, and Iowa. His populist message resonated with working-class Americans in these blue-collar states and districts. He is promising to bring jobs, higher wages, and development back to these areas that were bypassed during the recovery and haven't seen much economic gain in two decades.

Can he succeed? The left insists no. They say growth cannot get back to 3 percent and that Trumponomics will make things worse. They say that the factories that have left places like Flint, Michigan; York, Pennsylvania; and Toledo, Ohio, are gone for good. They say that the steel mills and coal mines aren't coming back. Trump is betting his presidency that he can create an economic revival in industrial-state America. It's a gutsy, risky strategy.

The two of us worked as economic advisors to Donald Trump in 2016. Steve traveled with him. We met with him and his political and economic teams regularly in the primaries and in the general election phase. We worked on his speeches and spent months representing him as surrogates for his campaign. We are currently members of the Trump Economic Advisory Council and meet with Trump periodically.

This book is not meant to be a celebration of Donald J. Trump or Trumponomics. We clearly have an admiration for

President Trump and support most of his policy goals, or we would not have agreed to serve as his economic advisors. And we wouldn't be helping him today if we thought he was deranged, dangerous, delusional, or unfit for office, as so many liberals seem to think he is.

At the same time, we have worked with governors, congressmen, senators, and presidents for decades, and there is one constant that we've discovered with nearly all of them. There is a good, a bad, and an ugly with politicians, and the goal is to help make sure that as often as possible, the good triumphs over the bad and ugly. So it is with Donald Trump. He can be brilliant, gracious, and insightful one moment and sophomoric, impulsive, and hurtful the next.

One of our favorite moments of the campaign was when we asked Trump if at an upcoming campaign rally outside Orlando, he could meet with a 16-year-old boy, John Michael, who a few months earlier had suffered from a horrific brain lock, which left him paralyzed and unable to speak. The boy had learned to communicate by typing out words on a computer by blinking his eyes. One of the first things he typed, and this is the God's honest truth, was: "Make America Great Again." When we told this story to Trump, he said he absolutely wanted to meet John Michael. He instructed his campaign advance team to make sure that everything was set up so that John Michael in his wheelchair could greet him when he arrived at the airport. When Trump walked down the steps of the plane, there was John Michael and his family waiting for him. Trump spent several minutes giving encouragement to this stricken boy and taking pictures with the family, as the crowd of thousands waited. The crowd started chanting, "John Michael, John Michael . . ." It was a tender moment that wasn't caught on the TV cameras.

When we asked the deputy campaign manager why Trump hadn't brought John Michael on stage, he whispered: "Donald didn't want to do this in front of the cameras. He didn't want people to think that he was exploiting this tragedy for political gain." This is the side of Donald Trump that many people are unaware of.

Trump also thinks big—really big. When we would advise Trump that his tax cut, deregulation, and pro-America energy policies could get America back to 3 or 4 percent growth, Trump would interrupt us and say, "I want 5 percent growth." This is a guy who shoots for the stars, and why not? When John F. Kennedy said he was going to put a man on the moon before the end of the decade, many scoffed and said it was technically impossible and fiscally unaffordable. Trump faces this same criticism from growth skeptics every day.

Donald Trump is *not* an ideological conservative. Reagan was far more schooled in conservative thought and was more dedicated to the principles of limited government. Trump is for common sense. He is an economic populist in many ways—he believes in addressing the plight of ordinary people. His business mindset was one of his greatest attractions as a candidate against a GOP field of 16 mostly career politicians, and is a great attribute as a president. With Trump, it is all about results.

In this book we define what Trumponomics is and describe how and why Trump has adopted the policies that he has. For the most part, we reserve judgment as to how well these policies will work. The verdict on that will come in the next few years depending on how the economy performs. We like the direction of things and are cautiously optimistic that America could be in for a good run of prosperity.

*   *   *

Originally this book was conceived by Steve, Arthur, and our longtime partner, Larry Kudlow. The three of us worked together as a team during the campaign in 2016 and then as outside economic advisors to the president on the tax bill and other financial and economic issues. We got almost halfway into the writing when an important event happened that changed everything. President Trump tapped Larry to be the head of his National Economic Council. Overnight Larry became, arguably, the most important economist in the world. When President Trump called Arthur on a weekend in April 2018, asking if he should choose Larry for the job, Arthur replied: "Sir, there is no better choice that you could make."

So we lost our coauthor, but the president got one of the best economists in the world to lead his team.

But Larry is almost a silent partner here. Readers will see that Larry was the major contributor in many of the meetings and strategy discussions with Trump and other key players in this story. We quote him liberally throughout and simply refer to him as Larry. Of course, he is not responsible for any of the text or any commentary about Trump or others. Those views are our own.

Meeting Trump

In early March 2016 the three of us (Arthur, Larry, and Steve) got urgent calls from our longtime friend Corey Lewandowski. Corey was a political activist and organizer extraordinaire, who had worked as the state director in New Hampshire for Americans for Prosperity, a major national taxpayer organizing group.

Corey had been tapped to be the campaign manager for the upstart, long-shot Donald Trump for president campaign. His message for us would change our lives. "Donald Trump would like to meet the three of you," Corey explained. "Could you meet him at four p.m. next Tuesday at his office in Trump Tower in Manhattan?"

Wow. That was unexpected. When Trump had announced his run for the White House—about six months before—we, like most people, thought it was mostly a publicity stunt.

Trump was saying some headline-grabbing things, throwing out a blizzard of populist policy ideas for the American people to chew over: "Build the wall." "Repeal NAFTA." "The biggest tax cut ever." Meanwhile he was drawing massive, excited crowds at his political rallies across the country.

Donald Trump, although politically inexperienced and disdained by the Mediocracy and the professional political class, was somehow connecting with millions of voters. Rival candidates (perhaps with the exception of Bernie Sanders) were in denial and ignoring the signs of voter unrest at their own political peril.

We were initially anything but devoted fans. He was part of the New York City scene and had never taken on a significant role in the conservative free market movement. Trump's statements seemed to us to be all over the map, a pastiche of conservative and progressive ideas. True, we were iconoclasts ourselves, and some of our own ideas—our advocacy of a more open legal immigration policy and our confidence that economic growth could balance the budget—were considered borderline heretical by some factions of the conservative coalition to which we belonged.

All three of us had written columns and research papers that had been critical of several of Trump's positions, especially on trade. We were and are staunch free traders. Larry and Arthur had met Trump on many occasions in the past and liked him very much personally. Steve had never met Trump and was somewhat turned off by his brash, media-hogging style.

But all three of us were intrigued by the grassroots political movement that we now know as Trumpism, which was building throughout the country. And we liked what he was saying about chopping tax rates and restoring American greatness. We had openly supported his big ideas on changing the IRS tax code. Trump (and Corey) had taken notice of our public praise.

In several early major primary events, Trump had called out Larry by name. "Larry Kudlow loves my tax plan," Trump had thundered several times in debates and rallies. Larry, on CNBC, was one of the first economic analysts to give Trump credit for some bold reform initiatives on taxes and rolling back unnecessarily burdensome government regulations. Similarly, Trump had gloated to conservative audiences: "I got my tax ideas from the great Reagan economist Arthur Laffer."

We also loved Trump's unyielding optimism about America's potential for much faster economic growth, which would pull us out of the slow-growth ditch the nation had careened into during George W. Bush's last years in office and Barack Obama's entire presidency.

Trump was proclaiming that we could get to 5 percent growth with the right set of pro-business policy ideas. Though we thought that 5 percent was overly optimistic (we thought 3 to 4 percent was definitely doable), we loved the aspiration! We recognized that Trump, as a real estate developer who built skyscrapers and five-star resorts, thinks very big and does not shy away from dramatic license. The October 6, 2016, issue of *The New Yorker* (in an obvious attempted character assassination just before the election) reported Trump saying to [architect Der] Scutt, ahead of a 1980 press conference, "Give them the old Trump bull[s*&%]. Tell them it is going to be a million square feet, sixty-eight stories . . ."[1]

We certainly agreed—wholeheartedly—that the economy could grow much, much faster than most economists believed. The standard trope on the left at the time was that 1 to 2 percent growth was the best America could achieve.[2] After all, if the left's political messiah, Barack Obama, couldn't get the economy moving faster, how could a mere mortal like Donald Trump presume to?

We were ecstatic that finally someone was frontally assaulting the tyranny of low expectations that sold America short. And we loved that Trump seemed to relish that the professional political class ridiculed his Make America Great Again (MAGA) theme. We did not agree with all Trump's policy prescriptions. That said, he certainly had all the right enemies attacking him.

So, yes, we told Corey, we definitely wanted to meet with candidate Donald Trump.

TRUMP TOWER

A few days later we arrived at Trump Tower in New York City and sifted through the massive security detail and what seemed like a tsunami of media cameras in the lobby, heading up to the twenty-sixth floor . . . and Donald Trump's personal office.

One thing especially impressed us immediately: everyone around him seemed to love Donald Trump. Trump treats his people well.

It wasn't an act. The Trump team displayed genuine affection for him, affection clearly mirroring his for them. You can tell a lot about a person from how he treats those who work for and with him every day. The vibe of deep mutual respect and obvious affection was telling.

We encountered no arrogance or stiffness. Team Trump was uniformly made up of polite and sweet people, all instantly likable, including our now good friend Rhona Graff, Trump's longtime personal aide and one of his greatest assets.

Donald Trump, also, was punctual.

Our meeting was scheduled for four p.m. At 4:05, Donald Trump came bounding out of his inner office and pumped our hands up and down with an affectionate handshake and a charming smile. While at the *Wall Street Journal,* Steve Moore had once interviewed the famous college basketball announcer Dick Vitale—the live-wire personality with boundless energy and enthusiasm about everything. Trump seemed to Steve to be a political version of Vitale. We were a bit humbled by this warmth.

We immediately felt at ease as Trump ushered us into his office and excitedly showed us around. Trump's office is like a museum filled with sports and entertainment memorabilia. He shared with us footballs and photos with (and many signed by) George Steinbrenner, Joe Namath, and other sports legends. The wall was also covered with dozens of framed magazine covers—from *GQ* to *Esquire* to *New York* magazine and on and on—featuring Donald J. Trump. The man loves his celebrity status—and no one has ever played the media better, as we would soon discover.

There were just us and Donald Trump in his office. He included no aides, no "handlers," no self-important people tapping on tablets. He wanted to take photos and sign books, and it was all very engaging. We were surprised that, though he was arguably the busiest person in America at that moment, he acted as though he had all the time in the world for us.

Then our host sat down behind his giant desk and hunched toward us—in his signature style. He began to pepper us with questions about the economy and what we thought of his campaign. "How am I doing?" he asked, as he always did throughout the campaign. He proved inquisitive about everything. "What do you think of my tax plan?" "Is the economy headed to a recession?" "Don't you think we have to worry about China?" "We're doing great in the polls, have you seen our numbers?" (Yes, Trump showed an obsession with the polls.) "What should we do about the deficit?" "Should I keep Janet Yellen at the Fed?"

Trump didn't lecture us. He asked for our opinions, straight up. He listened. When he disagreed with us, he would challenge us. Donald Trump, while open-minded, is nobody's pushover.

One of the first things Steve said to him was: "I just attended one of your rallies a few weeks ago and met a lot of the people there. Donald, I don't know if I love you, but I sure love your voters." Trump almost burst out of his chair. "I love these people too. They're the greatest Americans, aren't they? They love our country." (Now you know why he loves to do political rallies even as president. It recharges his batteries.)

The next thing we said to him was: "Thank you for sticking by Corey Lewandowski." Corey at that time was under attack from the left, unfairly so, for allegedly assaulting a reporter away from Trump at a rally. It was a preposterous charge, obviously designed to undermine Trump, by separating him from the talented and loyal Lewandowski. The sharks were out to get Corey.

To his credit, and astutely, Trump stuck with Corey through the thicket of slander. Shrewd move. In return, Corey helped mastermind one of the greatest upsets in modern American political history: Trump's winning the GOP nomination. History might show this to have been an even more herculean challenge than Trump's winning the general election.

We discussed trade. Trump knew full well we were on the free trade side, while he publicly and stubbornly declared that he was more for "fair" than "free" trade. A few months earlier Larry and Steve had penned a piece in *National Review* called "Smoot-Hawley-Trump," arguing that Trump could wreck the economy should he follow in the footsteps of Herbert Hoover, the last (and disastrously!) protectionist president.[3] Hoover signed the infamous Smoot-Hawley tariff. That bill exacerbated the Great Depression by inciting a global trade war.

Don't go there, Larry and Steve had unflinchingly written. It was a tough piece and he clearly knew about it. Yes, Trump is always attentive to any criticism—especially when it comes from his friends. (He reminded us a little bit of our late friend Jack Kemp, who took every criticism personally.)

Arthur had been nervous too. He had written an article later that year noting, "I know of no politician who understands a single word of the benefits of trade or even how to think about trade . . . trade is not about jobs at all or even about total employment, but instead trade is about the value of income." As you can see, free trade is something the three of us were and are very passionate about in the realm of good economic policy.

Trump briefly articulated his concern that countries like China and Mexico were "eating our lunch." When we suggested that he was flirting with protectionist tariff policies, he held out his arms and seemed slightly insulted. "I am not a protectionist," he insisted. "But China isn't playing fair." We weren't persuaded, but he had a point. For instance, both Japan and China utilize non-tariff barriers to trade and manipulate their currencies in ways that actually do hurt the U.S. economy. Trump wasn't just shooting from the hip. He knew his stuff.

Politely, we reminded him that he would want to steer clear of a trade war, an event that could crash the stock market and slow the economic growth on which he had so convincingly campaigned. We felt then and now that, at the very least, our arguments have given him some food for thought.

Trump wanted to talk in depth about taxes. We liked his tax plan. We wished to persuade him of the benefits of a more comprehensive tax reform that would also close loopholes. This was our message to all the GOP candidates. We had delivered this tutorial to every Republican presidential aspirant who had asked for our help on tax policy. The only notable exception in the field was Senator Marco Rubio, whose tax plan was tilted more toward tax credits than supply-side growth.

We assured Donald Trump that a business tax cut would help most dramatically to restore American economic growth. He asked how big of a tax cut we could afford. We told him to go as big as possible . . . to get the economy jumpstarted and to help middle-class workers. "Don't get stressed out by the phony numbers of Washington's bean counters," Larry instructed. "They are always wrong. And the benefits of a higher economic growth rate far outweigh the cost of short-term deficits."

This principle has become a pillar of Trumponomics. We strongly contend that it is the right way to examine tax policy changes. To paraphrase legendary football coach Vince Lombardi, "Growth isn't everything; it's the only thing."

Larry stressed repeatedly that the big winners from a business tax cut would be workers, who would command higher wages. If a company has 19 trucks and now, thanks to a tax rate cut, has the money to buy a twentieth, that's one more truck *driver* the firm will have to hire. Trump's a businessman. He got it.

Trump had already articulated the rough outline of a campaign tax plan. He told us that most of the ideas had come from the campaign's discussions with Arthur. We considered the plan to be a diamond in the rough and very much liked its broad outlines. The Trump campaign's rough sketch stressed a 15 percent tax rate on corporations and a lowering of rates for workers and small business owners. He said very emphatically—at least twice: "I'm for cutting the corporate tax, but I want to make sure that every small business in America also gets a tax cut." We admired his instincts on this. About two-thirds of jobs are created by small firms with fewer than 100 employees. Plus, as a matter of politics, Americans love small business, but they aren't too fond of corporate America—big business—which voters think too powerful, too fat, and too dumb and happy . . . often with good reason.

Then he cut to the chase: Could we refine his tax ideas so that the reforms provided the biggest bang for the buck but still included revenue-raising base-broadeners and loophole closings so that the numbers added up?

Sure, we replied. We would be honored to. We promised to get to work putting some meat on the bones of his tax plan and to crunch the numbers to make sure that this could all be done without unduly increasing the federal deficit. We assured him we would give him dynamic scoring, taking into account the larger national output and job base that one could reasonably expect as a consequence of the tax rate cuts.

Trump, ever the no-nonsense business exec, wanted us back to show him our calculations in a mere two weeks. Short fuse, but justified by the calendar imposed by the presidential campaign itself.

As we walked out, he put his hands across our shoulders, like a big brother . . . or a football coach. Like, for instance, Vince Lombardi.

CHARM OFFENSIVE

Our meeting had lasted about 50 minutes. We each felt strangely exhilarated. We know well two years later that the very charismatic Donald Trump has that effect on people. He isn't the bully or the egomaniac that he sometimes plays on TV or is portrayed as by his adversaries. (Yes, sure, he does crave affirmation, and he does have a big ego.)

We sensed that he instinctively "gets" what makes an economy work. Clear away the excessive government taxation, bureaucracy, red tape, and inane rules . . . and much faster growth is possible. Trump knows this not from studying economics books but from his own business background and his many interactions with government agencies in Washington and New York City. *Economists and politicians only study and talk about the economy, which is made up of Donald Trump and people a lot like him! It is doers and risk takers like Donald Trump who put our ideas into action.* Love him or hate him, Donald Trump has New York street smarts—and that's worth a lot.

This surely injures the vanity of the Ivory Tower snobs. Yet when it comes to getting the job done—creating jobs and economic growth—the voters were starting to show more smarts than the intelligentsia.

Sure, we disagreed with him on trade and on some of his tough-on-immigration policies. But in so many ways he sounded to us more pro-growth and more pro-business than any other presidential aspirant in the field. In fact, to us he sounded more pro-growth than any other candidate since Ronald Reagan.

And there was something else. The two of us have been around politicians all our working lives. We've met all the presidents since Reagan. Arthur goes back to President Nixon, whom he worked for in the White House under George Shultz. In fact, Arthur has a Camp David windbreaker given to him in 1971 when he was involved in the formulation of Nixon's "New Economic Policy," which included the temporary closing of the gold window.

As mentioned earlier, the three of us have worked with scores of governors, senators, congressmen, even mayors. We've vetted hundreds of candidates for public office. We have developed a pretty good sixth sense of what a winner looks like. Winners project a certain aura, a sense of confidence, and a connection with the voters.

Trump connects. The only three presidents with whom we've interacted who demonstrated that uncanny ability to connect—to light up a room when they walk in? Ronald Reagan, Bill Clinton, and Barack Obama. And now, Donald Trump.

Trump demonstrated to us that "X factor" so critical to winning elections and succeeding in politics.

After that initial meeting, Trump asked us to wait in the conference room adjoining his office so we could meet with a few others in the campaign. After about ten minutes Trump popped his head in the door of the conference room to say, "I just wanted to make sure you guys are doing OK. You need anything?"

"No, sir, we're just fine, thank you." We looked at one another and smiled as we blurted out the same line at the same time: "My God. This guy is for real. He can win this thing."

*   *   *

One last thing struck us from that first meeting.

Corey asked us to meet with his senior staff in the campaign office, a few floors down from Trump's personal office. When we got off the elevator at campaign central, we confronted a giant, cavernous office with tables, rows of cubicles, campaign posters on the wall, and Trump paraphernalia strewn everywhere. The campaign was entering the height of the primary season. We were astounded that there were perhaps ten people roaming around, plus a few tucked into offices. The rest of the campaign area was quiet and mostly empty. This was unexpected and extraordinary.

We looked at each other quizzically. *Where is everyone?* We were standing in the middle of the central nervous system of the campaign of a candidate who at that time was the unexpected front-runner in the Republican primary. And nobody was here. There was less buzz and activity than you would see in the campaign office for someone running for a local city council seat. Amazing!

"Corey, where is everyone?" Steve finally asked, puzzled. "This *is* the campaign staff," he replied. "You're looking at it." *Really?*

"Mr. Trump doesn't like to waste money," Corey explained patiently. Trump had promised voters in the primary he would take no special-interest money and fund his own campaign. He was attempting the biggest upset in presidential political history. And he wasn't squandering money in the process.

Corey explained that every month he would show Trump the expenditure report for the campaign in the previous weeks. Trump would rake through it and query this or that expense. At one point he asked Corey why they were paying eight field officers in Iowa. "Do we really need eight people?"

Corey responded, "Well, sir, it's a big state that we have to do well in." Candidates like Jeb Bush and Scott Walker had spent tens of millions of dollars in Iowa without success when the votes were cast, while the frugal Trump finished second, behind only Ted Cruz. Whatever his other services to the nation, Trump certainly deserves high praise for demolishing the myth that big money buys elections.

That visit to the campaign office confirmed two other admirable characteristics about Trump. First, he's frugal and watches every penny. Someone like this, we commented to each other, would have a field day going through the federal budget and rooting out the rampant waste, fraud, and redundancy.

Second—and we loved this—Trump's campaign completely bypassed the professional campaign consultant apparatus that makes tens of millions of dollars on pundits, field officers, pollsters, campaign advertisers, and the like. Trump rendered the consultants inconsequential. They didn't make a penny off him.

This fact goes a long way to explaining why the professional Republican political class detested, and still detests, Trump. He thwarted their protection racket. Trump wasn't paying the usual dues to the GOP's political mafia. Trump even ran few political ads on TV—which is how, via commissions, the consultants typically make their millions.

The consultants felt a need to destroy him, lest he set a dangerous (to them) precedent. This is why Bush and Romney operatives like Steve Schmidt, Stuart Stevens, and Rick Wilson denounced Trump week after week on TV. In the end the political class didn't destroy Trump. He destroyed them.

Couldn't have happened to a nicer group of people.

So that was our first meeting with the man who would be president, Donald J. Trump. It was the first step in our playing a much bigger role.

THE TRUMP PHENOMENON

It's worth recalling what was going on at this moment in the presidential race. It was perhaps the critical juncture of the bid for the GOP nomination.

Donald Trump had been enduring intense ridicule from the media and the intellectual class on the left and right. He was dismissed as a buffoon with zero political experience and no chance of winning the presidency. No less than Jeb Bush had said about Trump early on: "I guarantee you, Donald Trump is not going to be the nominee."[4] Many pros said he would be out after the Iowa caucuses. As our friend Kellyanne Conway, now a White House advisor to President Trump, used to tell us: "There is no more pervasive and self-serving lie in American politics than 'he or she can't win.'"

When Corey called us, Trump was causing a cardiac arrest within the GOP establishment because he *was* winning. It was still topsy-turvy, and Trump had suffered setbacks in a few early primaries. He lost Iowa to Texas senator Ted Cruz. The political insiders believed that the odds were still heavily stacked against him winning the primary, let alone the general election.

Remember, at this still early stage of the race, there were 15 other Republican candidates vying for the GOP presidential nomination. Many Republican operatives described this field as the best slate of candidates the Republicans had fielded in many years, perhaps ever. The contenders included Florida's former governor Jeb Bush, Louisiana governor Bobby Jindal, Ohio governor John Kasich, Texas governor Rick Perry, and Scott Walker, the Wisconsin governor who had become a hero of a few well-heeled conservatives for taking on the state employee union kingpins in Madison . . . and for not backing down under intense political pressure when the state capital came under siege from leftwing protesters.

Then there were the senators: Florida's Marco Rubio, Kentucky's Rand Paul, South Carolina's Lindsey Graham, and Texas's Ted Cruz. The social conservatives had their favorites as well, former Arkansas governor Mike Huckabee and Pennsylvania's former senator Rick Santorum. Some moderates quietly hoped that Mitt Romney would be a late entry into the race.

There were also two other initially formidable non-politicians in the race: neurosurgeon Dr. Ben Carson and former Hewlett-Packard CEO Carly Fiorina. At one point in the early primaries, the "anti-politicians"—Trump, Carson, and Fiorina—were first, second, and third in the polls.[5] This fact alone should have set off alarm bells in Washington, signaling the pervasive rage of voters who had come to recognize that the political class had steered America into an economic and cultural cul-de-sac.

By the way, as we discuss in Chapter Three, our view was that Americans—especially in the Rust Belt states of the Midwest—had full justification for their dissatisfaction with the political elite. America had badly underperformed, economically speaking, in Bush's disastrous last years in office.

The weak recovery under Obama was deeply disappointing and had flattened middle-class income growth. Average gross domestic product (GDP) growth was tortoise-paced over the past decade and a half. Jobs weren't coming back, except for low-paying menial and unskilled jobs. Obamacare was making healthcare unaffordable.[6] Annual federal deficits were averaging more than $1 trillion.[7] Big business bailouts and welfare handouts were becoming the norm.

The elites on the left and the right were so out of touch that they were flabbergasted to discover how unhappy Americans were with the state of affairs in America. They were oblivious to their own polls, which had shown for years that about two-thirds of voters believed the country was going in "the wrong direction."[8] Only two candidates in America seemed to recognize and capitalize on this voter unrest: Trump on the right and Bernie Sanders on the left.

The so-called experts in the GOP had all been assuring us that Jeb Bush would eventually emerge as the party's nominee—and we originally thought so too. This was the Republican Party after all, which over the course of history has unfailingly relied on "the next in line."

Think about it. In 1968 it was Nixon, Eisenhower's VP, then Ford, Nixon's VP, in 1976, then it was Reagan's turn in 1980, then George H. W. Bush, Reagan's VP, in 1988, then Bob Dole in 1996, George W. Bush in 2000, John McCain in 2008, Mitt Romney in 2012, and now the very successful and highly admired former two-term governor of Florida, Jeb Bush, son and brother of presidents, richly funded by family connections—the dynastic choice.

But Jeb, despite a treasure chest of $100 million from the Bush family political money machine, was languishing in the polls. Everyone was waiting for his big breakout, but it didn't happen. Trump had dubbed Bush "low energy," and the aura of his campaign so far certainly felt that way. Quite possibly the best image of the lackluster nature of Jeb's campaign occurred at the end of a speech in Hanover, New Hampshire. He pathetically urged the audience to "Please clap" for him after his closing remarks, which were initially met by crickets.[9] Jeb had just finished in sixth place in the Iowa Caucus.

The shocking and almost inconceivable leader of the pack was one Donald J. Trump—the brash real estate mogul and star of the TV hit show *The Apprentice,* who was most known by Americans for his memorable line, "You're fired!"

Everyone we knew—and we mean everyone—believed that Trump would be a flash in the pan. The polls couldn't possibly be right. Odds makers on betting lines still had his chances of winning the presidency at about 1 in 20. When he announced six months earlier his intention to run for the White House, he was the 100-to-1 underdog. A Hillary operative once told us that it was more likely that the New York Islanders would beat the New York Knicks in basketball than that Trump would ever beat Clinton.

But Trump was connecting with voters in a way none of us, or just about anyone in the media, had witnessed before. Those red-and-white Make America Great Again hats seemed to be cropping up on every street corner in Middle America far below the ivory towers of Washington, D.C., and Manhattan, those bastions of snobbery.

The more outrageous Trump's statements, the more his voters seemed to adore him. As we would soon learn firsthand, with Trump it was always "another day, another banner headline or lead cable news story."

Steve attended a Trump political rally in early 2016, mostly out of curiosity, but it was there that he had an epiphany about Trump. The crowds were large and boisterous—with the energy level of a Rolling Stones concert. But what was shocking was the type of people who attended. This wasn't the country club set.

These were people we now describe as prototypical Trump voters and whom Steve mentioned to Trump in that first meeting—blue-collar, working-class, culturally conservative folks not strongly aligned with either party. They were angry, patriotic, frustrated, financially stressed out, and searching for a great change of direction for a nation that they believed was showing all the symptoms of an economic and cultural breakdown.

There were schoolteachers, cops, construction workers, bikers (hundreds of motorcycles parked on the side of Trump rallies), soccer moms, grandparents, small businessmen and businesswomen. A surprising number of blacks and Hispanics were among this crowd of attendees. When asked what they liked about Trump, they said things like "He speaks his mind about what's wrong with America," "We need someone who will rattle the cages," "He will shake things up in Washington," "The fake news media lies about him," "I'm sick of politicians, we need a successful businessman." These were voters who didn't like Obama at all, but they also had little good to say about George W. Bush.

Neither party was paying attention to these voters, and when either party did pay attention, it was nothing more than a patronizing pat on the head. Many times we felt the same frustration with the political class.

What so many of these voters liked most about Donald Trump was that he would drain the Washington swamp.

The political left ignored and dismissed these voter complaints as irrational and witless—in the end to their own detriment. Hillary Clinton was so contemptuous of this voter uprising that she infamously told a group of her millionaire and billionaire donors that many Trump voters were "deplorables" and, even, "irredeemable." The left regularly ridiculed the Trump voters as xenophobes, Islamophobes, racists, misogynists, and homophobes who wanted to turn back the clock.

The view of most political elites—both Republican and Democratic—was that they were culturally, morally, and intellectually superior to the Trump troops. They had, and showed, contempt for working people.

When we would ask the folks at these rallies or later during the campaign what they thought about the Obama recovery, they would often respond with disdain: "What recovery? This is Michigan." Or Ohio. Or Illinois. Or West Virginia. Or upstate New York. Or Iowa. Or the other half of America not on the coasts and not connected to Hollywood, Silicon Valley, Wall Street, or Washington, D.C.

These voters were visibly giddy with excitement; they had typically waited three or four hours to see and hear Trump in person. Everyone was eager for the Mick Jagger of politics to show up. You couldn't help getting caught up by it all.

The more the left threw temper tantrums over Trump, the more voters he attracted. Leftism was in-your-face and reverberating across America—and you had to accept their ideas or you were a small-minded bigot. As columnist Peggy Noonan put it so well, it wasn't enough for Middle America with Christian values to accept things like same-sex marriage, now they had to bake the wedding cakes.[10] Trump stood up to the bicoastal elitists and challenged their political correctness and speech codes. It turns out he was speaking for tens of millions of what are now called the "forgotten Americans."

We learned as we attended more of these rallies that the routine was always the same. When the Trump plane arrived, it was bedlam. The plane would circle to a halt 100 yards from the rally, and then the door would open. Trump would walk out and stand at the top of the stairs, waving to the crowd and soaking in the adulation.

He was dressed immaculately—always. White shirt, red tie, and dark blue suit. He was theatrical and seemed bigger than life. In some ways, he was.

He would step out onto the stage to hysteria, as if Bobby Thomson had hit the game-winning home run to send the Giants to the World Series.

He would walk around with two thumbs up, wait a few minutes for the chaos to die down, hold his arms out as if a wide embrace were coming, and shout: "You are. My people."

That brought the house down again. Then he would roll out his campaign slogans. Build the wall. Who will pay for it? The crowd, in unison, in call-and-response mode: *"Mexico!"* End NAFTA. The biggest tax cut ever. Repeal Obamacare— every word of it. Put coal miners back to work. Rebuild our infrastructure. And then, of course, the closer: Make America Great Again.

He was P. T. Barnum. What a showman! What a gifted orator. Was there some demagoguery here? Sure. But it always made us laugh that when Trump said *Build the wall* he was denounced as a dangerous demagogue, whereas when Barack Obama promised to prevent the rise of the oceans, he was viewed like a Greek god as the media swooned over his stage presence and charisma.

We had a sense early on that Trump was breaking all the rules and conventions and . . . for better or worse, was on the verge of making history. And, of course, we wanted to be part of pulling it off.

BACK AT TRUMP TOWER

Exactly two weeks after our first meeting with Trump, we reconvened in Trump's office in Manhattan. We went through the same security screening and chatted amicably with his charming office staff. After a brief wait, Trump ushered us into his office.

At this meeting, Larry and Steve were joined by Stephen Miller, Trump's new and indispensable campaign policy director. We had known Miller from his time as the press secretary for Senator Jeff Sessions of Alabama. Miller came over to the Trump campaign when Sessions became the first major Republican national legislator to endorse Trump.

Miller is sharp, organized, policy savvy, an amazingly gifted writer, and as conservative as they come. On Capitol Hill he'd helped advance some of Senator Sessions's best budget ideas, welfare reforms, and a flurry of other money-saving ideas. In a short time, Miller had become the point guy who was pulling the policy strategy together. He traveled with Trump, crafted many of the speeches, knew Trump's voice, and instinctively understood his philosophy better than anyone. Trump could not have been better served.

We were still refining the tax and budget numbers for Trump's tax plan but had come with a briefing book of preliminary numbers and a series of policy options for Candidate Trump to decide from as he moved forward with a bulletproof plan. We recognized that this could be a make-or-break document for the Trump campaign, already under relentless assault from entities who claimed the plan would balloon the federal deficit.

The media was disparaging Trump's tax plan as "voodoo economics on steroids," as one critic put it.[11] Many deficit hawks were denouncing Trump's budget and tax plans as unrealistic. Trump had called himself the "king of debt" in business, meaning, of course, that he was a virtuoso at using debt financing to build enormous wealth. Now some of his political adversaries sought to twist the meaning of "king of debt" to imply profligacy rather than virtuosity.

But in this second meeting with us, Donald Trump didn't get into the weeds of the policy proposals. The first thing he asked was: "Where's Laffer, we need him here." We explained that Arthur was out of the country, but he was on board. We chatted about the latest in the campaign free-for-all, but it was clear he didn't want to talk about the contours of the tax plan at this meeting. Instead, he got right to the point. "I want the two of you and Arthur Laffer to serve as senior economic advisors to my campaign."

We looked at each other in a bit of shock over the offer. *Huh?* Larry broke the silence by saying, "Well, Donald, I'm not sure we can work for you, or even that you want us to. We are for free trade and you're a protectionist."

Trump's reaction was instantaneous. He first challenged our description of him as a protectionist. He responded as if he were slightly insulted. "First of all, I understand the benefits of trade. I just want a better deal for American businesses and workers. I want free and fair trade."

That was reassuring to a couple of free trade die-hards like us. Then he said something even more reassuring: "Guys, we can agree to disagree on trade. But I really need your help on taxes, energy, regulations, and other economic issues. I really want to blow out this economy."

That declaration revealed a lot about Donald Trump, revelations that many political elites have still not grasped. Trump does not require ideological loyalty. There could be disagreement on issues. That was fine with him. There was no "purity test," no dogma.

We didn't always win the policy fights, and we still have skirmishes with him and his team. Trump is not ideological like Reagan was—and that was frustrating to us at times. But he does encourage honest and fair-minded policy debates. This man is a commonsense conservative who is about producing results, not adhering to ideological litmus tests.

There is something else about Trump's personality that many don't appreciate. Donald Trump—whatever his many other virtues (and vices) might be—is hard to say no to. His enthusiasm and can-doism are highly contagious. These qualities are no small part of the secret of his success in business . . . and politics.

Trump is also no-nonsense. He wanted an answer right then and there. We thought about it for a minute or so, weighing our reservations. Then, enthusiastically, we couldn't help ourselves: we said yes. He jumped out of his chair and said, "Good, let's get going then."

We were off to the races. It was brutal and bruising and exhausting, but we had the time of our lives being part of what was arguably the greatest political upset in American history.

POSTSCRIPT

In passing, let it be noted that none of us asked for or received any compensation for our advice and counsel and research during the campaign. This was a matter of national service that we were proud to undertake at our own expense. We later joked that our compensation was four front-row seats in the Trump box at the U.S. Open tennis tournament that summer. (Steve took a four-month unpaid leave of absence from the Heritage Foundation think tank to work on the campaign.) This follows in the tradition of Arthur, who never took a paycheck from President Reagan. Arthur firmly believes that once economists start taking money for economic policy advice, the incentives are such that it is very easy to start ignoring simple truths in favor of complex falsehoods that will curry favor with political benefactors. Arthur also never took the official title that Larry and Steve took: senior economic campaign advisor.

When Trump won the election, we served in various roles in the transition to put the economic agenda together for the incoming president. Then we advised the president in informal roles throughout 2017. And, of course, in early 2018 the president honored Larry Kudlow by appointing him director of his National Economic Council, formalizing his role as advisor. Arthur and Steve were appointed members of the president's Economic Advisory Council.

2

Battle Scars from the Biggest Political Upset in American History

"Donald Trump is a demagogue. Period. The fervor of his crowds recalls Nasser's Egypt. His convictions are illiberal. His manners are disgusting. His temper is frightening. It ought to have been the job of thoughtful conservatives in this season to point this out, time and again. If they can't do that, what good are they?"

—BRET STEPHENS,
Wall Street Journal columnist, November 2016[1]

When the campaign made the public announcement in the spring of 2016 that Larry and Steve would serve as senior economic advisors to Trump, and that Arthur would be a member of Trump's Economic Advisory Board, we weren't at all prepared for the ferocity of the reaction. Many of our friends, colleagues, and intellectual allies expressed shock and even rage over our apparent apostasy.

The three of us still have the bruises from supporting Donald Trump.

It's hard to appreciate, looking back on the heat of the campaign battle, how fiercely passionate and visceral the anti-Trump faction was within the Republican Party. At this stage of the game, most conservatives were lining up behind Bush, Rubio, or Cruz. Most party regulars were organizing an "Anybody but Trump" alliance to derail him. In just two or three months he had gone from a joke to an existential threat to the entire GOP machinery.

Back in the spring of 2016, the Never Trumpers on the right were as vicious and vociferous in their disdain for Trump as the left is today. Our endorsement of Trump was described as almost traitorous. Trump was said to be "hijacking the party," and we were seen as aiding and abetting the crime. We lost many friends as a result. (Most we have won back, based on Trump's success—both in winning the election and his policy victories. Many of the Bush neocons have never forgiven our heresy and maybe never will.)

A common attack on the three of us in those early days of the campaign was that we had either lost our minds or lost our principles—maybe both.

A column by *National Review*'s Jonah Goldberg a few weeks after we made our pro-Trump announcement was indicative of the backlash we experienced. Jonah, long a friend and colleague, wrote:

> What a short, strange trip it's been for Donald Trump's conservative supporters . . .
>
> Consider Larry Kudlow and Stephen Moore. In August, the two legendarily libertarian-minded economists attacked Trump, focusing on what they called Trump's "Fortress America platform." His trade policies threaten the global economic order, they warned. "We can't help

wondering whether the recent panic in world financial markets is in part a result of the Trump assault on free trade," they mused. As for Trump's immigration policies, they could "hardly be further from the Reagan vision of America as a 'shining city on a hill.'"

Let not the irony go unnoticed of the *National Review*—one of the leading anti-immigration voices in the conservative movement—attacking Trump for being tough on immigration. Goldberg then highlighted our change to being Trump supporters, linking it to his improvement in the polls. "What explains such Pauline conversions on the road to a Trump presidency?" Goldberg asked. "One argument they and many other converts make is purely consequentialist. 'For me, Trump potentially represents a big expansion of the Republican Party, a way to bring in those blue-collar Reagan Democrats,' Moore told the Washington Post. 'That's necessary if the party is going to win again.' Instead of converting voters to conservatism, Trump is succeeding at converting conservatives to statism."[2]

In retrospect, didn't it turn out to be exactly true that Trump expanded the Republican Party by bringing in "those blue-collar Reagan Democrats"? And wasn't this necessary for the party to win again in states like Ohio, Pennsylvania, Michigan, and Wisconsin?

Many conservatives were also angry that Trump had promised not to cut Social Security or Medicare benefits. Our view was that Trump was shrewd in eschewing unpopular and politically unachievable cuts in programs for seniors. We had seen Republicans, in Pickett's Charge fashion, get slaughtered many times in this well-intentioned but fundamentally misguided crusade. We had advised Trump to steer clear of these cuts in popular entitlements. Democrats desperately wanted Trump to call for benefit cuts so they could run TV ads of Granny being rolled over a cliff in her wheelchair.

We have always believed that the shrewdest way to make the entitlement programs solvent is to restore rapid growth. With a 3.3 percent or greater sustained growth rate, the entitlement deficits turn into surpluses over 20, 30, and 50 years. In truth, the wise, practical, beneficial way to "reform" entitlements is by getting economic growth up over 3.3 percent a year, not by cutting benefits or raising taxes!

Many of the conservative think tank and political groups—the Cato Institute, the American Enterprise Institute, and the Club for Growth—were also regularly attacking Trump as a fraudulent free market conservative. Trump seemed plenty pro-growth to us.

Many political commentators on the right were certain that Trump would not prove a viable nominee. Most pundits were telling the media night after night that Trump would be defeated in a historic Hillary Clinton landslide. For example, Jonah Goldberg, less than a month before the election, said, "I still think Donald Trump will lose in at least an Electoral College landslide."[3] Republicans who got behind Trump, the theory was, were throwing away the presidency and handing the keys of the Oval Office to the odious Clinton machine.

The American Enterprise Institute fellows were so eager to lose that they arranged for Ohio governor John Kasich to give a speech in their auditorium three days after the election to perform a political autopsy report on the party's blowout loss. Kasich was to rise out of the ashes. This event was cancelled the day after the election.

The Heritage Foundation, where Steve is a Distinguished Visiting Fellow, was one of the only major right-of-center policy institutes not to criticize Trump, thanks in part to the foresight of then-president Senator Jim DeMint and its former president and influential trustee Ed Feulner.

Most problematic for Trump (and, candidly, for us) were the ongoing and almost daily attacks on Trump from the venerable *Wall Street Journal* editorial page, where Steve had worked for ten years and where we all had published op-eds regularly for decades on economics and tax policy. Trump was regularly characterized as a cad and an opportunist without core beliefs. The iconic editorial page editor Paul Gigot often rightly railed against Trump's support of tariffs and his hard-nosed stand against illegal immigrants. But the *Journal* also had the election figured all wrong. They regularly opined that Trump was probably "the only candidate who cannot beat Hillary," when our view was, and still is, that he was probably the only candidate who could have beaten Hillary.

Some of the concerns on the right were legitimate. Trump had, for example, reversed his public positions on abortion, taxes, global warming, limited government, and other important issues. He had over the years supported and written checks to the Clintons, the Cuomos, and other liberal Democrats.

There was a nagging worry, which we at times shared, that based upon this history of policy inconsistencies, he might prove a liberal in disguise and thereby betray the conservative movement and injure the Republican Party even if he won. We'd seen it before.

What was fascinating to us about this litany of complaints was that none of these concerns seemed to bother the Trump voters. His unorthodox style, his brash and combative behavior, his contempt for the Washington elites were viewed by Trump supporters as assets, not liabilities.

POLITICALLY INCORRECT

Though we are economists by trade, we—like so many millions of Americans—were attracted to Trump's clever, gutsy, and long-overdue assaults against political correctness. He refused to genuflect to the political correctness that had become a crucial tool of the left. At the same time, many traditional conservatives were appalled by his style.

If you were against gay marriage, you were indicted as a homophobe. If you were against transgender bathrooms, you were a bully. If you didn't want boys in the middle school girls' locker room, you were sexist. If you were worried about Muslims committing acts of terrorism, you were an Islamophobe. If you were in favor of border security, you were a xenophobe. If you opposed abortion on demand, you were a misogynist. If you told or laughed at an ethnic or off-color joke, you could be fired from your job or shuffled off to "sensitivity training classes."

If you were against raising the minimum wage, you didn't care about poor people. If you supported the police, you were racist. If you opposed athletes who disrespected the flag or the national anthem, you were a nativist yahoo. If you questioned the climate change agenda, you were a scientifically illiterate "denier."

Millions of Americans just kept their mouths shut while self-designated "social justice warriors" took over and shut down public spaces, often brutally. We remember one voter telling us at a Trump rally that he felt "we are living in the era of the Spanish Inquisition." The left's tolerance movement had morphed in Orwellian fashion into a new era of rampant intolerance.

Nowhere was this more evident than on college campuses, where free expression and the open exchange of ideas had been supplanted with intolerant speech codes, "trigger warnings," "microaggressions," "safe spaces," and claims of "white privilege." Conservatives were increasingly shouted down and shut up as left-wing "groupthink" crushed free speech, too often with impunity, too often with the connivance of elected officials and the cowardice of university presidents.

Trump treated the political correctness epidemic like the plague it had become and refreshingly violated the left's close-minded code of conduct and limitations on free speech at every opportunity. The more he antagonized the left, the more his vote totals rose among the forgotten Americans.

At last, we felt, a political leader was demonstrating courage. Here was the conservative who had the guts to call out the intelligentsia in the media, academia, government, and Hollywood, showing that the emperor has no clothes. The left reacted with fury and indignation that anyone would dare challenge their claim to owning the moral high ground.

What the left failed (and fails) to realize was that their over-the-top character assassination of Trump was taken as an assault on these conservative voters' own beliefs. This made them rally even more loyally behind Trump. The left, in violation of their own stated ethos of inclusion, created an "us versus them" mentality—driving many blue-collar Americans right out of their coalition. Although many political commentators denounced Trump as divisive and polarizing, they were blind to the fact that the left had already systematically and severely polarized America.

As we mentioned in the last chapter, Hillary reinforced this "us versus them" schism during a speech in front of her millionaire donors when she infamously ridiculed Trump supporters as "irredeemable" and "a basket of deplorables." Her liberal snobbish friends in the audience laughed uproariously.

The Trump rallies brought to light that for years many millions of Americans felt isolated by their views because their views had been ruled impermissible in public discourse. Trumpism allowed Americans to make contact with tens of thousands of others who broadly shared their views and could come to political rallies and feel connected. As one voter told us at a rally in Colorado Springs: "These events are so liberating."

A PARTY OUT OF TOUCH WITH ITS VOTERS

Perhaps the most important virtue that we saw in Trump was the voters who made up his political movement. They are patriotic, hardworking, culturally conservative, middle-income Americans of all races and backgrounds who are tired of being ignored and lied to by politicians. These were the Reagan Democrats reemerging as a political force whom both parties purported to stand with and behind, but never actually listened to. We loved the Trump voters.

Trump inspired these Americans, but just as importantly, they inspired him. As he said in his victory speech:

> As I've said from the beginning, ours was not a campaign but rather an incredible and great movement, made up of millions of hard-working men and women who love their

country and want a better, brighter future for themselves and for their family.

It is a movement comprised of Americans from all races, religions, backgrounds, and beliefs, who want and expect our government to serve the people—and serve the people it will.

Working together, we will begin the urgent task of rebuilding our nation and renewing the American dream. I've spent my entire life in business, looking at the untapped potential in projects and in people all over the world.

That is now what I want to do for our country. Tremendous potential. I've gotten to know our country so well. Tremendous potential. It is going to be a beautiful thing. Every single American will have the opportunity to realize his or her fullest potential.

The forgotten men and women of our country will be forgotten no longer.[4]

Why were so many people inside the party clueless about this rising political force and even contemptuous of it? Many in the party viewed the Trump base as uneducated and "low-information voters." Michael Gerson, a former George W. Bush speechwriter and a columnist for the *Washington Post,* described Trump voters as those who "hold an absurdly simplistic anti-establishment attitude."[5] This is the kind of unseemly superiority complex we encountered all the time.

No one exemplified it more than Mitt Romney. In his disgraceful rant against Mr. Trump in March 2016, Mitt Romney made it clear that he thought Trump unfit to serve as president and said that nominating Trump would cause the nation's chances of being more prosperous and more secure to be "greatly diminished." He called Trump a "phony" and a "fraud."[6] Jealousy is an ugly thing.

This was what we were up against. And frankly, these criticisms were far harsher and further below the belt than anything that Hillary Clinton would publicly say about Trump.

Romney and Bush supporters even briefly conspired to steal the nomination from Trump at the Cleveland Convention by keeping him from getting a majority of the delegates, and then allowing these delegates to choose someone else, like . . . Mitt Romney. Never mind that millions of voters had cast a ballot for Trump and that he was winning most of the state primaries by large margins. Ironically, advocates of this shady tactic included some of the same people who were critiquing the Democrats for rigging their nomination process in favor of Clinton over Sanders.

To our dismay, we eventually recognized that it wasn't Trump who was out of touch with voters, but rather his elitist critics. How many Trump haters ever got out of the cocoon of the Washington Beltway and attended a Trump rally? How many of them met and talked to the truck drivers, the soccer moms, the veterans, the taxicab drivers, the construction workers, and the disaffected millennials, rather than hanging around RNC meetings with millionaire GOP donors and arrogant political consultants? As the election results confirmed, it was the party elites who were mystified about the concerns of real Americans. Trump was in touch.

Trumpism as a political phenomenon wasn't a big mystery to us. We had lived through two terms of a mostly failed Republican president in George W. Bush (whom we like as a person but who didn't leave America better off than he found it), followed by eight years of a largely failed Democratic presidency. Over these 16 years, Middle America hadn't seen a pay increase. Meanwhile, Republican political consultants raked in millions as a reward for incompetence. The fact that the five wealthiest counties in America—out of over 3,000 counties—are Washington, D.C. suburbs said volumes to voters about who was benefiting from a $4 trillion federal government.[7]

Our view was that the Republican Party apparatchiks had only themselves to blame for the working-class revolt. These voters, horrified by what President Obama was doing to them, naively put their faith in congressional Republicans to fix things—or at least to try—and had been sorely disappointed.

The exit polls from most of the primaries in 2016 showed that, in states across the country, an overwhelming number of GOP primary voters felt "betrayed" by the Republicans in Washington.

Why wouldn't they feel betrayed? The persistent lack of jobs and upward income mobility—the very stuff of the American dream—under both parties' control of both the White House and the Congress was a message that the System had betrayed the people. We, too, felt betrayed.

Even worse, the political establishment kept ignoring the voters' concerns in favor of those of the billionaire check writers who funded its super PACs. Super PACs had become a curse for the party—a way for the special interests to impose their will on both parties' selection process, the voters be damned. Ultimately the super PACs were proven to be impotent. And yet wealthy donors were dumb enough to dump another $50 million into the corrupt political consultant sinkhole. Some people just have to learn the hard way.

The same party elites who had patronizingly patted conservatives on their heads for years and told us that we must take one for the team and vote for Dole or Bush or McCain or Romney now threatened to bolt the party if Trump were the nominee. They were more than willing to hand the election to Hillary—even while accusing Trump voters of doing just that.

In short, in the spring and summer of 2016, the GOP was fighting a civil war over the soul of the party. On one side was the establishment with its big donors and consultant class, and on the other were the workers, cultural conservatives, and rank-and-file voters of America.

What was especially galling to us was the accusation that Trump was unprincipled and would sell conservative principles down the river.

Did they mean we might get a president who is asleep at the switch before the biggest financial crisis in 75 years? Or a president who runs up multitrillion-dollar deficits? Or bails out big investment banks, insurance firms, and energy companies with hundreds of billions of dollars of taxpayer money? Regulates our lightbulbs, toilets, and washing machines?

Oh, wait. That was George W. Bush and Barack Obama.

Ironically, for those who craved an "insider" who knew how government works, there was no better candidate in all of America than Hillary Clinton, America's consummate insider. She spent nearly $1 billion of special-interest money to trash her primary rival, who wanted to toss over the apple cart in Washington. That billion dollars did not come from the "common people" extolled by Ben Franklin.

We discovered that it was the Trump movement, more so than Donald Trump himself, that was an existential threat to the establishment elites of both right and left. These "forgotten Americans" are the frontline victims of big government policies run amok. The elites pretended to serve these folks, but they were so out of touch with working-class Americans, they forgot to ask them what they wanted and needed and how they felt about the direction of the country.

DID WE *REALLY* THINK TRUMP WOULD WIN?

Virtually every member of the entire political-industrial complex in Washington was wrong about the 2016 presidential race. Even on election night, pollsters confidently predicted that, based on the exit polling, Hillary had a 95 percent chance of winning. Three hours later all the crystal balls were shattered and the pollsters should have been sued for professional malpractice. It's a good thing for them that this profession doesn't get paid for results!

Why were the pollsters—those supposedly basing their calls on empirical data—so shockingly wrong? We think it was the undercover Trump voters whom we encountered all over the country. As one bumper sticker we saw in Tampa, Florida, put it so beautifully:

Vote for Donald Trump:
(Nobody Has to Know)

We are often asked: Be honest, did you really think Trump was going to win? Larry and Steve thought that Trump *could* win, but we doubted at times whether he *would win*. Our view was that Trump had the voter base to win the GOP nomination that summer and then it would be a very close general election race that could go either way.

Arthur, prophetically, called the election to his clients at Laffer Associates in May 2016. Here was the headline of his analysis:

To save you the agony of plodding through this infor-
mation-rich paper, I'll get straight to the point: Donald
Trump will be the next President of the United States after
having won an easy victory over Hillary Clinton in November 2016.[8]

Um, it wasn't exactly an "easy" victory, but Arthur was
one of the very few who called the election outcome early and
correctly. It's worthwhile to explain why Arthur predicted a
Trump presidency. His five reasons, which appear prescient
today:

1. The essential characteristics of the narrative for the
   Trump campaign and the Reagan campaign of 1980
   are surprisingly similar, which would point to a
   Trump victory.
2. The economy is in a poor state, as measured by the falling employment trends, poor economic growth, and
   falling new home sales data. These measures strongly
   indicate a Trump victory.
3. Using historical data for the Gallup poll question "are
   you satisfied" and presidential election dates points to
   an overwhelming Republican win in November 2016.
4. Relying on voter turnout data this year versus earlier
   years and party selection, the Republicans have a large
   advantage coming into the fall election.
5. Taking careful measure of what both Hillary Clinton
   and Donald Trump are talking about on the campaign
   trail, Trump has the economic issues on his side.

Donald Trump did face the longest of odds when he started
his campaign odyssey. He had zero political experience. He

said, and tweeted, some outlandish things. Nobody could be sure about what he believed in. There was a sneaking suspicion, based upon rapid-fire self-contradictory statements, that even *he* didn't always know what he believed.

He first had to beat the field of 16 very talented, mostly experienced Republican aspirants and then knock off the formidable preeminent figure in the Democratic Party, Hillary Clinton, with her billion-dollar war chest.

It's astonishing and admirable to us, given the long odds he confronted, that Trump threw his hat into the ring in the first place, subjecting himself to the high possibility of ridicule and humiliation. We admired his courage and his willingness to take the risk. We always root for the underdog!

THE TRUMP GAMBLE

Backing Trump was certainly a big gamble. To be perfectly honest, at the start of the presidential cycle, we were less worried about whether he could win and more worried about whether, if he did win, he would stick to his campaign promises. We were hopeful, but we never tried to oversell him to our friends and colleagues. What we said about Trump from the start was that he is "pro-business"—and that would be a radical departure from the zealous anti-business philosophy of the Obama administration. We were fairly certain that after eight years of Obama, and with Hillary Clinton looming as the heir apparent, America could do a lot worse than Trump.

Having worked with literally scores of candidates and elected officials, we can say this with more than a little experience. In 2015, we formed a group called the Committee to Unleash Prosperity. Its mission was to educate the political class of candidates about growth economics. We worked with more than a dozen of the 2016 GOP presidential hopefuls at one time or another.

We reiterate this to emphasize that we weren't naive. We knew from experience that, more often than not, politicians wind up frustrating and disappointing you. That's politics. The elusive goal is to search for the diamond in the rough, the man or woman who won't let you and the voters down. There really is no guarantee on who will keep, or break, their campaign promises. You just have to make an educated gamble, and Trump, for us, was a smart bet.

In the late spring of 2016 the attacks on Trump were intensifying, even as he racked up impressive primary victories in the Northeast and many of the western states. Rick Dearborn, who had worked as chief of staff for Trump ally Jeff Sessions and was one of Trump's most trusted campaign advisors, asked us to issue a joint statement of why we supported Donald Trump for president. We were joined by our friend and colleague Andy Puzder, a successful businessman who ran fast-food restaurants throughout the country and had been a great and trusted surrogate for Trump on the campaign trail.

Our joint statement drew huge exposure in the media. We believe that it helped legitimize Trump's economic game plan—and, thus, Trump as a viable candidate—with many skeptical Republicans. Two years later, we think it was rather prescient. Here is what we wrote:

Why We Support Donald Trump

While the four of us were proud to provide economic and policy advice to nearly all 17 Republican presidential candidates this year, none of us endorsed a particular candidate believing the voters should make that choice.

They have. Donald Trump won the race fair and square, receiving more votes than any Republican primary candidate ever has, garnering support from Republicans as well as Independents and cross-over (Reagan) Democrats.

One reason for Trump's success has been the failure of President Obama's economic policies, particularly for middle- and working-class Americans. Bill Clinton was right; the last seven years have been "awful." Economic growth has been anemic producing the weakest "recovery" since the Great Depression. The middle class is disappearing and the working class has seen virtually no gains with average household income slightly negative in real terms since Obama took office. Unfortunately, Hillary Clinton wants to continue with Obama's economic bromides, as if a double down on failed policies will heal the economy.

The voters aren't that stupid.

But what is Trump offering as an alternative?

First, the biggest pro-growth tax cut since the Reagan cuts in 1981, 35 years ago. He proposes simplifying the tax code while significantly reducing marginal tax rates on individuals and businesses. His proposed corporate tax rate of 15 percent would make it easier for American businesses to repatriate earnings, bringing capital into the US and making our nation a more hospitable place to invest. It is a pro-growth, supply-side tax plan that would generate economic growth and do more for working- and middle-class families than any plan to redistribute income.

Second, entitlement reforms. Some conservatives complain he won't reform these. Nonsense. Obamacare is the fastest growing entitlement program. He promises to repeal and replace it with a consumer-choice health plan.

He has also said he wants to restore work requirements for welfare programs, perhaps the single most important entitlement reform.

Next, while Hillary would put tens of thousands of coal miners out of work, Trump supports a pro-growth energy policy that will use all of our abundant energy resources—oil, natural gas, and coal. That's a great idea since we have more fossil fuels than any other nation. Trump's plan could make America the world's number one energy producer within five years—producing millions of new jobs and trillions of dollars of extra output each year.

Yes, we also have policy differences.

We are pro-immigration and see the foreign born as an enormous asset. While Trump is portrayed as a close-the-doors nativist, there is a difference between being anti-immigration and anti–illegal immigration. Trump has said he favors legal immigration. There is nothing inherently wrong with viewing immigration policy through the lens of protecting our national security and the interests of American workers. We can be compassionate while preserving our sovereignty.

Given that voters have been demanding action on illegal immigration for years while politicians did nothing, Trump's proposals to build a wall, increase enforcement of our laws, return criminal aliens, defund sanctuary cities, and reduce visa overstays are reasonable and sensible.

Nonetheless, we do believe that deporting 11 million people is an unworkable idea. We should only pursue deportation when an illegal immigrant has committed a felony or is collecting government welfare benefits and has become a "public charge." This is fully consistent with our historical immigration policies.

The four of us are also free traders and oppose punitive tariffs. But, Trump is right that many of our free trade agreements have been poorly negotiated. His pledge to negotiate with the Chinese from a position of strength makes sense. There is nothing protectionist in insisting that China uphold intellectual property laws and cease their practice of compelling U.S. companies to release proprietary technology as a precondition to entering China's markets.

Free-trade purists are missing a practical political point. Working-class Americans believe they have disproportionately borne the burdens of lax enforcement of our immigration laws and "free trade" deals. Taking a tougher stance on trade with nations like China and Mexico may be a necessary precondition to restoring public support for the comparative advantages of free trade going forward.

Finally, there is a concern that Trump is a showman, temperamentally unsuited for the job. We disagree. Running a large and successful enterprise is an excellent qualification for serving as president. Trump has had prolonged business success. He didn't fake that. We find it so refreshing and uplifting that middle- and working-class voters don't envy Trump's success or view him as an evil rich man. Rather, they admire and want to emulate his success.

Some will point to Trump's business failures, but one of the great things about this nation is that people have the ability to fail and to rise above those failures. Henry Ford and Steve Jobs did and they changed the world. Despite the occasional failure, Trump has maintained a level of success few people ever achieve.

Americans across the political spectrum know it's time for a change. In fact, they're insisting on it. It is time for Republicans to put the bickering and infighting aside and support Mr. Trump. If that happens, both he and the American people will win.[9]

Today, in light of all that has happened, we wouldn't change a word of the statement.

There were also purely practical reasons for climbing aboard the Trump express.

First, we honestly believed that his populist, pro-growth message was the platform that stood the best chance of defeating Hillary. We believed the conventional wisdom voiced almost daily by our friends at the *Wall Street Journal* editorial board—that Trump was the only candidate who would lose to Hillary—was exactly backward. After spending some time with Trump and attending a few of his rallies, where we heard his unconventional message and rousing presentation and saw how the voters connected with him, we began to believe that he might be the only Republican who could beat her.

We thought the Trump strategy, conceived by Steve Bannon, of crashing through the blue wall in the economically depressed midwestern states was pure genius. Trump's blue-collar appeal could deliver crucial electoral votes and steal members of the electorate who either rarely voted or had cast ballots for Obama in 2008 and 2012. We had met and chatted with many of these voters firsthand. They previously had been known as the "Reagan Democrats," and we knew from their discontent the right message could bring them back.

Trump had an electoral strategy that made sense. Steve Bannon, who became a confidant of Trump's and later his campaign CEO, told us something that made sense—especially when we saw what we saw at the Trump rallies. There was a populist revolt brewing in America against the incompetent power structure that had misruled America for twenty years. Voter discontent manifested in the surprising momentum of Bernie Sanders on the left and Donald Trump on the right.

There were two slogans throughout the United States that seemed to spark voter enthusiasm: "Make America Great Again" and "Feel the Bern." Not coincidentally, Trump and Bernie shared the view that the invasion of Iraq was a tragic and expensive mistake, that trade deals were hurting America, and that political insider trading within Washington's power structure was redistributing income from the working class to the rich.

Corey Lewandowski and Steve Bannon were brilliant tacticians. They discerned the unrest of the 2016 electorate better than did career political consultants of both the right and left. "We have to make sure this populist uprising tilts to the right, toward Trump," Bannon told us, "not to the left, toward Bernie Sanders."

At that moment it wasn't at all clear which way the populist uprising would tilt. We were in total accord with Bannon's commitment to tilt it right. We couldn't allow the "Sandersnista wing of the Democratic Party," as Larry referred to the radical left, to triumph. A Sanders victory could have doomed America's free market capitalism as we know it.

There was another factor that influenced our decision. We found Donald Trump extremely likable and enjoyed working with him. He proved to be a great listener—unlike many stuffed-shirt candidates in politics who are too full of themselves to really pay attention—and, gratifyingly, he often took our policy advice. We were worried about being used as props, but that wasn't the case. We didn't always win the policy arguments with Trump or his other advisors—the most influential of whom were, justifiably, Jared and Ivanka—but our views often prevailed and almost always were at least taken into account. Incidentally, we came to view all of Trump's family members as amazing assets with great political instincts (like their father).

Our view back in the spring of 2016 was that Trump had real flaws and we disagreed with him, sometimes passionately, on certain issues, notably trade and immigration. But on the most crucial policies, such as regulation, energy, tax cuts, economic growth, and creating a respectfully pro-business climate, Trump had the right schematic in his head. He also had the right enemies: leftists who mocked, sneered at, and vilified him. In Washington, making the right enemies is a badge of honor.

IS IT NOW THE PARTY OF TRUMP?

Three days after the general election, while the country and the GOP establishment were still in shock—and truthfully, we were a bit in awe too—that Donald Trump would be inaugurated as president on January 20, Steve spoke under the Capitol dome to the House Republican caucus on the GOP economic agenda going forward. He had been invited by Republican House Majority Whip Steve Scalise, the meeting scheduled weeks before the election when it seemed probable that we would be confronting President-elect Hillary Clinton.

It was supposed to be an autopsy report. Now that Trump had won, the room was overflowing with members and staffers eager to hear what the Trump election meant for the agenda of the Grand Old Party. So few had thought that Trump had a prayer of winning that this was a truly novel question.

At that breakfast meeting Steve made some (unintentionally) controversial comments that surprised many of the attendees. The meeting was supposed to be off the record, but it got leaked to the press—proving that nothing is ever really off the record in Washington. A few hours after the meeting was over, *The Hill* ran a story with a banner headline:

> Trump adviser tells House Republicans:
> You're no longer Reagan's Party

The article discussed a closed-door presentation during which Steve told a group of leading Republican lawmakers that they no longer belonged to the conservative party of Ronald Reagan but to Trump's populist working-class party. According to a *Hill* source, lawmakers were reportedly "taken aback" by Moore's comments. The source put the reactions in context this way: "For God's sake, it's Stephen Moore! . . . He's the guy who started Club for Growth. He's Mr. Supply Side economics." *Politico* then went on to quote portions of an interview with Steve:

> "Just as Reagan converted the GOP into a conservative party, Trump has converted the GOP into a populist working-class party," Moore said in an interview Wednesday. "In some ways this will be good for conservatives and in other ways possibly frustrating.
>
> "Having spent the last three or four months on the campaign trail, it opens your eyes to the everyday anxieties and financial stress people are facing," Moore added. "I'm pro-immigration and pro-trade, but we better make sure as we pursue these policies we're not creating economic undertow in these areas.

"Elections have consequences," Moore added, "and I do think Donald Trump has a mandate."

... "Reagan ran as an ideological conservative. Trump ran as an economic populist," he said.

"Trump's victory," Moore added, "turned it into the Trump party."[10]

This article sparked a brief wildfire of anger and resentment. One friend commented to the press that Steve Moore "must have been drunk when he said these things." He wasn't.

But let us put to rest the misunderstanding that any of us would ever in any way denigrate Reagan or Reagan's legacy. Far from it. We each worked for Reagan in one capacity or another. He won the Cold War, defeated the Evil Empire, rebuilt the American economy, and caused a quarter-century-long boom in wealth creation and prosperity nearly unrivaled in American history. (Chapter Five discusses this economic resurrection in further detail.) His face belongs, in our eyes, on Mount Rushmore.

What Steve actually said to the House Republicans rings even truer today than in the afterglow of the Trump victory. Reagan's legacy, like Lincoln's, enriches the soul of the GOP. Hopefully it always will. That said, we live in a different era than the one we entered in 1980. The baton has passed from the Reagan era to a new generation, one led by the populist Donald Trump, who brings a similar kind of optimistic populism to the office of the president as did Reagan. That isn't apostasy. It is a truism.

We, under the banner of Trumponomics, believe that Republicans must prioritize delivering jobs and economic development to regions of the country like the industrial Midwest, in states like Michigan, Pennsylvania, Ohio, Indiana,

Wisconsin, Iowa, and Missouri. These are places that for the most part never fully participated in the meager Obama recovery and where blue-collar Reagan Democrats took a leap of faith and came back to the Republican Party for the first time since 1984.

The GOP will be judged—in 2018 and 2020—on whether it delivers results for this part of the country and for the forgotten working men and women whom the Democrats abandoned economically and culturally. This, too, is a political truism.

What drew the ire of some of our conservative friends was Steve's statement that "Trump has converted the GOP into a populist America First party." Let's address that.

Trump handsomely defeated 16 GOP rivals—a field that was touted as the most talented field of wannabes in modern history. GOP voters opted for his new breed of economic populism. Then he won the general election by a wide electoral margin.

Liberals and the few remaining Republican Never Trumpers can pretend that a political sonic boom didn't happen. But it did. The voters spoke with a thunderclap.

The GOP will be a lot tougher on illegal immigration and a lot more skeptical of lopsided trade deals. America will be a lot warier of foreign entanglements. We will spend more on infrastructure. We will put America's economic and security interests first. Trump was unequivocal, not at all ambiguous, about what he intended.

Those on the right and left who are still confused by what happened and why it happened should go back and read Jude Wanniski's classic book *The Way the World Works*. It is a book that shaped the Reagan Revolution and is no less valuable today. Wanniski reminds us over and over again of the lesson of history that there is great collective wisdom in the decisions made by the American voters. It is core supply-side doctrine to listen respectfully to what the electorate is saying.

THE REAGAN PARALLEL

This brings us to the final reason we were confident that Trump was the right man to back early in 2016. Though Trump is not Reagan, we recognized right away uncanny similarities.

As Arthur, who served on the 1980 Reagan campaign advisory board, has noted many times, Ronald Reagan was disrespected and abused by a significant segment of the Republican establishment. Reagan was called an empty suit, a trigger-happy California cowboy, only an actor, a person who spoke words others wrote, a racist, a bigot, a divorcé, a warmonger, and the man who would start the Third World War.

The Democratic Party "éminence grise" Clark Clifford privately referred to Ronald Reagan as an "amiable dunce." President Jerry Ford, never a fan of Reagan's, accused his nemesis of "a penchant for offering simplistic solutions to hideously complex problems."[11] George H. W. Bush, chosen as Reagan's VP, had denounced Reagan's supply-side tax cut agenda as "voodoo economics."

Then, as in 2016, the whole Reagan group received virtually no support from the Republican Party's elders. It wasn't until Reagan had finally defeated Bush, Howard Baker, Phil Crane, Bob Dole, and John Anderson in the primary that there was any attempt to be conciliatory to Ronald Reagan's presidential campaign.

At the convention in Detroit, the party's establishment conspired to browbeat Ronald Reagan into accepting Gerald

Ford as his co-presidential running mate. Then as now, the establishment was absolutely certain that Ronald Reagan would be blown away by Carter in November 1980 and so would the down-ticket Republican candidates. Reagan would get so blown out, they thought, that he would prove to be more devastating to Republicans than the Goldwater defeat of 1964.

Of course, none of that happened. Reagan handily defeated Carter, even though the Gipper was behind in the polls as recently as a week before the election. On Election Day Reagan swept 44 states and 50.7 percent of the popular vote to Carter's 41 percent and Anderson's 6.6 percent.

Arthur's theme was simple. The Reagan saga of 1980 looked a lot like the Trump story today.

The consensus opinion in 2016 was that Hillary was going to win one of the greatest landslides in the history of American politics and that even deep-red Texas might go Democratic. *New York* magazine called Trump "the crudest and most vacuous presidential candidate in human memory." Then a "Dream Team" of celebrity economists piled on and trashed Trump's economic agenda as a recipe for "another great depression" and a "stock market crash."[12]

Yes, Trump was saying and tweeting crazy things sometimes. He would exaggerate. He would put his foot in his mouth. And yet, Trump kept winning and winning, and with each improbable victory, the pundits assured us it wouldn't happen again and that this was surely the beginning of the end.

But the end never came for Donald Trump.

How did it happen? Craig Shirley, one of the best Reagan biographers, recently slipped us a big part of the answer, reminding us that "one major similarity between Reagan and

Trump is that both were always underestimated by their political adversaries."

The first "simpleton" won two landslide presidential elections, resurrected the stagflation-ravaged economy of the 1970s, and won the Cold War. The second pulled off the most improbable political upset in American history.

Donald Trump, on November 8, 2016, toppled the legacies of two family dynasties, the Clintons and the Bushes, and halted the leftward drift exemplified by Barack Obama. Our hope then and now is that Trump represents a modernization of the Reagan legacy of prosperity, optimism, and peace through strength.

3

Obamanomics and the Assault on Growth

*"Economists agree that unemployment benefits re-
main one of the best ways to grow the economy. . . .
For every dollar spent on unemployment benefits,
the economy grows by, according to one estimate
$1.52; by others $2."*

—Nancy Pelosi, 2009[1]

When Arthur used to meet occasionally with then-president
Ronald Reagan, he used to joke: "Sir, you were blessed
by the incompetence of your predecessors." Then he would
add, "After following Jimmy Carter into the Oval Office, how
could you *not* be a success?" Reagan would glow knowingly.

But there was truth here underneath the humor. One important life lesson is that in business and in politics, you always want to succeed a failure, not a success. Without Jimmy
Carter and raging inflation, there is no Ronald Reagan. Without George W. Bush and the financial meltdown, there is no

Barack Obama. And without the failed economic policies of Barack Obama, Donald Trump is not elected president.

Trump understood this fully. He wasn't running just against Hillary Clinton and her closet overflowing with scandals, but the Obama economy as well. He was running against Obamacare. He was running against the regulatory assault on business. He was running against the tax hikes and faulty trade deals. He was running against Obama's climate change fanaticism. He was running against opioid addiction, the plague of crime in inner cities, the $10 trillion rise in the national debt, and income stagnation.

One time on the campaign plane when Trump was working on an economic speech, about four of us, including Steve, Larry, Steve Miller, and Hope Hicks, had an impromptu and wide-ranging discussion about the state of affairs in America and the palpable voter unrest. Trump was convinced that Americans were enraged over Obama's failed policies. What would the economic revitalization plan be? Steve Moore summarized the game plan to Trump succinctly: "Donald, just look at all the things that Obama has done on the economy over the past eight years, and then do just the opposite." Trump generally agreed that there really wasn't much worth keeping.

When Trump thundered at rallies "Make America Great Again!" it was a not-so-subtle punch in the solar plexus to the Obama presidency. Obama used to wince at Trump's "Great Again" theme because he of all people understood that it is an implicit indictment of the Obama record. In other words, the 2016 election was a silent referendum on Obama's economy.

Obama used to counter Trump's campaign theme by protesting that "America is still great." For tens of millions of Americans, it didn't feel quite that way. The left had deluded themselves into thinking that all was well in America—further evidence that they had lost touch with the very voters the progressive movement professed to represent. The Democrats and the media also spun a fairy tale of the most liberal president in America, Obama, who heroically lurched the nation aggressively to the left and saved the country from economic ruin.

But they forgot to ask Americans whether they liked what was happening. Was the country on the right track? As we stated earlier, about two-thirds said no. How many rated the economy as good or great? Fewer than one in three. Did Americans think the American dream was intact? More than half said no. Voters, in short, were grumpy in 2016—and for good reason.

To fully understand why voters took a gamble on Trumponomics, we need to present the facts of the failures of its predecessor: Obamanomics.

PARADISE LOST

In mid-2008—right on the eve of the housing and stock market crash—the two of us (with Peter Tanous) released a book called *The End of Prosperity*. We don't always get our predictions right, but this was a bull's-eye hit. We forecast a potential stock market crash, but also a long slosh of low growth and stagnant incomes.

As we wrote then, "Why do we now forecast the End of Prosperity?"

> The short answer is that we aren't just optimists, we are first and foremost realists. And we are now witnessing nearly all of the economic policy dials that were once

turned toward growth now being twisted back toward recession. The problem is . . . that our politicians . . . are getting everything wrong—tax policy, regulatory policy, monetary policy, spending policy, trade policy. We call this the assault on growth. The political class seems almost intentionally steering the United States economy into the abyss—and, to borrow a phrase from P. J. O'Rourke, the American electorate, alas, seems ready and willing to hand them the keys and the bottle of whiskey to do it"[2]

We were horrified by the disastrous policies Bush enacted in his last year in office, which in some ways were worse than anything Obama gave us—bailouts, stimulus plans, and so on—but even more so by what the Democratic nominee for president, Barack Obama, was advocating. We cited as Exhibit A this famous exchange in early 2008 with Charlie Gibson on ABC News:

GIBSON: Senator, you have said you would favor an increase in the capital gains tax. You said on CNBC, and I quote, "I certainly would not go above what existed under Bill Clinton," which was 28 percent. It's now 15 percent. That's almost a doubling, if you went to 28 percent.

But actually, Bill Clinton, in 1997, signed legislation that dropped the capital gains tax to 20 percent.

OBAMA: Right.

GIBSON: And George Bush has taken it down to 15 percent. And in each instance, when the rate dropped, revenues from the tax increased; the government took in more money. And in the 1980s, when the tax was increased to 28 percent, the revenues went down.

> So why raise it at all, especially given the fact that
> 100 million people in this country own stock and
> would be affected?
>
> OBAMA: Well, Charlie, what I've said is that I would look at
> raising the capital gains tax for purposes of fairness . . .
>
> GIBSON: But history shows that when you drop the capital
> gains tax, the revenues go up.
>
> OBAMA: Well, that might happen, or it might not . . . [3]

This depressing interchange left us scratching our heads and wondering whether this gifted orator who was filling stadiums with 20,000 or more adoring fans and followers and said that he was promoting "the audacity of hope" had even the slightest clue about how economics works in the real world. How jobs are created. How entrepreneurs and risk takers create wealth. Senator Obama admitted that he would raise a tax even if the revenues would fall—because this is the "fair" thing to do. Fair to whom?

We had a multitude of other concerns. Obama seemed more obsessed with tearing down the rich than lifting up the poor.

We were convinced that tax rates were going to go up across the board over the next few years—income tax, capital gains taxes, dividend taxes, and estate taxes. Obama's tax plan on his 2008 campaign website endorsed tax rates on income going back to as high as 50 to 60 percent. (He raised them to only 40 percent.) Senator Obama said that income taxes had to be raised "so that we can pay for universal healthcare and other initiatives." Who would want to invest in those headwinds?

Arthur had advised governments around the world to cut their tax rates—and many, including Ireland, Britain, Russia, and even Sweden and France, listened and did so. If America began raising tax rates on investment, savings, corporate profits, and stock ownership while the rest of the world was cutting them, this story couldn't end well.

While all this was going on, Bush and the Pelosi Congress passed nearly $1 trillion of Keynesian "stimulus spending plans" and counterproductive bailouts of insurance companies and banks that had made risky loans. As our friend John Allison, then CEO of BB&T Corporation, explained to us, the feds engaged in a mob-like shakedown in the fall of 2008. "Treasury Secretary Hank Paulson locked us [major bank CEOs] into a room in Washington and put a [figurative] gun to our heads and forced all of us to take the bailout money whether we wanted or not." It sounded like a macabre scene out of a Batman movie. Free market economics was tossed out the window. At the height of the crisis, Bush reportedly said: "I've abandoned free market principles to save the free market system." The stock market crashed further.

Our prediction was that the combination of Bush's disastrous bailout policies in response to the financial crisis and Obama's catalog of anti-growth interventions was going to capsize the world financial markets and turn a temporary financial trauma into a full-scale deep recession. Which is exactly what happened.

Obama and his supporters take credit for saving the economy from "a second Great Depression." Academics have already bought into this narrative. A recent survey of historians ranked Obama one of the ten greatest presidents—which, alas, tells us more about historians than it does about presidents.

Our view is that Obama surely didn't start the Great Recession, he inherited it. But he inadvertently stoked the flames of panic on Wall Street and ensured a lengthier contraction and a much weaker recovery because of his wrongheaded policy prescriptions.

Markets are forward looking. In the midst of the financial market meltdown, investors, employers, and average Americans were listening intently to what Obama was saying. Investors all over the globe became convinced that the American people were going to elect to the presidency a youthful and charismatic community organizer who in a short time had become the most liberal member of United States Senate. There was a high likelihood that he would implement a slate of anti-growth and redistributionist policies—much like we had in the 1930s under FDR.

Our point is that the fear of this cauldron of bearish policies contributed to the financial panic and the massive sell-off of stocks in 2008. Ironically, Obama contributed to the very financial panic that he was elected to reverse.

We were fairly certain that if Washington turned away from tried and tested pro-growth policies, just as sure as the sun rises in the morning, the U.S. economic growth machine would grind to a halt. Prosperity doesn't happen by accident, and growth is not the natural course of events. It has to be nurtured and rewarded.

History was clear on this. When we got our policies terribly misaligned in the 1930s during the Great Depression under Hoover and FDR, the economy didn't recover for 12 years, and then only after we entered a world war and the economy became a military emergency mobilization operation with 2 million men in uniform. The Great Depression was a result of trade protectionism, high tax rates, a contractionary monetary policy, and a New Deal mishmash of government programs that were well intentioned but made things worse, not better.

Then in the 1970s during the era of malaise and stagflation, the overregulated, overtaxed, and overinflated U.S.

economy sank from the exhaustion of carrying around these economic Quaaludes and the stock market went helter-skelter. We should have learned from these eras of despair that policymakers can do a lot of harm to financial conditions, family incomes, and American competitiveness—and they can rain down destruction in a hurry.

In the 1980s and '90s, the economy soared because most of the impediments to growth were cleared away. Taxes, tariffs, regulations, and inflation weren't eliminated, but they were tamed. Yes, there were policy mistakes along the way. There were periods of irrational exuberance in tech stocks and housing and savings and loans. But the unmistakable trend over the period (of Reagan and Clinton) was toward stable prices, a dependable and strong currency, lower and flatter tax rates, freer trade, a lighter hand of regulation in key industries ranging from financial services to transportation to telecommunications and energy, welfare reforms that rewarded work over dependency, and eventually a balanced budget and a reduced debt.

The economy blossomed and U.S. industries reawakened from the wicked spell of stagflation. The United States was unquestionably the global winner in the race for capital. America soaked up some $4 trillion in capital investment from around the world. Smart money got parked in America, and the net worth of the nation exploded from $18 trillion in 1982 to $60 trillion in 2000.

HOPE AND CHANGE

In November 2008, at the height of the financial meltdown, Barack Obama won a resounding election victory. Voters opted for the optimism of "hope and change." A secret to Obama's success was his charm and youth and the fact that most Americans—and we include ourselves in this group— loved the idea of electing our nation's first black president.

Who could not be inspired by Obama's political rise to the top? We certainly were. He was reared by a single parent and without wealth or family fame or political connections but was elected to the White House. What an inspiring "only in America" story. He has a great wife and children, is a model husband and father, and, on the occasions we have met him, is engaging and likable.

Some conspiracy theorists on the far right used to ask us about Obama's policies: Is he intentionally trying to hurt the economy? We always rebuked the question and questioner. We have no doubt that President Obama adopted a policy path that he believed would bring prosperity back to the middle class and help lift the poor out of poverty. We were rooting for Obama to succeed. Our purpose here is not to bash Obama—someone we admire and like personally.

But the full-throttled experiment in "progressive" economics failed (predictably) to produce the kind of broadbased recovery that Americans hoped for.

It's important to get this factual history straight because we need to learn from the mistakes. That's doubly valuable, because progressive ideas still hold great sway in politics, academia, the media, and the broader American culture. Dead ideas that history long ago discredited—Keynesianism, Malthusianism, redistributionism, socialism, collectivism, and so on—were brought back into vogue under Obama. Why these bankrupting ideas remain so alluring to the intellectual elite is one of life's great mysteries.

A CRISIS IS A TERRIBLE THING TO WASTE

Let's travel back in time to the very beginning of the Obama presidency. Many will remember the declaration of Obama's first chief of staff, Rahm Emanuel, who said shortly after the inauguration in 2009: "A crisis is a terrible thing to waste." Liberals who then controlled the White House and both houses of Congress took that advice to heart and capitalized on the crisis to do the things liberals had wanted to do for years. As David Horowitz, a former leftist turned social commentator, put it: "This was the moment the radical left had been waiting for so many years."[4] *Time* magazine put Mr. Obama on its cover with a cigarette and a top hat looking like a dapper Franklin Roosevelt. It was fitting because Mr. Obama had in mind a supersized New Deal.

The infamous $830 billion "stimulus" plan with its "shovel-ready projects" was passed in Obama's first months in office. When looking at the details of the plan, it's clear that the objective was less to resuscitate the economy and more to spread tens of billions of dollars to left-wing interest groups. There would be money for the National Endowment for the Arts (this stimulates the economy?), Head Start, unemployment insurance, food stamps, renewable energy subsidies, high-speed rail, billions for federal bureaucrats to purchase a new fleet of cars, a bailout of the pork industry (how appropriate), tens of billions for new labor union jobs. Oh, and then there were billions more for the Washington zoo, a mouse eradication project in Nancy Pelosi's district, food stamps for illegal immigrants and college students, and money for electric car companies that have almost all subsequently declared bankruptcy. What an "investment."

The stimulus spending was supposed to be for roads and bridges and other "shovel-ready infrastructure." But only 15 percent of the money was for such brick-and-mortar projects. Most of the rest of the money lined the pockets of the groups that made the 2008 election possible.

The government sprang back to life and Washington got rich. Government spending as a share of GDP soared from 21 to 24.5 percent of GDP. Some agencies saw their budgets double. It was manna from heaven.

The height of the folly came with the Obama administration's Cash for Clunkers program, which paid Americans $3,000–$4,000 to trade in their old cars and buy a new car with better gas mileage. The program of free money for clunkers was wildly popular as Americans rushed to new car showrooms to get their check for often ten times the trade-in value of their car.

Of course, destroying hundreds of thousands of cars so people will buy new cars is as economically illiterate as paying Americans to burn down their houses so that construction crews can be put to work building new ones. The logical fallacy here was exposed in Henry Hazlitt's unforgettable book, *Economics in One Lesson.* Hazlitt reminded Americans that there is no wealth created by taking rocks and sledgehammers and breaking the windows of every building, so as to put people to work building new ones. But in the first years under Obama, all economic logic was tossed aside.

The 2009 economic stimulus was the biggest Keynesian spending and borrowing binge in modern times—Keynesian economics on steroids. But it produced anemic results; the economy performed worse in 2009, 2010, and 2011 than it would have if the government had done nothing at all! This is not *our* conclusion. This is based on the Obama administration's *own* numbers from 2009. Amazingly, the unemployment rate was higher every year with the stimulus spending than Obama's economist told us it would be without the stimulus. Trillions of dollars were spent and borrowed only to make the economy perform worse than if left to its own devices.

One excuse for these failed results came from Paul Krugman of the *New York Times*, who argued that the unemployment rate stayed at record-high levels because we didn't do enough stimulus spending and borrowing.[5] Five trillion of debt apparently wasn't enough; we should have borrowed $10 trillion, Krugman and many others advised. Scary stuff.

Harvard economist Robert Barro has ridiculed the Krugman pathology: "Every time heightened fiscal deficits fail, the policy advice is to choose still larger deficits." He concluded, "The results from following this policy advice are persistently lower growth and an exploding ratio of public debt to GDP."[6] Think Greece or Puerto Rico.

THE WORST RECOVERY SINCE THE GREAT DEPRESSION

The economy did start to get better and jobs mercifully started to reappear by 2011 (after nearly all the money was spent), but it was a turtle-paced recovery.

In 2014 we published a highly publicized study, called "Obamanomics Versus Reaganomics," that was summarized in the *Wall Street Journal* and which found that the recovery from the recession under Obama was the weakest in modern times. Worse, median family incomes continued to fall through 2014—five years after the recession began. The trajectory of the Obama recovery was far from the historical norm.

Democrats used to disparage the Reagan expansion as nothing special, but we found that the average annual growth rate from the end of the recession under Reagan was 4.7 percent, versus 2 percent under Obama.

How much does this matter? If we had grown at just an average pace of recovery, GDP in 2015 would have been about $2 trillion higher. If we had performed under Obama as the national economy had during the Reagan recovery, growth would have been almost $3 trillion higher. This growth deficit is the combined annual output of Michigan, Ohio, and Pennsylvania.

It is certainly true that every recession is different in cause and severity. But the comparison between Reagan and Obama is instructive for two reasons. First, they both inherited the worst economic conditions since the Great Depression. When Reagan was inaugurated, the economy was

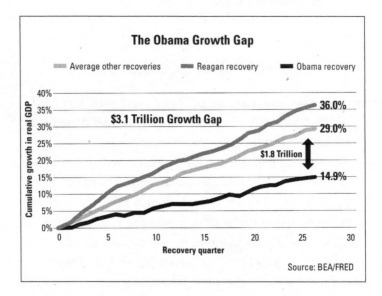

Source: BEA/FRED

crippled by stagflation—high unemployment and high inflation giving the nation a "misery" index of nearly 20 percent.
The stock market had lost more than half its value relative to
inflation in the previous dozen years. Obama also inherited
a severe financial crisis that had thrown 7 million Americans
into unemployment lines and crashed the stock market and
the housing market.

THE MISSING $3,300 PER PERSON

In 2015 the Joint Economic Committee (JEC) of Congress
dug deeper into the numbers to determine how the weak
Obama recovery was affecting average families. It examined
GDP growth on a per capita basis. The Reagan recovery was
abnormally strong in part because it occurred as millions
of baby boomers were swept into the workforce, adding to
job growth. But even on a per capita basis, under President
Obama real GDP grew only 9.0 percent, versus 18.8 percent
during the average recovery. That is the lowest of any post-
1960 recovery.

The committee also found that 95 million people in
America over the age of 16 weren't in the labor force. The unemployment rate fell impressively in Obama's second term,
but much of this decline was a result of millions of Americans dropping out of the workforce—and not just older retir-
ees. (This continues to be a major problem for the economy
under Trump.)

With fewer people working, the workweek shrinking
(thanks to the huge rise in part-time employment), and economic growth atypically low, incomes weren't growing.

That's the real sorry story of the Obama era. If the
Obama recovery had been just average, the JEC calculated

that "after-tax per person income (in 2015) would be $3,339 (2009$) per year higher." Americans were hungry for a change in direction in 2016, we submit, because they were feeling the impact of the slow-growth economy right smack in the wallet.

The JEC's dreary conclusion summarizes the real legacy of Obamanomics: "On economic growth the Obama recovery ranks dead last."

PUNISHING WORK AND REWARDING WELFARE

One reason for the anemic recovery was that Obama failed to get Americans quickly off welfare and into work. It's very simple: you can't improve your economic lot in life if you are on the government dole and not earning a paycheck and building useful skills. Obama regularly boasted about how many people were being helped by Medicaid, food stamps, and unemployment benefits. Obama's welfare agencies ran TV and radio ads (with taxpayer dollars) urging people to sign up for food stamps, Medicaid, Obamacare, and other federal welfare programs. They told Americans not to feel "shame" for signing up for welfare. In many cities food stamps were so widely available they became almost a second currency. We opened this chapter with then–House Speaker Nancy Pelosi's nutty belief that food stamps were an economic stimulus—and there were several economics professors who backed her up on this. If that was true, we should have really stimulated the economy by letting in millions of illegal immigrants and putting them on food stamps too.

It was sad to us how far from economic sensibility the Democratic Party had strayed. Bill Clinton took a bow for getting millions of Americans *off* welfare, while the Obama administration crowed about how many people they put *on* welfare. By the end of the Obama presidency, the number of people on welfare exploded and hardly came down at all during the recovery.

Casey Mulligan, an economist at the University of Chicago, found that the size of these benefits was so large that poor households had very little incentive to find a job.[7] In many cases the poor could lose as much as 50 cents of welfare benefits for every dollar they earned from a paycheck. Welfare could pay the equivalent of a $40,000-a-year job, according to the Cato Institute.[8] Why work? And lo, big surprise that people who had lost jobs didn't rush back into the workforce.

Just as the benefits for not working were raised, the cost of working, investing, and operating a business rose. Obama raised tax rates on businesses and investors (in the name of fairness), and this too poured cold water on the recovery. The capital gains tax that Obama had promised to raise back to the Clinton-era rate of 20 percent instead soared from 15 to almost 24 percent, a 60 percent tax hike on investment. The rate of new business start-ups crashed and more businesses were failing than getting off the ground. Firms were terrified of the next shoe to drop on their head under Obama's anti-business climate. Business investment was shockingly weak in the Obama years. If you tax something, you get less of it.

MINORITIES AND WOMEN HURT THE MOST

Don't forget that as part of this parade of liberal experiments, there were also three minimum-wage increases from 2007 to 2009. Well intentioned? Maybe. But these came at the absolute worst time—when the economy was already contracting.

The black teenage unemployment rate surged to 30 percent in 2011 as unskilled workers were priced out of the labor force and start-up jobs dried up. Our analysis showed that the black teenage labor force participation rate had fallen to an all-time low by March 2009. (Under Trump in 2018, total black labor force participation has risen to pre-Obama levels and black unemployment has fallen to a 46-year low. And yet Trump is accused of being a racist.)

In Obama's last year in office, the Congressional Budget Office released a stunning and depressing report on the status of black youths in America. It found that in 2014, nearly one in six American men between the ages of 18 and 34 was jobless or incarcerated, up from about one in ten in 1980. It was even worse for young black men, among whom nearly one in three was jobless or incarcerated. The CBO suggested several reasons for the significant increase in the number of jobless young men, including numerous state and local minimum-wage increases that raised the costs of hiring and means-tested welfare programs that discouraged young men from working.[9]

Under Obama, poor single women and minorities fell behind the most. According to Sentier Research, single women, with and without children, saw their incomes fall by roughly 5 percent in the five years following the end of the Great Recession in 2009. Black heads of households saw their income tumble by 7.7 percent, while Hispanic incomes fell 5.6 percent.[10] In other words, many of these groups experienced greater income reductions than the average voter. Happily, incomes rebounded in 2015 and 2016, but not enough to make up for the lost ground.

We shouldn't have been too surprised by this Keynesian "multiplier" experiment yielding unhappy results. The same thing happened in Europe, if anyone was bothering to pay attention. Our own research shows that those nations that doused their domestic economies with the largest Keynesian spending and debt had the slowest recoveries and those that mostly ignored the Keynesian debt and spending prescriptions healed the fastest. Greece was a massive spender and borrower—which only accelerated its tragic fall from grace.

A fair question would be: If things weren't working under Obama, how did he win reelection? First, Americans weren't willing to go to back to the policies of the Republicans, who had flattened the economy in the first place. It didn't help that Mitt Romney was one of the least inspiring presidential candidates in modern times. And second, Obama's 2012 political team, led by the brilliant David Axelrod, did a masterful job of persuading the American people that the disappointing recovery should be blamed on the hangover from the George W. Bush years and not on Obama. Post-election polls found that a large majority of Americans believed that story line, and despite a lackluster economy, he won reelection with 51 percent of the vote—but unlike Reagan, who won 49 states in his 1984 reelection, Obama's vote shrank in 2012 from 2008.

SECULAR STAGNATION

Even throughout Obama's second term, however, the economy continued to sputter, and the "blame Bush" excuse for a slow-growth economy became increasingly unpersuasive. In not one year out of Obama's eight in office did the economy hit 3 percent growth—which is a modest target to begin with. The growth rate in Obama's last year in office fell to 1.5 percent—so there was no acceleration, but deceleration when Obama exited stage left.

One standard explanation for the underperforming recovery was to cite a study by Carmen Reinhart and Kenneth Rogoff of recessions and depressions the world over, which concluded that when nations suffer a financial collapse like the U.S. banking system faced in 2008, it takes a decade or more to recover fully.

The problem with this explanation is how does it explain the Reagan boom? Reagan inherited one of the greatest financial crises, with massive inflation and high interest rates that had tanked the stock market by 60 percent in real terms in the prior 15 years. Economists like Nobel Prize winner Paul Samuelson had predicted it would take eight years to end the inflation plague. Reagan and Paul Volcker, the Fed chairman at the time, squashed inflation in 18 months, and the economy healed in two years—not a decade.

Another popular excuse for the feeble economy was popularized by former Obama chief economist Larry Summers, who theorized at the end of 2013 that America was suffering from what he called "secular stagnation."[11] This was a fancy way of saying that the economy can't grow faster than 2 percent anymore no matter what we do.

This was almost a laughable claim, because Larry Summers and other Obama economists were the same people who told us that 4 percent growth was easily achievable in the early Obama years.

Every one of the first six Obama economic forecasts predicted between 3.4 and 4.5 percent annual growth as a result of Obama policies. Year after year, they told us to expect robust growth. Joe Biden ran around the country on a "Recovery Summer" tour. By the end of the Obama administration, we were still waiting.

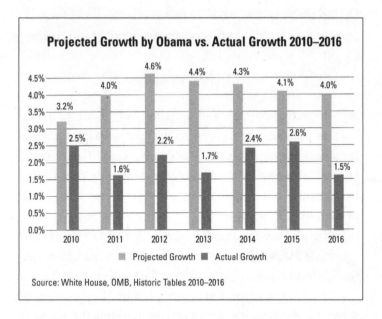

Projected Growth by Obama vs. Actual Growth 2010–2016

Source: White House, OMB, Historic Tables 2010–2016

Reality check: we *never* once got growth above 3 percent under Obama, and the average growth was 2 percent. So the economy performed at about half as well under Obama as we were promised. It is rich for these folks to then say that 2 percent was the best the nation could do. We told Trump over and over, "Sir, this is the best *they* can do. You can do much better with the right policies."

The left's computer models defied common sense. They told us that tax increases would create 4 percent growth, but tax cuts can't get us to 3 percent growth. No wonder they call economics the dismal science.

If the economy *had* grown at the rate Obama predicted, our national debt over a decade would have been about $5 trillion *lower*. Oh, and the 3 percent growth that they said was an impossible goal in 2016? Trump got us just about there (2.9 percent in Q4–2017) in the fourth quarter of his presidency!

FREE LUNCH ECONOMICS

So here were the simple and unhappy facts: Even with more than $4 trillion of debt spending in three years, by early 2011 the unemployment rate still stood at 9 percent. Counting the number of Americans who were working only part-time or had recently given up looking for work, it was still near 15 percent (the U6 number).[12]

Why did the Economic Recovery Act and so many other Obama initiatives fall on their faces so miserably? How were we able to so accurately predict that the model wouldn't work?

Because the entire Keynesian premise that government spending on make-work projects will spring the economy back on its feet again was highly suspect theoretically and historically incorrect. It didn't work in the 1930s for FDR; it didn't work in the 1970s for Nixon, Ford, or Carter; it didn't work for Japan in the 1990s; it hasn't worked anywhere at any time as far as we can see.

Keynesian economics has survived, despite the lack of empirical support, because the theory created a new role for politicians and the economists who would advise them. The Keynesian theory, in a nutshell, says that the government has a duty to smooth out the business cycle, and politicians are more than eager to claim the role of economic arbiter. It's great campaign material, after all. The reason for the repeated failures is, as our late, great friend Milton Friedman taught us all: there ain't no such thing as a free lunch.

The money the government hands out has to come from somewhere. Government obtains dollars to spend in three ways: taxing, printing money, or borrowing. And each of those options for getting money to spend has negative consequences that often outweigh the positive consequences of the government spending.

First, the government can raise taxes to spend the money. This means that $1 is taken from a productive worker (Mary) who earned the money with her hard work and is given to people (Jane) who didn't earn the money. So here the net effect of the redistribution scheme is negative: our own research shows there is a 20–40-cents-per-dollar deadweight cost to the economy of collecting taxes. So yes, Jane may spend that money at McDonald's or Walmart to create a multiplier effect. But it costs Mary $1.20 to earn the money to give it to the tax man—and she may just give up working and get in line for the handout with Jane.

Another option is for the government to print the dollars. But printing paper money only reduces the value of all other dollars. In other words, if the government were to magically double the supply of money, the value of every dollar would be half what it was before. If printing money made nations rich, then Argentina, Bolivia, and Mexico would be rolling in prosperity.

THE DEBT BOMB

Finally, Congress can finance government spending by borrowing the money—as Bush and Obama did to the tune of $10 trillion. That may sound like a free lunch, but someone has to buy the bonds that the government issues so that the money can be spent. So every dollar the government borrows and spends is taken out of the economy from the person who buys the bonds. (Yes, it's true that about half of those bonds are bought by foreigners, but there are costs associated with foreign ownership of debt as well that may even be worse.) So at best the net effect of borrowing on stimulating the economy is zero.

Obama ran deficits as high as $1.5 trillion and almost 10 percent of GDP. These debts have to be repaid by taxpayers in the future. To millions of Americans, this isn't just an economic issue, but a moral one as well. It turns out that both parties like to spend and borrow. Trump is now running deficits near $1 trillion a year that were largely inherited from Bush and Obama—but there is no plan to control spending to get these deficits down. Liberals who had no problem with Obama's trillion-dollar deficits are complaining mightily. And vice versa for the Republicans who hated the Obama deficits, but are now doing the same.

Our view about the impact of debt and deficits doesn't fit in the conservative or liberal basket. We are not opposed to debt per se. As Larry would say to Trump on several occasions, perhaps with a little exaggeration: "This country was built on debt." But Trump, the self-described "king of debt," understood what he meant by that.

If the debt is used to finance growth, then it can make sense and the borrowing can benefit future generations. Ronald Reagan tripled the national debt in the 1980s. But that debt accomplished two missions of spectacular long-term consequence. First, the borrowing helped finance the Cold War military buildup that defeated the Soviet Evil Empire and helped liberate the world from communist tyranny. Second, the debt financed tax rate reductions, which helped rebuild the U.S. economy after the dreadful stagflationary 1970s. The debt rose by $2 trillion, but national wealth increased by at least $8 trillion.

This was a debt that was well worth the cost many times over, just as the borrowing to win World War II was obviously a good use of money.

Which brings us to the $10 trillion of debt under the Bush and Obama administrations. Was that worth it? Our argument is a definitive no.

At the end of the day, what do we as a nation have to show for the $10 trillion of borrowing? Not much. We didn't build the interstate highway system, we didn't put a man on the moon, we didn't win the Cold War, and we didn't supercharge the economy. Instead we put people on food stamps, Medicaid, and disability, created a ruinous health insurance system, and poured money into failed green energy programs. Amazingly, we borrowed $10 trillion and the state of our military was in worse shape in 2016 than it was a decade earlier.

Will Obama's debt exact a cost on future generations? We will let then-senator Barack Obama answer that question. This is the almost poetic oration from the newly elected Senate superstar in a 2006 speech on the Senate floor about the perils of raising the debt ceiling and a nation that does not pay its bills:

> Mr. President, I rise today to talk about America's debt problem. The fact that we are here today to debate raising America's debt limit is a sign of leadership failure. It is a sign that the U.S. government can't pay its own bills.
>
> It is a sign that we now depend on ongoing financial assistance from foreign countries to finance our government's reckless fiscal policies. Over the past five years, our federal debt has increased by $3.5 trillion to $8.6 trillion. That is "trillion" with a "T."

That is more money to pay interest on our debt this year than we will spend on education, homeland security, transportation and veterans benefits combined. It is more money in one year than we are likely to spend to rebuild the devastated Gulf Coast in a way that honors the best of America. And the cost of our debt is one of the fastest-growing expenses in the federal budget.

This rising debt is a hidden domestic enemy, robbing our cities and states of critical investments in infrastructure like bridges, ports and levees; robbing our families and our children of critical investments in education and health-care reform; robbing our seniors of the retirement and health security they have counted on.[13]

THE UNAFFORDABLE CARE ACT

Finally, we must address the impact of what Obama believes was his greatest accomplishment, the Affordable Care Act, or Obamacare.

The ACA was signed into law by President Obama after it was rammed through Congress without a single Republican vote in the House and the Senate. Obama was right that there were giant deficiencies and holes in our healthcare system, and we applaud him for the goal of getting millions more Americans insured to cover the cost of healthcare emergencies. But the fundamental flaw of the new law is that it moved more toward government control of healthcare and away from the model of free enterprise, choice, and competition. In every other industry this model leads to lower prices and better services. But we adopt command-and-control when it comes to one of the most important industries of all: medical services. How dumb is that?

We predicted at the time, as most free market economists did, that Obamacare would drive up medical costs, and regrettably we were right. It is true that millions more Americans have health insurance, thanks mostly to dramatic expansions of Medicaid—one of the worst insurance systems in the world. But the costs to the economy and families have been enormous. Consider these healthcare broken promises:

Obamacare was supposed to save the average family $2,500 on insurance costs. Yet in May 2017 the Department of Health and Human Services reported that average health insurance premiums had doubled since 2013. The lowest-costing ACA silver plan cost as much as $33,000 per family in 2017.[14] The national premium increase from 2013 to 2017

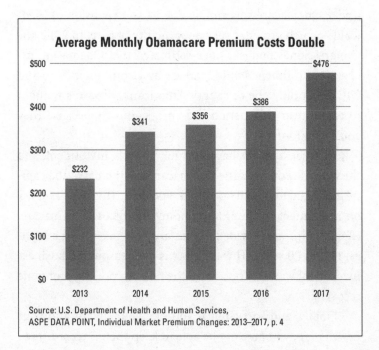

Average Monthly Obamacare Premium Costs Double

Source: U.S. Department of Health and Human Services,
ASPE DATA POINT, Individual Market Premium Changes: 2013–2017, p. 4

was nearly $3,000 per year. In 2018 costs are expected to rise by another 30 percent.[15] One reason average family real wages and salaries didn't budge at all under Obama's presidency is that higher healthcare costs crowded out pay raises.

Obamacare has not "bent the healthcare cost curve down." The year before Obamacare was fully implemented, healthcare amounted to 17.2 percent of U.S. GDP. Last year that tab grew to 18.3 percent—an increase of almost $200 billion in health spending. And the latest forecast for 2025 is that healthcare spending will reach almost 20 percent of GDP.

Obamacare has not eliminated the problem of the uninsured. Even with the massive cost of the program, Obamacare will still leave 30 million Americans uninsured in a decade, and that is assuming costs stabilize. Almost 90 percent of the reduction in the number of uninsured Americans under Obamacare was simply due to an expansion of Medicaid—which provides very poor quality of care. In 2012, the Congressional Budget Office estimated that Obamacare exchange enrollment would increase by 11 million in 2016 and 2017.[16] But only one of twenty Americans who were thought to enroll over that period did enroll—mostly because they couldn't afford it.

Obamacare taxes have hurt job growth, investment, and the overall economy. The Obamacare law increased the capital gains and dividend taxes by 3.8 percent. This is a direct tax on investment in the U.S. economy. Thanks to Obamacare, capital gains and dividend taxes are now taxed at the highest rate in 20 years. This high tax is one reason that business investment was only one-third the rate of a normal economic recovery.

Finally, and sorry, but if you like your doctor and your health plan, you may not be able to keep them. According to federal and state data of insurer exchange options per county, over 50 percent of our nation's towns have only one insurer in 2018. Over 30 percent of additional counties are limited to two insurers. This means that four of five counties will have either just one or two insurers to choose from. So much for choice and competition.

Other than that, Obamacare is a fabulous success.

In private, liberals whom we have met with and who were involved with drafting the Obamacare lemon admit that the system was always structurally deficient and would fall apart over time. Their plan was to fix the bill later, just as Democrats were going to read the bill after they passed it. Our prediction is that the inevitable Obamacare death spiral—with sick people signing up for coverage and healthy people dropping out—will continue to drive insurance costs up and millions more Americans out of the health insurance market altogether.

The critical choice in front of us is whether Trump can save healthcare with free market and consumer choice reforms before Bernie Sanders can achieve his dream (shared by most congressional Democrats) to drive all Americans into a single-payer health insurance system run by the government.

RISING DESPAIR

One other factor has been underappreciated when it comes to the voter disfavor with the Bush and Obama years: despair. Among other factors, the collapse of economic opportunities and the stall in upward mobility—which had been hallmarks of the U.S. economy in the 1980s and '90s—have been taking a heavy toll.

In 2015 a major, jaw-dropping report by Princeton University's Anne Case and Angus Deaton found, "Middle-aged white Americans are dying younger for the first time in decades, despite positive life expectancy trends in other wealthy countries and other segments of the US population."[17] The rise in mortality rates was especially acute for those with lower education levels. This reversed a century of progress that, among others, Steve and Julian Simon had documented in their book *It's Getting Better All the Time*. That book highlighted the stunning improvement in incomes, health, wealth, nutrition, and living standards throughout the twentieth century.

Especially disturbing was the finding by the Princeton scholars that a major factor behind the higher death rates was a surge in "deaths of despair—alcohol, drug overdoses, and suicide." As an aside, the statistics are a little skewed here because death rates from smoking (also a drug of despair) have fallen dramatically, and that is not accounted for in this study. What is undeniable is that these death rates have nearly doubled in a little less than 15 years.

Among the factors responsible for the disturbing trend are "worsening job prospects over the past several decades, the decline of stable marriages and family life, and a rise in bad health habits, such as obesity." As Deaton and Case concluded: "To manage their despair about the gap between their hopes and what's come of their lives, they've often turned to drugs, alcohol, and suicide."

Our point isn't to blame Bush and Obama for the rise in despair. But it is to note that the economic stagnation we saw for the middle class between 2000 and 2015 exacted a heavy toll. Money can't buy love or happiness—that's for sure. But when the tide isn't raising boats, many are pushed underwater—into bankruptcy, loss of self-respect, a feeling of worthlessness, idleness, a sense of not being loved (tied to divorce and family breakup). This is one of the reasons that we (and Trump, we believe) feel so passionately that government assistance cannot become a way of life and that work requirements are critically important—not so much for the taxpayers, but for the recipients themselves.

Obama promised hope and change, and sadly, many millions of Americans by the end of his two terms in office were feeling hopeless and powerless to change things.

This perhaps in a small way explains why so many elites were clueless about why the half of America that they didn't recognize or come in contact with wanted a radical change in direction in 2016. It helps explain the roots of the Trump phenomenon and the allure of his pitch to "Make America Great Again."

Trump has launched a major program around the country to reduce the opioid addiction epidemic, and we hope it works. But better job opportunities and less financial stress on middle-class families can't help but replace despair with real hope.

TRUMP'S TURN

When Steve worked at the *Wall Street Journal* he used to meet routinely with the men and women who run so many of the great American Fortune 100 companies. Throughout the first five years of the Obama presidency, he would often ask these CEOs: "Your company is profitable, the stock price is doing well, you've got a lot of cash on hand, so why aren't you reinvesting this money into growing your company?"

The answer was almost always the same: that four-letter F word, *fear.* They were worried about what Washington would do next to them. These companies had lived through a machine-gun torrent of policy bullets aimed at their balance sheets. Tax increases. A regulatory assault. Obamacare. Trillions of dollars of increases in government spending and debt. And, then, of course, came the attitude of dripping contempt that Washington held for successful businesses. This was articulated clearly by Barack Obama with his famous declaration that "you didn't build that."

So employers understandably hunkered down. Yes, they came out of the Great Recession with an almost savage obsession with efficiency and profitability. They got better at what they did in an amazingly transformative way. The best-run companies in the world today are generally American firms—and that clearly wasn't the case a decade ago. That's a very good thing that happened in the Obama years.

What made this recovery so continuously disappointing, ending with a turtle-paced 1.5 percent growth in 2016, was what might have been. Companies didn't build new factories or plants or laboratories, they didn't purchase new equipment or invest in computers and other technology. Even Hillary Clinton noted this shortcoming of the recovery. "Businesses have lots of cash," she said, "they just aren't investing it." Instead they sat on the money and bought ten-year Treasury bills at 2 percent interest rates. They bought these bonds even when the real interest rate went negative. That is severe risk aversion. That is fear.

This has been a problem that has paralyzed the economy for almost 15 years. From 1950 to 2000, annual business investment grew at 5.5 percent. From 2000 to 2015, it grew at a meager 2.5 percent. (Thankfully, now investment rates are very healthy again.)

One 2014 study by the National Association of Manufacturers found that on average, regulations cost American steel

producers, car manufacturers, computer makers, construction companies, and so on as much as $18,000 per job.[18] Is it
any surprise that the companies hopscotch over to Canada,
Mexico, or China? They could easily save $10,000 per worker
just on the easing of regulations.

Here is how one of America's greatest investment gurus,
Stanley Druckenmiller, put it in 2018 in a piece in the *Wall
Street Journal* titled "Where's the Invisible Hand When You
Need It?":

> Statists in America are more impressed by foreign top-
> down designs than with the far superior track record of
> free market capitalism here at home. Capitalism is under
> attack.
>
> For eight years the Obama administration disparaged
> the efficacy and fairness of capitalism. Government's in-
> fluence grew in every aspect of life. The cost of regulations
> doubled, corporate America was attacked to engineer so-
> cial equality, and our healthcare system was made even
> more inefficient.[19]

We will close this chapter with something that Larry
Kudlow said often during the campaign when debating
Obama economists like Austan Goolsbee or Jason Furman:
"We tried it Barack Obama's way for eight years. You gave it
your best effort. You meant well. But it didn't work. Now it's
time to give Trump's ideas a try."

There are no certainties that Trump's policies will turn
the tide. But Trump does have history and economic logic on
his side.

So now let's examine those Trumponomic policies in
some detail.

4

What Is Trumponomics?

"We will defend American jobs. We have to look at it almost like a war."

—Donald Trump, 2015

So just what is Trumponomics all about? Does it have any cohesive theme, or is Trump just making this all up as he goes along?

We wish we had a bitcoin for every time we've been asked that question.

Trump's own answer when we queried him about his economic philosophy was that it all boiled down to this: "I'm not running as a typical Republican. I think there're obvious problems with the way Republicans relate to working-class Americans—which is why they lose and lose." Other times he would simply respond, "Our strategy on the economy is to always put America first."

We are fairly certain that some of this vision for a new economic template for the GOP came from the former Breitbart CEO Steve Bannon. The controversial Bannon wasn't just the campaign CEO over the last months of the campaign, his involvement with Trump came years earlier. There was even talk of getting Trump to run for president in 2012. It's not clear to us whether Bannon had the populist ideas first and sold Trump on them, or whether Trump had cradled these ideas for a long time and finally found an advisor in Bannon who agreed with his predispositions.

What is clear is that from the start of their partnership— such as it was—they were largely of like mind on how to sell the American people and conservatives on a new economic populist paradigm.

At the very least, Bannon shared Trump's world vision from the start, and they both are disruptors. We found Bannon to be more pessimistic and Trump more optimistic about the future. Bannon talked a lot about the "wrecking ball" strategy. Trump talked about building things up. "You've got to understand that the GOP was out of touch with voters almost completely for the past couple of decades," Bannon explained to us during the campaign. "They haven't been addressing a tide of middle-class concerns about trade, immigration, the culture, and expensive and unwinnable wars. Most voters had just completely tuned out both parties. Trump is a nonpolitician who was promising a paradigm shift."

That's the understatement of this still-young century. Trump didn't run as a Milton Friedman–Reagan free marketeer. He is not a libertarian—far from it. He also didn't run as a "kinder and gentler" Bush neocon.

Trump upended two decades of stale Republican dogma with a freshly minted populist agenda. What was shocking was how many millions of independent and Republican voters—and even some populist Democrats—found Trump's approach to economic policy refreshingly attractive or at least worth a try.

THE MAN AND THE MESSAGE

Before we describe the principles of Trumponomics, it is critical to point out that this "populist" agenda—he used to like calling it "popularism"—couldn't have been pulled off by just anyone. The message required the right messenger. What made Trumponomics sell was a brilliant salesman. We have already made note that Trump is arguably the greatest marketer of modern times. This is the key to his success in business. But it is even more so the key to his success in politics.

What made Trump such a natural and believable messenger was that he never hid his wealth and success—instead he wore it as a badge of honor and even flaunted it. He donned beautifully tailored suits. He drove around in limos, hung out in swanky resorts, flew around in his own plane, and built tall buildings. He boasted about his success (many times excessively) with a bravado that was somehow endearing to his voters.

We are convinced that he pulled off the populist message so well because he was the un-politician. Hillary was smooth, brilliant, prepped, and almost infallible in her presentations. Obama too.

Trump talked like a real person at a sports bar or a neighborhood party (we won't say like men in a locker room), not someone programmed with a teleprompter. Hillary was Madison Avenue. Trump was Brooklyn. It was Trump's authentic street fighter persona—which admittedly many Americans found highly off-putting—that was pivotal in selling the populist message. When people ask us what Donald Trump is really like in person, the one word that we found best described him was "authentic." What you see is what you get.

One other thing we firmly believe about Donald Trump—a belief that his voters clearly share—is that he genuinely cares about the middle class and helping them better their lives. Many criticisms of Trump are legitimate. But we never believed for one minute that he was in this to further enrich wealthy people like himself. He already was rich.

THE PRINCIPLES OF TRUMP POPULISM

Now let's get right down to it. Trumponomics revolves around a handful of core principles.

First, always put America first. Reject globalism. This isn't to say that America will not continue to be the most generous and charitable nation in the world when it comes to rushing to the aid of a friend. But it does mean that we will put America's and Americans' interests above those of other nations.

The left snubs its nose at this idea as outdated "nationalism." Wrong. The entire basis of our nation is self-government and consent of the governed. World government and multinational governing bodies are dangerous and misguided solutions. Globalism is out. National greatness is in.

Second, restore American patriotism. Trumponomics is predicated on the core belief in the fundamental greatness and goodness of America. America is a special place, and Trump believes that to his core. To quote Reagan: "Divine providence put us here as a beacon of freedom for the rest of the world."

Many of the leaders of the intellectual left are contemptuous of the idea of American triumphs. Liberals tend to highlight America's failures and shortcomings, not our greatness. There is a subversive "blame America first" attitude about the American experiment—starting at the very birth of the United States. Our founding fathers, for example, are now portrayed as immoral slave owners and patriarchs, not heroes of the world's greatest freedom revolution.

Third, empower Americans to make decisions for themselves. This is a rejection of government paternalism. Relying on the forces of competition and choice will foster better outcomes than rules, regulations, and mandates. People can decide for themselves.

The left has adopted the opposite philosophy: people aren't qualified to make their own decisions about healthcare plans, or schools, or pension investing. It was always disheartening to us that the Trump Cabinet secretary whom the left hated the most was Secretary of Education Betsy DeVos. Her unforgivable sin was a plan to empower minority parents with more options for educating their kids. The left believes that poor parents would make poor choices and that competition would hurt public schools in inner cities—as if they could possibly be any worse.

Fourth, rebuild America's inner cities. This means eradicating crime, violence, drug abuse, corruption, and joblessness. Trump exposed to the American people that liberal governance had failed to keep its promises of helping the poor and distressed communities. Trump has unflinchingly revealed the flaws of liberalism for its failures in cities like Baltimore, Newark, Chicago, Detroit, and Cleveland. He famously asked inner-city audiences—mostly minorities: What have the Democrats in the inner cities done for you and your neighborhoods? The answer was nothing.

One of Trump's big urban initiatives is the designation of 50 enterprise zones—mostly poor areas in inner cities—that will be targeted for lower capital gains taxes, regulatory relief, and the clearing of other barriers to development.

Fifth, secure and protect our borders from drug runners, terrorists, illegal immigrants, and criminals. A nation without borders, Trump said many times, is not a nation. The left's response was sanctuary cities, and charges of racism and xenophobia. The public was with Trump—and they remain so solidly. As a side note, we always urged Trump to talk about high, protective walls, but with big gates for people to enter legally.

Sixth, promote and support American business. Donald Trump is an unapologetically pro-business president—which is a major reason the stock market soared when he won the election. The modern Democratic Party, by contrast, has become reflexively anti-business, in part because of its preoccupation with income inequality. Liberals love jobs, but they hate job creators. As Trump likes to say: you can't have one without the other.

Seventh, reject identity politics. The prevailing liberal mindset is that Americans are inherently divided by race, sexual orientation, ethnicity, and class and that there is a zero-sum game being played among all those divisions. No. We are one nation under God, *indivisible*. Everyone can be better off, and the gain of one person does not necessarily equal the infringement of another. All Americans should be treated as individuals, not members of a class, and should be treated equally under the law regardless of their race, gender, and income status. *E pluribus unum* means "out of many, one," not "out of one, many."

Eighth, reject declinism and celebrate that America's best days lie ahead. This means rejecting the limits to growth, secular stagnation, and the environmental doomsdayism (climate change) that animate the left today. Trumponomics is predicated on a faith in the future and a confidence that America can solve any problem through innovation, invention, technology, and a healthy dose of just plain American can-doism. To quote John Lennon in "Mind Games": "Yes is the answer." The solutions to the social, economic, and environmental threats and challenges that will confront our society in the future—from poverty to addiction to cancer—are solvable in the next generation, if not sooner.

Ninth, America's most valuable role in the global economy is to lead by example. Our most important gift to the world is to export the virtues of democratic capitalism and free enterprise. When we get it right, the rest of the world follows. Trump often said, "Strong at home, strong abroad," and that was almost a duplication of a core Ronald Reagan belief.

The spread of freedom and economic liberalism across the globe in the 1980s and 1990s happened in no small part because nations started to emulate the Reaganomics formula for growth. When we cut taxes, the world started cutting taxes. When we deregulated and privatized, the world followed our lead. When we stabilized and strengthened the dollar, other nations got control of inflation as well—many times by linking to the dollar.

Trump is right that the best way to promote prosperity abroad is to fix America's problems first. Then we can serve as a beacon of freedom and opportunity for nations around the globe. If we lead, the rest of the world will follow.

FINALLY, GROWTH, GROWTH, GROWTH

The final and we would argue the most important principle of Trumponomics and restoring American prosperity is this:

Growth is everything. Faster economic growth is a necessity if America is to fix its socioeconomic problems.

As a White House bulletin put it in early 2017: "Over the next 10 years, 3% growth instead of 2% will yield a nominal gross domestic product that is $16 trillion larger, federal government revenues $2.9 trillion greater, and wages and salaries of American workers $7 trillion higher."[1] The good news is that at the time of this writing, the economy has already posted quarters with annualized growth as high as 3.2 percent—much higher than the 1.5 percent growth in Obama's last year in office.

While the left is more obsessed with income inequality, the way the economic pie is divided, Trump's view is the bigger pie gives everyone a bigger slice. The left's response to the roaring stock market under Trump in 2017 was that since 1 percent of Americans own over half of the stocks, only the rich will benefit. Our view is that a more prosperous and financially secure nation is better for everyone—including the 100-million-plus Americans who own stock through pension and 401(k) plans.

One underappreciated dividend from this higher permanent pedestal of economic growth is that, if Trump succeeds, it will help largely solve the long-term funding crisis of Social Security and Medicare. With 3 percent economic growth, up from the 1.8 percent predicted by the Social Security and Medicare actuaries, the compounding effect over 50 years means more than $50 trillion of revenues into the Medicare and Social Security trust funds, largely dissolving the funding shortfalls of these programs—and perhaps leaving them in long-term surplus, not deficit.

TRUMPONOMICS IN ACTION

Now we have to address the issue: How do these Trumponomics principles translate into real-world policy solutions? We have had many discussions with Donald Trump on this front over the past two years. In some cases, we've helped steer his thinking on these policy directives.

Another highly influential voice in defining Trumponomics in action has been Mick Mulvaney, the hyperactive (in a good way) former GOP congressman from South Carolina and Trump Office of Management and Budget (OMB) director. We met regularly with Mulvaney during the transition period and early months of the new administration, as he constructed Trump's first two federal budget requests from Congress. Mulvaney has been one of Trump's shining lights in the Cabinet when it comes to promoting sound economic policy ideas.

We have always liked the way Mulvaney outlined what he calls MAGAnomics, which is shorthand for Make America Great Again economics. So we will borrow liberally here from Mulvaney's formulation, with a few of our own additions and refinements.

1. Cut unnecessary regulations

Rolling back unnecessarily burdensome regulations means lower costs to businesses and consumers. As we describe in Chapter Six, the regulatory beast had become one of the greatest deterrents to investment here in America and a faster pace of job creation. As Mulvaney puts it: "Requiring realistic and fact-based cost-benefit analyses of regulations will help protect both the environment and American jobs." For example, the Environmental Protection Agency (EPA) found that the benefits of the Clean Air Act regulation exceeded the costs by a factor of 30 to 1.[2]

The World Bank says the United States ranks number eight in the world in having a sound regulatory environment. Trump wants to get to number one.

2. Improve American competitiveness by slashing tax rates and burdens

Lower tax rates—as JFK, Reagan, and others have proven throughout history—lead to more growth, more investment, and more jobs. Trump always saw this through the lens of American competitiveness. "We have put our businesses in a deep hole. I want us to have the tax advantage, and for America to go from worst to first on tax competitiveness." He scoffed at the left's notion that taxes don't impact behavior. "Taxes had a big impact on every economic decision I've made," he told us early on.

He wasn't alone. For decades, growth in private-sector jobs and wages has correlated with growth in private business investment. When businesses invest in new plants and equipment, they tend to hire more people, who produce more and get paid more.

3. Replace welfare with work

Growth will require more able-bodied Americans getting off welfare and into jobs. Although the labor pool is aging, we are also seeing people who could be working but are staying home.[3] Welfare payments can often exceed in generosity the take-home pay from most starter jobs—and that isn't fair to those who do work for low wages, for taxpayers, or for the long-term economic mobility of those who could be working. In some states like Hawaii, a full welfare package could give a family the post-tax equivalent of a $50,000-a-year salaried job, according to a 2014 Cato Institute study.[4] Welfare—which includes cash assistance, public housing, food stamps, disability payments, unemployment benefits, and Medicaid—needs to be a hand up, not a handout.

4. Use America's abundant natural resources

America has well more than $50 trillion of natural resources that are accessible with existing drilling and mining technologies. This is a vast storehouse of wealth that far surpasses what any other nation is endowed with. We are not running out of these resources, and the technology to discover them and put them to use for American industry and consumers—such as fracking and horizontal drilling—continues to improve rapidly over time, which means these resources are for all intents and purposes inexhaustible. We can access hundreds of years' worth of these resources—minerals, rare earth metals, oil, gas, coal, timber—*with existing technology.*

Using our natural resources enriches the United States in every way. It increases our national output by tens of trillions of dollars over time; it raises trillions of dollars of income tax revenues and lease and royalty payments—for the federal government and the states; it enhances our national security by making us less dependent on the Middle East, Russia, China, and other bad actors across the globe; and it can create millions of high-paying jobs for American workers. The left's philosophy is "keep it in the ground," while ours is drill, mine, and recover resources to help make the United States the world's preeminent natural resource powerhouse.

The Trump White House says that "cheaper, cleaner, more abundant energy will increase investment and employment across dozens of industries, from chemicals to automobiles. By ensuring reliable supplies and stable prices, the president's energy plan will reduce uncertainty, especially in the manufacturing sector, thereby reducing the risks associated with building new plants in America." Trump is exactly right.

5. Modernize America's infrastructure

Trump has called for $1–2 trillion in added infrastructure spending. But he isn't talking about traditional and expensive make-work, "shovel-ready projects" that aren't valuable to Americans over time. He wants to leverage private and state dollars to rebuild our traditional public infrastructure—including roads, bridges, schools, airports, and ports.

We often advised Trump that America's most important infrastructure needs are private—factories, warehouses, research centers, office complexes, laboratories, and so on. Those are largely incentivized by the Trump tax cut and the immediate capital expensing of improvements to these facilities that are privately owned and operated. We also need a new generation of twenty-first-century infrastructure that is public in benefit, but can and should be privately operated. We are talking about pipelines, liquefied natural gas (LNG) terminals, energy refineries, airports, the electric grid system, broadband development, satellites, space rockets, and so on. By simply deregulating these areas, Trump envisions a future with American investment exploding, with few taxpayer dollars necessary. Look at what Space X is doing with private rocket launches as a prototype for what the private sector can do in infrastructure in dozens of other areas.

6. Encourage twenty-first-century healthcare and education based on choice and competition

No modern policy failure highlights the failure of one-size-fits-all government policy more than the bankrupting Obamacare program. Obamacare denies patients the ability to tap into two forces that work to improve products and lower costs in other industries: choice and competition.

Compare this situation with the response to the crisis in 2017 at Facebook, which has promised to change its behavior regarding privacy and content controls, once its customers learned of its misbehavior. Facebook must change its practices, or it risks losing tens of millions of customers who can scramble to find other social network platforms. Consumer power works.

But in healthcare and education, the model is driven by monopolistic structures that are costly, bureaucratic, customer-unfriendly, and molasses-slow to innovate. These two industries have experienced by far the largest increases in prices over the last two decades. In education, more spending has led to flat results. That would never be tolerated in a model that forced schools to compete. Trump wants a competition model in healthcare and education that will revolutionize how we get our healthcare and how we choose our schools. At the time of this writing he has suggested allowing Americans to shop around for very low-priced health insurance packages that will save their families up to 50 percent on insurance costs. Needless to say, the bureaucracy and incumbent powers are putting up mighty resistance.

7. Promote free and fair trade deals

Trump believes that the United States is frequently abused when it comes to international trade deals. He has called

NAFTA the "worst trade deal in the history of the world" and pulled the United States out of the multilateral Asian trade pact known as TPP. He wants renegotiated trade relationships—especially with China—in order to stop cheating, stealing, and other misbehavior by trading partners. The Trump administration estimates $600 billion of intellectual property is stolen each year by our trading partners through nonpayment for use of our computer software, drugs, vaccines, technological innovations, patents, trademarks, entertainment, music, and so on. His Council of Economic Advisers reported in 2017 that most other nations have trade barriers "and nontariff tariffs" that block American companies' access to foreign markets. The latest Global Trade Alert report said that there were 2,420 protectionist measures in effect that harm U.S. commercial interests at the end of last year.[5]

Trump is banking on the threat of tariffs and other penalties against our trading partners to reduce IP theft and force nations like Japan and China to open up their markets. It is a dangerous game, and it is a highly unconventional approach to trade policy. Some indications that nations like China and South Korea are willing to further open up their markets to American firms suggest that Trump's trade confrontations could end up enhancing the volume of American international trade rather than impeding it.

8. Reduce government spending

Trump promised on the campaign trail that he would cut government spending and balance the budget. It's a good goal. Milton Friedman taught us that the real "tax" on American businesses and families is the amount the government spends, not the amount it taxes. This is because at some point, all government spending has to be paid for one way or another.

Trump's first two budgets requested a massive downsizing of government with the cancellation of dozens of spending programs that are no longer necessary or cost-effective, if they ever were. Trump also endorsed the "Penny Plan": cut one cent of spending for every dollar an agency receives for each of five years. After a decade, this simple formula would balance the budget. But the reality so far is that Trump has signed two budgets that have inflated debt spending as a means to rebuild the U.S. military budget. "When government spends a lot," Mulvaney says, "it takes money away from private investment. And private investment is always a more efficient allocator of capital than government." Unfortunately, so far Trump's goals of spending restraint have been ignored by Congress.

9. Implement a pro-America immigration policy

Overshadowed by Trump's call for "the wall" and some cuts in our family-based immigration system has been his call for a "merit-based immigration system." This visa system would select immigrants based on their skills, talents, investment capital, English-language ability, and education level. These characteristics all presage success in America. We used to tell Trump that these immigrants are very desirable because they are the world's "brainiacs."

Given that almost all international migrants want to choose the United States as their destination, this new merit system could create dozens of new Silicon Valley tech centers across the country, giving the United States a giant advantage over China, Germany, Canada, and other nations that want to challenge American economic and industrial superiority. These immigrants are more likely than American-born citizens to create new businesses, new patents, and new American-made consumer products. The United States would still allow immediate family members—spouses and children—to gain visas, but most others would be chosen based on how they will benefit the United States.

One potential problem is that Trump wants to (unwisely in our opinion) reduce the total *number* of visas awarded each year at a time when more young foreign-born workers are necessary to cover the costs of our aging population in the United States.

CAN IT WORK?

So far, Trumponomics has encountered ferocious resistance by the left. This is apparent nearly every day. Let's face it: the philosophy of Trumponomics assaults the basic framework of command-and-control policies, globalism, the righteousness of the political class, and the victimization thesis of modern-day liberalism.

For example, a core tenet of modern-day liberalism is the victimization narrative. In short, this narrative says that women, blacks, Hispanics, immigrants, inner-city residents, and the disabled can't get ahead in America because of discrimination, a lack of opportunity, or other insurmountable barriers to success. While there is certainly some truth to this, it has become in too many cases a self-fulfilling excuse factory for people to fail or, worse, not to try at all.

We have found ourselves in general agreement with most principles of Trumpism. On immigration and trade, we are more in favor of expansion rather than restriction. As advisors to Trump, we have always felt it is vitally important to tell him (mostly in private) when we thought he was right and wrong. In some cases, we have publicly criticized Trump's policies. He wasn't happy when we argued on TV and in print against his steel tariffs in early 2018. We also tried to persuade him to veto the 2018 omnibus spending bill—which we regarded as obese and economically unwise. He has told us subsequently that he wishes he'd taken our advice on that spending bill.

But on the big-picture priorities, it was our belief, and remains so today, that Trump had the right political and economic take on what was wrong with America and how to fix it. Trumponomics was the right game plan and Trump was the right man to sell it.

In the chapters ahead, we describe how Trump implemented these daring policies and how it has worked out—so far.

5

Designing the Trump Tax Plan

I want this to be bigger and more beautiful than Reagan's tax cut. The biggest ever. Can you guys help me do that?"

These were practically the first words that Donald Trump said to us when we sat down with him at our first formal policy briefing in Trump Tower in March 2016. At that meeting were Steve, Larry, and Stephen Miller, then the campaign policy director for Candidate Trump. While Arthur was not present, Trump had said the same exact thing when the two met earlier in the year.

Donald Trump himself was in a jubilant mood at that meeting. He was relaxed and super-confident. For a very good reason: he was on a political roll. He had just won the Florida primary. That victory was a virtual knockout punch to two of his rivals for the GOP nomination: Jeb Bush and Marco Rubio. Both of these men hailed from Florida. Trump had routed two of his most formidable adversaries on their home turf.

Things weren't going well for the Democrats, either. Hillary Clinton found herself in a knock-down drag-out fight with a U.S. senator from Vermont, Bernie Sanders. Sanders was punching Hillary hard on her ties to rich Wall Streeters, the suspicion of corruption during the Clinton presidency, and her own support, as U.S. senator, for the Iraq War.

These were many of the same attacks that GOP nominee Donald Trump would use against Hillary. What was even worse for the Democrats' electoral prospects? The economy was tanking again. The economic growth rate in this election year was barely above 1 percent. Job creation was mediocre. The percentage of the population who desired to work and who could find a job—the "labor force participation rate"—remained woefully low.

Companies were making profits but were sitting on them. Businesses just were not adding capacity. Business confidence was ebbing.

This raised the political stakes for and the urgency of a well-constructed tax plan. We had to make the tax plan both exciting to voters and politically bulletproof from the well-armed critics.

This was especially critical because at the time, even the Republican establishment was treating Donald Trump as a political pariah and searching for reasons to toss him and his upstart voters over the side of the boat in favor of a more conventional and lower-risk party standard-bearer. Everyone we encountered seemed to want Trump to fall flat on his face.

The more primaries Donald Trump put in the win column, the more seriously people were investigating his economic game plan. Many left-leaning economists, whose opinions typically dominate the elite media, were dumping on Trumponomics. Gene Sperling, who had served as the head of the National Economic Council under Bill Clinton and as a campaign advisor to Hillary Clinton, told *Politico* in early May that "this is the most risky, reckless and regressive tax proposal ever put forward by a major presidential candidate."[1]

Even some of the tax experts on the right were making wild charges. Ryan Ellis, who had helped construct the flawed Rubio tax plan, slammed the Trump tax design as a proposal "that drags down the entire effort at conservative tax reform to a circus level." Then he added: "There is no amount of entitlement reform that can pay for that and there is no amount of base broadening that can pay for it."[2]

We too were under increasing attack for being among the first major economic voices to validate Donald Trump's candidacy. As Shane Goldmacher wrote in *Politico* on May 11, 2016: "Kudlow, Laffer and Moore are well known voices in conservative economic circles. . . . The group's imprint could help add credibility on the right to a revised Trump tax plan, after his original proposal came under attack from some Republicans as unrealistically large."[3]

Our primary mission in helping Trump was to hand him a revised plan that was large and pro-growth, but far from "unrealistic."

THE ORIGINS OF THE HISTORIC TAX CUT

Recall that when we arrived on the scene, Trump had only the outline of a plan that he had been citing throughout the early campaign season.

It was a rough sketch—what we described as the first drawing of a grand and audacious architectural design to tear down the 60,000-page tax code edifice and rebuild it with something brand new. All we had to work with at that time was a single-page document with five tax cut initiatives laid out in bullet points. This first plan had been released rather hastily at the end of September 2015.

Trump had shown voters the outline of his big vision of tax reform, appropriate for the early stages of the campaign. At that time voters simply wanted to know from candidates: What direction will you take us? Will my taxes be going up or down?

Let's start, though, with the original plan. Given the historical significance of that original architectural design of a new tax code, it is curious that no one seemed to know for sure where it came from. Trump told us that he "got a lot of the ideas from long conversations with Arthur." Trump had held lengthy discussions with Arthur in the weeks preceding the plan's release.

But just who put those exact bullet points down on paper in that original memo is still a mystery. Roger Stone, an early consultant to Trump, reportedly had a hand in the construction of the memo. So did Corey Lewandowski, then the Trump campaign manager, who had arranged for Trump to get guidance from Arthur, among others. Corey handed the document to Trump for his final stamp of approval.

Another unsung hero here was the brilliant and loyal economic policy analyst for Trump from the very early days in Iowa—Sam Clovis. Clovis played a lead role on everything economic at the start of the campaign and through the primaries—both in formulating and selling these ideas on TV and to the grassroots activists. Sam became a good friend and ally of the three of us, and Trump was smart to have chosen him as his policy director.

So just what was in that original tax memo? There were five recommendations:

1. Anyone who is single and earns less than $25,000 or is married and jointly earns less than $50,000 will not owe any federal income tax. This would remove nearly 50 percent of households in the country from the income tax rolls, quadrupling the standard deduction.

    (Trump joked at a press conference in late 2015 that tax filers would all have to do one thing: "They get a new one-page form to send to the IRS saying, 'I win,'" according to the plan, which was posted on Trump's campaign website.)

2. A "simpler" tax code with but four brackets—0, 10, 20, and 25 percent. Let it be noted that this would reduce the highest tax bracket to the lowest level in living memory.

3. Cut the business tax rate from 35 percent to 15 percent. No business in the United States would pay more than 15 percent of its business income in taxes—from a Fortune 500 to a mom-and-pop shop to a freelancer living job to job.

4. Bring back money that corporations are holding overseas to avoid taxation by imposing a one-time reduced 10 percent tax. That would return an estimated $2.1 trillion to the United States. An immediate tax would be imposed on American companies' overseas earnings—taxes that can currently be deferred.

5. Eliminate the marriage penalty, the alternative minimum tax, and the estate tax.

What was being proposed here was a giant cut in taxes. When the plan's first bare-bones template was unveiled, Trump promised in his typical hypercharged speeches throughout the campaign: "This will simplify the tax code. . . . It will save the average family $1,000 a year. And it'll grow the American economy at a level that it hasn't seen for decades."

He told the press and rally attenders that the plan would not increase the deficit because it would raise growth rates to "3, or 4, 5, or even 6 percent."

It is uncanny how closely Trump's original outline resembled the tax cut that he would sign into law a little over two years later.

Double the standard deduction. Check.

Cut the corporate tax rate. Check.

A 10 percent repatriation tax on foreign earnings. Check.

Simplify by reducing loopholes. Check.

Eliminate the marriage penalty. Check.

THE REFINEMENT

We were impressed with the conciseness and simplicity of what Trump was saying and dedicated ourselves to the task of keeping these original priorities in the 2.0 plan. He seemed to be pushing all the right growth buttons. The design wasn't perfect, but voters liked that Trump was thinking big. Our view was that the economy needed a big boost to get its natural mojo back. The line that we used to use with Trump in our discussions of the plan was "Go big, or go home."

The three of us loved the flat tax that our colleague Steve Forbes had made famous in his own presidential run 20 years before. That said, Trump's plan represented a major positive step toward improving the tax code in ways that would permit the American economy to once again blossom. When Trump's memo came out, we agreed that we should work to help him get elected president, and then to get the tax plan passed into law.

Trump had the right overall strategy, but the plan had no revenue-raising offsets for the tax cuts. What was needed were some base-broadeners to help pay for the rate cuts. We had no doubt that the growth and jobs impact of these cuts would be highly beneficial and could even get the economy to 3 percent growth and maybe 4 percent for a while. But the media and the left-of-center think tanks such as the Tax Policy Center were hammering Trump for a plan that would dramatically increase the federal deficit. Their multi-trillion-dollar estimates were wildly excessive, but the media was reporting them as gospel truth.

Our starting premise, as we reviewed the plan, was to assess what policies would have the most power to push the American economy above a sustained growth rate of 3 percent. This was the goal Trump had been—very correctly—emphasizing on the campaign trail.

Trump gave us fairly wide latitude to refine the tax plan. But right from the start he insisted on maintaining three features of the original plan. He mentioned these as nonnegotiable terms in nearly every meeting with him in those early months.

First, Trump was insistent on the 15 percent corporate rate. "Don't bother to come back and tell me we can't get 15 percent," he would growl. We certainly could live with 15 percent and always remained excited that he wanted America to go from the highest rate in the world to one of the lowest—overnight.

He didn't need our cheerleading on this point. He couldn't be budged and wouldn't listen to naysayers who counseled him that getting that was a political impossibility. This became a running gag we had with Trump after he was elected president: "Remember, Mr. President, no backing off on the 15 percent rate."

He always nodded knowingly and gave the thumbs-up sign.

Second, Trump said that he wanted to make sure that small businesses got the same rate as Fortune 100 corporations. "Small businesses have to be included, guys. Don't take that away." This was a sound policy, but it added immensely to the cost. There are roughly ten times as many small businesses in America as there are corporations.[4] And we were going to sharply cut the small business tax rate for successful companies from 40 percent to about 15 percent.

No other candidate had suggested a tax cut that deep for small so-called pass-through companies. They were called "pass-throughs" because the earnings from the company pass through to the individual owner's tax return and taxes are paid at the rates set by the individual income tax. The corporate income tax applies only to C corporation income. (Of course, when the corporation pays dividends to its owners, those dividends get taxed again at the individual recipient's rate, but that's a separate matter.)

This discussion with Trump only intensified our appreciation for his uncanny political sixth sense about voters. Corporations are not popular with voters. Americans tend to think that corporations are faceless and greedy behemoths. Americans tend to think that CEOs get richer and richer by paying their workers the bare minimum required and cozying up to politicians to get special favors, favors that aren't available to the rest of us. Most Americans weren't convinced that, as the old saying goes, "What's good for GM is good for the country."

American uneasiness with big business was especially intense in the wake of the financial crisis of 2007–09, when corporate misbehavior had driven the American economy into a meltdown. American workers got clobbered—7 million of us lost our jobs. Meanwhile, many of the corporate bad guys got obnoxious golden parachutes and taxpayer bailouts to cushion their fall. We agreed with most Americans: unfair.

At the same time, polls showed unequivocally that most Americans love small business and the little guy taking on the corporate raiders. That's the memorable theme of *It's a Wonderful Life*—the tale of the heroic George Bailey, played by Jimmy Stewart, whose tiny neighborhood Bailey's Building and Loan takes on the villainous Henry F. Potter, whose big bank is trying to swallow up any small competitor that dares compete with him. It is part of our national folklore. It's in America's DNA to admire and cheer for those who risk everything, put out the shingle, and start a small business based on a few thousand dollars, lots of sweat equity, and a good idea.

Not just that. Almost two out of three Americans are employed by small businesses, not by the government and not by IBM or other giant enterprises. So most Americans could relate to the benefits of providing a financial lift to the small businesses for which they work. Less money for the government and more money for the business would mean more jobs, higher pay, and more generous benefits.

NO TAX CUTS FOR THE RICH

Trump's third instruction to us will probably surprise many people. "I want to make sure that this isn't a tax cut for rich people like me," he proclaimed. He was most adamant about this. He made this declaration to us literally dozens of times. And he proclaimed this during the campaign debates as well.

Now, skeptics may sneer at this Trump declaration as an insincere and delusional request given that we were sharply cutting tax rates across the board, including for those in the highest income tax bracket and for the owners of companies. We kept proclaiming that the most economic-growth bang for the buck comes from chopping punitively high tax rates imposed upon the most successful.

A 10 percent tax rate means there is an after-tax incentive rate of 90¢ per additional dollar earned by working harder or investing more. However, with a 50 percent tax rate, the after-tax incentive rate is only 50¢ per additional dollar earned by working harder or investing more. In the extreme—yet still within the bounds of actual top marginal tax rates faced in the United States at times throughout our history—a 90 percent tax rate has an after-tax incentive rate of only 10¢ per additional dollar earned. Big difference!

Our main goal was to maximize growth by providing a bigger incentive for working, hiring, starting or expanding a business, or saving more. While the tax cut would surely keep more money in the pockets of middle-class workers and families, we explained, the ultimate benefit to workers would come from higher wages, more job opportunities, and a more productive overall American economy.

But Trump really believed that millionaires and billionaires like himself didn't need or deserve a tax cut. He also was rightfully fearful of the political optics. He didn't want the Trump middle-class voters to think that this plan was self-serving—a charge the left loved to make.

MAKING THE NUMBERS ADD UP

So we huddled up to figure out how to cut the tax rates without lowering the overall tax burden paid by the rich. It was no easy task given the scope of the tax cut Trump was proposing. Over the next several weeks the media was on our tail. What were we up to?

Reporters from *Politico* and the *Wall Street Journal* had somehow learned of our meeting with Trump and of Trump's instructions that we should refine the plan.

We told these reporters that we weren't rewriting the Trump tax plan but "tweaking it" to make sure that all the numbers added up. The big challenge—as per the candidate's instructions—was to find ways to pay for the tax cuts' large cost and ensure that the wealthy weren't getting a windfall.

One mathematical "solution" would have been to add a higher tax rate for the very wealthy. We were always nervous that Trump would go for that "populist" option. Trump had been somewhat ambiguous on this point on the campaign stump and with the media. In May 2016, while we were deliberating on how to raise the necessary revenues, Trump went on ABC's *This Week* and said: "I am willing to pay more [taxes]. And you know what? The wealthy are willing to pay more."[5] He said this again on NBC a few days later.

Trump had asked us about the wisdom of a higher tax rate on millionaires. Under the early plan, the highest tax rate would fall to 25 percent from 40 percent. But he was flirting with the possible idea of a surcharge tax rate for the super-rich of 42 to 45 percent. One of the people who thought this was a good idea was political consultant, later Trump campaign CEO, and eventually chief White House strategist Steve Bannon. Bannon suggested a higher capital gains and a higher income tax rate, perhaps as high as 45 percent.

We always had a friendly relationship with the controversial Bannon and respected his keen understanding of politics. He had helped persuade Trump to run as a nontraditional Republican, a pro-worker populist and against the big business–Wall Street elites. Bannon also was instrumental in persuading Trump to challenge long-standing GOP doctrine on liberal trade and immigration, seen by blue-collar workers as undermining their economic security.

Now Bannon was pushing Trump to break with the Republican (and supply-side) commitment to lower tax rates and to call for a higher rate on the very wealthy. The thinking went: the wealthy can afford it. Soaking the rich polled as popular with voters. Why not?

We were completely opposed to that approach. It would have made the tax system less growth-oriented, defeating Trump's, and our, entire objective. We tried to explain this with Arthur's classic example of what would happen if you had a system that taxes people at 30 percent for working on Monday, 40 percent for working on Tuesday, 50 percent for working on Wednesday, 60 percent for working on Thursday, and 90 percent for working on Friday.

How many people would go to work on Friday under this system? If you tax the wealthiest people and subsidize the least wealthy people, you're going to end up with more poor people and less wealthy people.

We also told Trump that he couldn't possibly win the class warfare game with Hillary or Bernie or any Democrat.

If Trump suggested a 45 percent tax rate, the Democratic nominee (and the media) would be for 50 to 60 percent. If he proposed a 50 percent tax rate, they would be for 70 percent. As Arthur put it, "You need to be for growth; let the Democrats be for redistribution. Americans always choose a bigger pie over a smaller pie cut up differently."

Then we showed Trump a few historical graphs to prove that higher tax rates don't necessarily lead to more taxes paid by the rich but, rather, less taxes paid. Under Reagan, for example, the highest income tax rate fell from 70 percent to 50 percent and then to 28 percent. But the share of taxes paid by the top 1 percent nearly doubled by 1990, from about 19 percent to about 35 percent. At lower tax rates you get less sheltering of income. That yields a bigger tax base, more economic growth, and more wealth flowing into the United States—all things that raise tax receipts from the wealthy.

Both John F. Kennedy and Ronald Reagan, two presidents Trump respected and hoped to emulate, had cut tax rates on the rich and seen more revenue flow into the Treasury. As JFK put it so eloquently at the Economic Club of New York in late 1962: "It is a paradoxical truth that tax rates are too high and tax revenues are too low, and the soundest way to raise the revenues in the long term is to cut the rates now."[6]

What we did agree to—at the end of the day and with great reluctance—was a highest tax rate of 35 percent rather than 25 percent. Arthur was highly opposed to this change— which he argued made the Trump tax plan "a lot worse, not better." He argued that we were compromising with ourselves—and there was something to that. If Trump had stuck with 25 percent, we might have ended up with a highest rate closer to 30 percent, not 37 percent when all was said and done. However, we just couldn't get anywhere near revenue neutral with a 25 percent tax rate for the Congressional Budget Office, which would eventually be scrutinizing the plan.

Another idea floated was to add some kind of new tax, such as a wealth tax, but that too would have negated the positive effects of the rate reductions. We also have generally opposed introducing new taxes, such as sales taxes. Europe demonstrates that these taxes get ratcheted up and up over time and lead to expanding entitlement and welfare programs. "Free everything"—as Bernie Sanders might aspire to. So we rejected that option. "Let's not be the tax collectors of the welfare state," Steve had warned, borrowing a line that Newt Gingrich had used about Bob Dole.

BROADEN THE BASE AND LOWER THE RATES

Lore has it, when the Reagan administration did the transition handoff to the incoming George H. W. Bush administration, the Reaganites left a blackboard in a Treasury Department conference room with four words scribbled on it: "Broad Base, Low Rates." That was a lesson that Team Bush neglected. Just a year and a half later, Bush raised the income tax rate, including raising the highest tax rate to 31 percent from 28 percent. He lost the next election, of course, partly as a result of reneging on his marquee "Read my lips, no new taxes" GOP convention speech pledge.

But for us the "broad base, low rates" formula was the first building block of a good tax system. Low rates, few loopholes, and the tax system won't intrude on economic decision-making and will ensure that everyone—regardless of how rich they are and how many tax accountants they have—pays their fair share.

Deductions and exemptions increase tax complexity, which is an invitation for tax avoidance. We knew that however the plan turned out, it had to be less complex than the current taxing system. In April of 2016, Arthur gave oral testimony at a congressional hearing for the Joint Economic Committee on the damaging economic impact of tax complexity, laying seeds for the battle that was to come a year and a half later.

It hasn't been just Republicans who have believed in this principle. We went back to the ideas of a past generation of pro-growth Democrats—people like Senator Bill Bradley of New Jersey and House majority leader Dick Gephardt of Missouri. These Democrats had worked together 30 years earlier to propose and advance the bipartisan 1986 Tax Reform Act. They were competing with the Republicans, led by Jack Kemp, to see who could offer the lowest tax rates! (Those were the good old days!)

The Reagan, Kemp, Bradley, Gephardt plan of collapsing tax rates to 15 percent and 28 percent with minimal deductions led to a reform that passed overwhelmingly in the House and Senate. This tax structure served the nation well until the lobbyists started carving in new loopholes and progressives began raising the top rate from 28 percent in 1986 to nearly 40 percent in 2016.

We wanted to borrow from the 1986 bipartisan framework. So we contacted the very fine economists at the Tax Foundation and asked them to solve this equation: How much can we cut the tax rate for people who make over \$1 million if we take away all their deductions except the charitable write-offs?

They cranked up their computer models based on IRS data on taxes paid by income groups and came back to us with the answer. We could get the rate down to about 35 or 36 percent and take away all the tax write-offs for the Donald Trumps, Bill Gates, Warren Buffetts, and Tom Bradys, and these richest, the top 1 percent, would still as a group pay the same amount of taxes.

Voilà. No tax cut for the rich.

We proposed a cap of $100,000 on deductions per tax filer. Ninety-eight out of every 100 voters would fall well below the cap. Only families with incomes above about $400,000 a year would be affected. Ingenious! This would drive the special interests crazy by closing sacred cow loopholes . . . but only for the extremely affluent. Middle-income Americans could keep all their customary write-offs such as charitable contributions, mortgage interest, and state and local taxes.

Even better! By doubling the standard deduction, 90 percent of tax filers wouldn't have to worry about mortgage deductions, or state and local tax write-offs, or keeping track of charitable contributions. Most of us would pay a lower tax just by checking the box and getting the first $24,000 of income tax free and hassle free.

Doubling the standard deduction was a big simplification win, one that put a wooden stake in the heart of the special interests. The housing industry tried to argue that doubling the standard deduction would hurt housing because fewer would take a deduction.

Big "Charity" complained too. They seemed to be favoring higher taxes on the middle class so that they could get their special-interest break. We also showed persuasively that when tax rates come down, housing activity and charitable contributions go up because the economy does better.

When we took this idea to Donald Trump, he instantly liked it. He insisted that we keep the charitable deduction for high-income people so that the charities wouldn't complain. So we did that. By the way, Steve and Larry had to drag Arthur along, but in the end, he agreed.

As a real estate developer, Trump was also uneasy about any cap on the mortgage deduction. That said, in the end, he didn't object to the parameters of the plan.

One other feature of our refined Trump plan, needed as a "pay-for" on the business side of the tax code, was to take away the deductibility of interest on business debt in exchange for allowing companies to expense all capital purchases.

Ending the deductibility of interest was a nonstarter. Trump expressed hatred for the elimination of write-offs for interest payments. *No way,* he said. We were a little surprised at how firm he was in this rejection. But after we argued for five minutes he put his foot down. "Look, I've spent my whole life doing real estate deals. Every one of them was financed by debt. I hate this idea."

End of argument.

THE BATTLE OVER BUSINESS EXPENSING

Right from the start, Larry Kudlow was a pit bull on the importance of capital expensing—the immediate deduction of capital expenditures (business plant and equipment that would last for years rather than being immediately consumed). Larry and Steve were in constant contact with Arthur and other economists such as Steve Entin, a former Reagan Treasury official who was an expert on the economics of tax policy.

Entin played a big role in 1981 in convincing Reagan that in addition to cutting tax rates, Congress needed to index the tax brackets for inflation to protect the middle class from the "bracket creep" caused by the high inflation of the 1970s. Inflation kept pushing working-class Americans into higher and higher tax brackets—brackets originally devised for the affluent—even though their real income wasn't rising.

Entin had shown us persuasive tax modeling results demonstrating that for every dollar of revenue loss by expensing, the economy would grow by $2–3. This research persuaded us that expensing was crucial to getting the economic growth rate up to 3 percent or higher, our holy grail.

We had also consulted with business executives like Fred Smith, the CEO of FedEx, who had told us that with expensing "we will purchase hundreds of new trucks and planes almost immediately." This would, of course, generate jobs for auto and aerospace workers.

Under the current tax law, businesses had to comply with complicated depreciation schedules, which would spread out the deductions over 10, 20, or 30 years for the costs of buildings, plants, equipment, computers, research and development expenditures, and so on.

Dick Uihlein of Wisconsin, the CEO of Uline, who recently built a 1.1 million square-foot warehouse, told us that the tax laws were entirely out of date with current business practices in twenty-first-century America. "The economy is changing so rapidly," he told us at his home office. "We're lucky if a warehouse has a 10- or 20-year useful life. But the government tells us we have to take 30 or more years to write it off. It is the dumbest thing, but no one in Washington has a clue."

We were persuaded that, bang for the buck, nothing would provide a bigger stimulus for the real economy than full and immediate expensing for business. For that reason, we put this provision at the top of the revised plan for Trump's review. Candidate Trump and campaign finance chairman Steven Mnuchin—who would later be named Treasury secretary—loved the idea. It stuck, and we are proud of it as one of our major contributions to the final tax plan.

But we were still left with the herculean task of finding several trillion dollars of revenue to cover much of the cost of the plan.

MAKE AMERICA GROW AGAIN

In July 2016 Larry Kudlow and Steve Moore flew with Donald Trump and a small group of his most influential campaign advisors from LaGuardia to Detroit for his campaign's major economic speech. This was about three months after Arthur had just made his now-famous prediction that Trump would win the election.

Donald Trump had sewed up the nomination. Thus, the media fascination with the Trump economic plan had reached a fever pitch. We guarded the details of the tax plan like we were carrying the code for the nuclear football. There were no major leaks of the grand announcement.

On the Trump campaign plane, Trump would typically sit at a table in the plane's middle section with a select group of advisors. (When he needed a rest, he would retreat to his bedroom in another section of the plane.) Trump always had one eye on the big-screen TV. Normally this was tuned to Fox News. He paid close attention every minute to the latest national news—especially as it related to the campaign and the Democratic nominee.

It was surprising to us how much important policy work got done in the middle cabin of Candidate Trump's airplane. We soon saw, firsthand, that Trump was an efficiency expert. He didn't waste a minute. Given how rigorous his travel schedule was, the only time available to sit back and think about policy and strategies often was from 25,000 feet.

The discussion on this trip was devoted to the economic game plan.

Trump wanted Larry and Steve aboard with trusted advisors Newt Gingrich, Steve Mnuchin, and the ever-present Jared Kushner so we could finalize the crucial specifics of the tax plan. Everyone sat on the couch and hunkered down for over an hour to review the latest version.

Trump signed off on almost all the proposals that Larry and Steve offered, with the important exception of rejecting any cap on the mortgage interest or charitable deductions.

Candidate Trump felt that while this cap might be good economics, it might subject him to an avalanche of criticism that it would hurt important charities and the housing market, which had finally gotten back on its feet after the crash of 2007–09.

At one point Candidate Trump wanted to add a story to the narrative. His instinct was brilliant. Mr. Trump asked if any of us had seen a story buried in one of the back sections of one of the New York newspapers—either the *Times* or the *Post*.

The story related how poorly the upstate New York areas—like Buffalo, Syracuse, Rochester, and so on—had been faring in recent years. The upshot was that these areas had become places of economic despair with lost jobs, lost factories, and lost hope.

Trump said, "Wait a minute. This is shameful that no one has done anything to help with economic development in these areas for 20 years." Then he connected the dots to Hillary. She had been the U.S. senator from New York. Yet she had done nothing to alleviate the spiral of decline in these areas. Trump added a line to the speech, saying that Hillary would do to the country what she allowed to happen in upstate New York.

This was a fair and devastating shot across the bow at Hillary that the rest of us probably should have thought of. Though a newcomer to politics, Donald Trump often demonstrated more acute political instincts than his advisors.

That was one of those moments when we realized Donald Trump is a natural.

The theme of the Detroit Economic Club speech was "A New Chapter in American Prosperity." The lunchtime speech—which touched on all the economic issues, with a special focus on taxes—was delivered to a packed house.

TV cameras from networks around the world were crammed three and four deep across the back of the auditorium.

The speech was brilliantly delivered. Trump is one of the best speech-makers we have ever witnessed. That speech also turned out to be an inflection point for both the campaign and the tax reform battle. It was almost universally hailed on the right as a policy tour de force—even among groups and pundits who had been highly skeptical and even critical of Trumponomics.

The *Wall Street Journal* editorial board, for example, which had been hypercritical of Trump up to that moment, heaped the speech with praise—while warning against a trade protectionist agenda, which it feared would be "a jobs killer." But the editorial the next morning praised the Trump economic revival plan as "a major leap forward in the Trump agenda on taxes and regulation." At a time when "60 to 70% of Americans think the country is going in the wrong direction," said *Wall Street Journal* associate editor Dan Henninger, "this speech gave voters a sense of hope and optimism."[7]

As if emphasizing Henninger's point a few days after the speech, the *Journal* featured the latest worker productivity numbers, which had been publicly released and which were dismal . . . again fueling the conviction that the country's economy was stalling out.

For the first time in the campaign there was a sense that conservatives' icy resistance to Trump was thawing—in part because of the inevitability of his nomination, but also because everyone loved the tax cut and deregulatory agenda Trump was campaigning on.

We estimated the plan would lose $3 trillion over a decade in static terms—assuming no growth from the plan. But when we dynamically scored the tax plan with the assumption of 1 percent faster annual growth—not just from the taxes, but the deregulation, energy policies, and so on—we had credible statistical estimates that the plan would achieve revenue neutrality.

For middle-class workers we estimated 25 million new jobs and a 10 percent increase in real wages over a decade. If these numbers were even near accurate—and it is always difficult to estimate what will happen in five or ten years—this would be the most pro-growth initiative out of Washington since the Reagan tax cuts of 1981.

PARTY UNIFICATION

From a political point of view, the tax plan at that stage of the campaign was a home run. The Trump campaign was still struggling mightily to unify a resistant party behind the prospective nominee. The NeverTrumpers were in an angry and subversive mood. Many backers of Ted Cruz were bitter that their constitutionalist conservative had lost the nomination to a populist conservative. The tax plan brought many in the conservative movement around to Trump, even if begrudgingly at first.

Arthur was on the cable news circuit on an almost daily basis calling the plan "the best tax plan I've seen since Reagan. It will supercharge growth." This helped credential Trump with many economic conservatives who had been skeptical about the nominee's economic conservative bona fides.

Larry and Steve went on the road to speak to countless influential conservative groups to sell the more-often-than-not-skeptical audiences on Trump. At one impactful meeting before the prestigious Council for National Policy (CNP)—a highly selective group of high-powered conservative donors and thought leaders—Larry and Steve presented the economic case for Trump with our friend and CNP board member Bill Walton, CNP's vice president. Walton later became one of the top members of Trump's transition team for the economy.

We never tried to oversell conservatives on Trump or to blur the nationalist elements of his agenda that were at odds with established free-market doctrine in matters like trade and immigration. But the tax plan brought almost all the hundreds present over to Trump's side, or at least to keeping an open mind about Trump. The consolidation of the party behind Trump was greatly facilitated by the attractiveness of the Trump tax plan.

Tax reform was like a rite of passage, and Trump was, at long last, admitted into the conservative fold, even if on probation.

The Democrats' designated presidential nominee, Hillary Clinton, lashed out immediately against the reform as "trumped-up trickle-down" economics. The left called it the most financially irresponsible tax cut in American history. To Trump's credit, and to our delight, Trump never wavered on taxes throughout the next 18 months.

THE CROWN JEWEL OF THE TAX PLAN

The corporate tax rate reduction from 35 to 15 percent had nothing to do with any Trump love affair with corporate America. The goal was always twofold:

1. Enhance America's competitiveness on the global stage, and
2. Lift the wages of middle-class workers.

Larry was especially insistent that "a corporate tax cut is a middle-class tax cut." He patiently connected the dots for those in the media and the electorate who could not. GDP growth comes from two, and only two, factors: how many people are working and how productive they are. Per capita GDP growth, which determines how much each of us is better off, all comes from productivity growth. The more productive we are, the more valuable we are, the higher the wages (plus bonuses and promotions) a worker commands. Period!

Wages, like all other prices, are organically determined by supply and demand, not by government-imposed wage controls like a statutory minimum wage. That thinking might as well be make-believe. If the government, by law, demands that a business pay me more than the value I am contributing, the business will eliminate my job by, for example, automating it. It has to! Businesses can't stay in business if they lose money, and forcing a business to pay its employees more money than it makes spells doom both for that business and for those jobs. To think otherwise is to embrace a fantasy that leads to only misery.

Better wages come from better productivity. Better productivity comes from better tools. And better tools come from capital investment. Supply-side economics isn't "trickledown." Supply-side economics, very much including its incarnation as Trumponomics, is an "artesian well surging up!"

Thus, first, lower corporate tax rates mean more capital investment by businesses in the United States. Companies invest based on the after-tax return on the investment. If you lower the tax penalty on investment, businesses will invest more—all other things being equal. This isn't theoretical. We saw right out of the gates in 2017 a big boost in business investment in the wake of the tax cut.

Second, capital investment is a major factor in making workers more productive. Workers who work with computers, diagnostic equipment, technology, tractors, fork lifts, and robotics, etc., can produce more than a worker without such tools. A steel mill today produces twice as much steel with one-third as many workers compared to 50 years ago.

In 1900 almost one in three Americans was employed in agriculture. Today three in 100 Americans are employed in farming, yet they produce four times more food using one-third as much land. Why? Because of farm equipment, better irrigation, better seeds, bigger fruits, fatter cows that produce more beef and milk, and a multitude of new modern farming techniques that yield more food per acre, and on and on.

Third, worker productivity is the major driver of higher salaries and benefits to American workers.

Although we have fewer manufacturing workers today than 30 years ago, the ones we do have are better paid than those of the 1950s and '60s. A worker who has a computer in front of her has about twice the salary of one without a computer. That's the true magic of productivity, which grows the pie and provides more for everyone. From Q4–1982 through Q4–1999, the increase in real hourly compensation to workers in the nonfarm business sector rose at an average annual rate of 1.1 percent, tracking the ebb and flow of productivity growth, which grew at an average rate of 2.1 percent.

Alas, those gains stalled out after 2000 under Presidents George W. Bush and Barack Obama. Living standards have stagnated for a generation. And when you compound that stagnation year over year, it means that Americans are somewhere between one-third and one-half as well off as we would have been had the federal government stuck with a policy mix that sustained the growth rates of the 1980s and '90s.

That is why the tax cut was so urgently needed: not merely to let people keep more of what they earn, but to rekindle the economy to generate the equitable prosperity that is the heart and soul of the American dream.

Even the stodgy CBO confirmed our belief that workers were bearing the brunt of the cost of our excessive corporate tax. According to a 2006 CBO report, based on what it called "reasonable assumptions, domestic labor bears slightly more than 70 percent of the burden of the corporate income tax."[8] In other words, cut the corporate tax burden, and middle-class Americans will reap the rewards in higher paychecks and more better-paying jobs.

THE REST OF THE WORLD WAS LAUGHING BEHIND AMERICA'S BACK

It's hard to exaggerate how economically debilitating America's business tax system had become. The U.S. top federal corporate tax rate of 35 percent (almost 40 percent with state and local taxes) was the highest of all the nations we compete with. The rest of the world had been slashing their business tax rates in half for about 20 years. By 2016 the average rate internationally was closer to 20 to 25 percent. Some nations like Ireland had cut their top corporate rates to as low as 12.5 percent. (Arthur would pun with an Irish accent that Ireland was always a good place to invest because "the capital was always Dublin.'")

Trump was right that the rest of the world was laughing at us behind our back. We were effectively putting a tariff on our own goods and services. What country does that?

Steve and Larry had been lamenting that our business tax in America was nothing more than a 20 percent "Head Start program" for every country that America competes against.

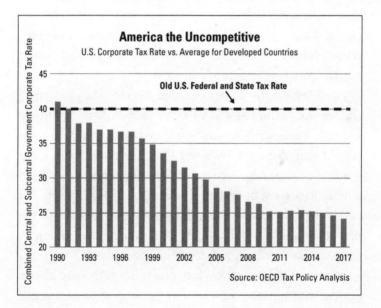

Plus, the corporate tax was complicated, unfair—because some industries paid much higher rates than others—and in the end raised less than $400 billion annually.

The very definition of a bad tax is one with an excessively high rate—thus distorting economic activity—shot through with big loopholes and exemptions, leading to not much tax revenue. Worst of both worlds! Amazingly, from 2010 through 2015, the U.S. top corporate tax rate was the highest in the OECD (35 countries), yet the United States had the ninth-lowest average corporate tax revenues as a share of GDP.

The reason for the differential between the statutory and the actual rate paid to the Treasury was that many industries—such as wind and solar power companies—paid no tax at all. Where is the fairness in that?

Our argument was: let's get the rate down to 15 percent and make sure that everyone is paying it. We had seen companies like Burger King, Medtronic, Pfizer, and dozens more leave or threaten to leave the United States in search of lower tax rates abroad. In 2016 as we were putting the tax plan together, Johnson Controls announced a merger that would send its company and its jobs abroad.

Left-leaners like to pretend that the U.S. tax rates aren't chasing out businesses and jobs. But they could never answer a simple question: Why are so many nations slashing their rates if they don't see a benefit? Over the past 25 years, the international average corporate tax rate has come down from almost 40 percent in 1990 to closer to 20 percent by 2016. For two and a half decades the U.S. rates didn't budge, while the rest of the world kept chopping. Any wonder the American economy has been sluggish for a full generation?

Putting aside the left-wing ideologues who were always against cutting tax rates for any reason, most reasonable people seemed to recognize the problem of our sore-thumb tax rate, but nothing got done to fix it—not under Bill Clinton, not under George W. Bush, and not under Barack Obama. Even President Obama's own tax reform commission, headed by former Fed chairman Paul Volcker, found "deep flaws" in the corporate tax. It concluded:

> The high statutory corporate tax rate reduces the return to investments and therefore discourages saving and investment. . . . The tax acts to reduce the productivity of American businesses and American workers, increase the likelihood and cost of financial distress, and drain resources away from more valuable uses.[9]

As for the stimulus value of our proposed corporate tax cuts, the Tax Foundation found that immediate expensing and cutting the business tax rate are the best short-term strategies for generating more growth. Here is how the foundation put it: "A cut in the corporate tax rate would have large effects on GDP, but minimal effects on federal revenue in the long run."[10]

In the revised plan, we retained the Trump idea of pairing the vital pro-growth business tax cuts with relief for middle-class families. This wasn't as easy as it sounds, since almost 40 percent of families weren't paying any federal income tax. We wanted to provide relief for those making between about $40,000 and $125,000 a year. There were three main benefits to the middle class:

1. A doubling of the standard deduction so that the first $24,000 of earnings for a married couple and $12,000 for an individual would not be taxed.

2. A doubling of the child tax credit from $500 to $1,000. This meant a family with two kids would see an immediate $1,000 tax cut.

3. Lower tax rates for those who earned less than $125,000, meaning that the tax on every extra dollar earned was reduced.

Our analysis revealed that the average family would save about $1,500 to $2,000 from their federal tax bill as a result of these changes. We also determined that the increase in growth rates and productivity would boost before-tax wages by about $4,000 over time. This meant that the percentage reduction in taxes was higher for the middle class than the rich—despite all the headlines to the contrary. We were offering big gains in after-tax income for a big segment of the American population that had been running faster on an economic treadmill just to stay even for the past decade and a half.

THE MYTH OF THE $6 TRILLION TAX CUT

None of this, of course, stopped Democrats from immediately and relentlessly attacking the Trump tax plan as too expensive and too tilted to the rich. This is what Democrats had been saying about virtually every GOP tax cut proposal since Reagan campaigned on a 30 percent across-the-board tax rate cut. Attacking it as "too expensive" often worked with voters because many Republicans put a balanced budget and deficit reduction above all.

Hillary hollered that the plan would "blow a $6 trillion hole in the debt." This was rich in irony coming from someone who worked with an administration that nearly doubled the national debt in eight years. Confounding neo-Keynesian dogma, she claimed that the cut would cost jobs and could even "cause a recession." Given that Democrats are mesmerized by the Keynesian idea that deficits stimulate the economy by putting more money in people's pockets, this was an astonishingly weird claim by Trump's rival for the presidency. Its outlandishness certainly undermined any credibility on job creation to which Mrs. Clinton may have aspired.

We struck back hard against the left's internally contradictory argument that taxing businesses at a lower rate and letting them keep more of their earnings would capsize the economy. They combined this nonsense with other imaginary horrors. Meanwhile, Hillary was threatening a $1.5 trillion tax hike, which, in the Bizarro World economics of the left, was somehow going to *create* jobs.

Sure, and injecting Elmer's glue into your veins is a good way to prevent a heart attack. The left-leaning media fell for it. The voters saw right through it.

Democrats and left-leaning economists were also rewriting the history of the 1980s. They were arguing that the Reagan tax cuts hadn't really fixed the economy from the malaise and income losses in the 1970s, and had only burdened the U.S. economy with "massive debt." We quickly reminded every journalist who would lend us an ear that the deficits as a share of GDP in the Obama years were almost twice as high as those in the Reagan years, but the Reagan recovery was almost twice as strong as Obama's.

Reagan had borrowed to finance America's victory in the Cold War. Reagan's tax rate cuts had set the stage for a vibrant U.S. economy for nearly two decades. The Obama deficits had financed food stamps, unemployment benefits, "green" energy boondoggles, and largely nonexistent "shovel-ready projects."

The difference in the two recoveries was nearly $3 trillion more output gains (in 2016 dollars) under Reagan than Obama. Similarly, the John F. Kennedy tax cuts got us 5 and 6 percent growth. JFK was right: the best way to raise revenues is to "cut tax rates now." Even President Clinton agreed to a capital gains tax cut, which led to a gusher of new federal revenues.

The Trump tax plan was stellar compared to the mishmash of tax hikes that Hillary wanted to serve up. We prepared for the Trump campaign, which was widely circulated in the following weeks. It showed that the Trump tax plan would cause a rise in after-tax income by about $4,000 for the average middle-class household, while the Hillary plan would shrink family income. Hillary's plan, under close inspection, would actually make the middle class poorer.

Hillary's economics team argued that more growth would come from spending more tax dollars on . . . expensive freebies. This was the residual effect of the Bernie Sanders maverick presidential campaign. Sanders was running as a soft socialist. Heathcare should be free. College should be free. Job training should be free. Day care should be free. Paid leave should be free.

Hillary latched on to many of these ideas in the general election to preempt and neutralize Senator Sanders's surprising appeal to the Democratic base. She desperately firmed up some support of the party base by running as a fiscal Sandersnista. It worked, but at great cost. She squeaked through getting the nomination but irretrievably damaged her own credibility as a fiscally conscientious Democrat in the general election.

Hillary was offering tens of billions of dollars of subsidies to the solar industry and other green energy enterprises.

When Hillary accused Trump of advocating "trickle-down" tax cuts, we countered that Hillary was offering the American people "trickle-down government." When had that ever worked?

In the end, millions of voters, endowed with mother wit and common sense, agreed with Trump. Notwithstanding historically hostile media coverage, Trump won by carrying the traditional red states in the mountain regions and in the South, while crashing through the blue wall of the Midwest, where the economy had long been underperforming. The pro-jobs tax cut message along with Trump's populist call to fight for American jobs in trade deals swept the South and mountain states and turned Michigan, Ohio, Pennsylvania, Wisconsin, and Iowa . . . red.

Now Trump had to deliver the goods. The tax plan that he ran on was even more anticipated in the months after he won the election. In January of 2017, Arthur traveled in secret to Trump Tower to meet with David Malpass, Anthony Scaramucci, Gary Cohn, Steve Bannon, and, of course, Trump himself to talk about the prospects of the tax plan and how to reduce burdensome federal regulations. Trump made it clear to Arthur that he wanted to move quickly on the tax bill and that he would need Arthur's help to pass it. To Arthur, the corporate tax cut component was crucial, and over the next year, he would become its champion.

6

The Tax Cut Heard Round
the World

Once Trump was sworn into office, he was ready to hit the ground sprinting, as is his signature style. But Congress sure wasn't on board. The tax bill couldn't have gotten off to a worse start on Capitol Hill. There were many times throughout a tumultuous 2017 when it looked like the tax bill was a lost cause. That said, as Ethel Lina White wrote in *The Wheel Spins*, "Lost causes are the only causes worth fighting for."

A big part of the problem was that the Trump White House decided to defer to Republican congressional leaders, who made a lousy decision right out of the gate. Speaker Paul Ryan and Majority Leader Mitch McConnell decided to pursue Obamacare repeal first, deferring the tax cut to the second half of 2017.

This made us nervous. We argued against it, to no effect.

Arthur and Larry had lived through the 1981 tax battle and remembered the lessons many in the party had evidently forgotten. Reagan had smartly announced that his historic tax cut would come first, and then the budget battle and other priorities thereafter.

Had Reagan reversed his priorities, the tax cut, and with it the booming prosperity that ensued for seven years, may never have happened. It was the tax cut that helped create a ferocious economic comeback, which helped Reagan amass enormous political capital, and then led to his landslide re-election in which he won 49 states—the biggest blowout reelection in modern times. Follow the Reagan political formula, we urged.

We were very much in favor of repealing every word of the disastrous Obamacare experiment, one that had the opposite effect of making healthcare "affordable." That said, we didn't see why Congress couldn't walk and chew gum at the same time.

Time was not on the newly elected president's side. Any delay in passing the tax bill risked slowing the path to real economic recovery. The longer the delay, the lower the odds of getting a tax cut passed at all. Presidents who got their agendas passed did it right away. Reagan led with his tax rate cut and signed it into law in August 1981. Obama signed his enormous $787 billion "stimulus" bill four weeks after taking office. The political capital from winning a presidential election needs to be deployed fast lest it dissipate.

In our meetings with Trump and the White House brain trust, we urged that Trump weigh in and call for a tax cut to come to his desk in the first 100 days of his administration. We felt that a robust debate over tax reform on the Senate floor would be a good thing, forcing members to deliberate, offer alternatives, and vote.

Republicans were flinching from the "tax cuts for the rich" attacks by the Bernie Sanders crowd. But such claims could be countered effectively. The president's new chairman of the Council of Economic Advisers, American Enterprise Institute economist Kevin Hassett, had assembled solid evidence showing that business tax rate reductions would mostly benefit workers through higher wages.

Upward income mobility for workers was the president's primary objective. It was our objective. It was what the American people wanted and voted for. It's an argument we were certain we could win.

So bring on this debate, and the sooner the better. But the delays continued, and Wall Street and the business groups were getting nervous. By early summer, the business lobbyists and the financial gurus were betting that tax cuts wouldn't even happen in 2017. In a meeting with White House and congressional tax writers in the early summer, we took a tough stance and scolded GOP leaders for dragging their feet. Our pitch was that a delay until 2018 would hurt the economy, hurt the financial markets, and put the Republicans in a precarious position for the midterm elections. That got their attention. For a while.

WHOSE TAX BILL IS THIS ANYWAY?

Another hurdle we had to clear was dealing with the congressional leadership in the House. Speaker of the House Paul Ryan, whom we had worked with and admired for years—dating back to when he was a junior staffer working for the great Jack Kemp—had written for House Republicans something called the "Roadmap" to tax reform the year before the election. House Ways and Means Committee chairman Kevin Brady of Texas was also totally committed to tax reform and a pit bull in getting it done, and deserves enormous kudos for his leadership, right through to the final victory, working hand in hand with Paul Ryan.

The House Roadmap plan was a bold wholesale revamping of the tax system. Most of the ideas were sound, though some were controversial. The problem was that no one had ever heard of the Roadmap. It was different in many ways from what Trump had campaigned on. So there was a political disconnect between what Trump had promised during the campaign—presumably what the voters had elected him to do—and Paul Ryan's unsung Roadmap.

Ryan was intent on enacting his Roadmap, not the Trump plan. There was much overlap but major differences on rates and deductions. The Roadmap was more grandiose, and it had more moving parts and more controversial items, including the wholly novel border-adjustment tax. The House Republicans were also obsessing about revenue neutrality. We worried that this undue emphasis was a trap, given that, calculated on a static basis, tax cuts raise deficits.

Our view was that the House should run with the plan that got Trump and so many other Republicans elected and not start throwing curve balls.

What really threw a wrench into the tax cut roll-out strategy was that the GOP was busy botching Obamacare repeal. Congressional leaders had told Trump to let them handle Obamacare repeal (as they were doing on tax reform). They promised to deliver a first-rate repeal to his desk for signature.

The Republicans failed to repeal Obamacare because they couldn't agree on an alternative. The process bogged down and then broke down.

By the spring and through midsummer, tax reform wasn't even out of the gate. We were in a state of extreme agitation. What was supposed to be a first 100-day policy victory was nowhere to be seen 200 days into the new administration.

The defeat on Obamacare repeal in the Senate (by one vote), combined with Trump's rising anger about his signature tax reform languishing, wound up being a turning point. There was no room for swinging and missing on tax reform after whiffing on healthcare reform.

Failure would be a political and policy catastrophe. Trump had to take the reins away from Congress. Trump was needed as the chief spokesman and negotiator or tax reform wasn't going to happen.

THE BORDER-ADJUSTMENT TAX IMBROGLIO

Then there was the giant distraction of the border-adjustment tax. The highly controversial issue almost brought down the entire tax cut effort.

A few weeks after the election, Steve was giving a talk at the Economic Club of Minneapolis to discuss Trumponomics and the economic agenda of President-elect Trump. The night before the speech, he received an urgent call from the Economic Club president asking if he could have breakfast the next morning with Hubert Joly of Best Buy and Brian Cornell of Target—two of America's most respected national retail chains.

It was flattering that they wanted to meet. He readily agreed.

After ten minutes of pleasantries, they made their real agenda clear. They wanted to talk about the border-adjustment tax, aka the BAT.

This was the House proposal to impose a tax on U.S. imports and exempt U.S. exports. This would be a big tax break for U.S. manufacturers and very bad news for importers—i.e., retailers like Target and Best Buy. These two gentlemen walked Steve through the math.

Retailers were getting squeezed by online competition from Amazon. The big-box stores had very slim margins. A 15 percent tax on the cost of their merchandise would potentially put them into bankruptcy. This was live-or-die for these firms, they argued. It would lead to higher prices for consumers.

It was a friendly conversation, and their case struck Steve as somewhat exaggerated. Yet there was no doubt retailers were fearful and would fight to the death to prevent this tax from happening. They mentioned that Walmart was in a complete go-to-the-mattresses mode on the BAT. The Retail Federation would spend whatever it took to defeat it.

Putting aside the merits of the opposition, as a political calculus, how were we going to pass a tax bill through the Senate when there were only 52 Republicans and two of them were from Arkansas, home of Walmart?

We had a giant political headache on our hands.

House Ways and Means Committee chairman Kevin Brady and House Speaker Paul Ryan—two of the true heroes of the tax reform epic—saw the border-adjustment tax as the trillion-dollar "pay-for" to offset the cost of expensing and rate reduction. Because we import about a half-trillion dollars more than we export (the merchandise "trade deficit"), by taxing imports and exempting exports, the government would raise about $1 trillion more revenues over a decade. This would significantly reduce the net deficit impact of the tax cut.

Conservatives were split on the issue. In fact, Arthur, Larry, and Steve couldn't even agree on it—and we generally agreed on almost all tax issues. A family fight was brewing just at the time when a unified front became crucial.

Steve was for the tax as a matter of policy. Arthur was for a value-added tax model that would replace taxes on personal and corporate income and incorporated a BAT, but he also saw a preclusive technical flaw in the BAT. In a research paper Arthur published in March, he made the point that "the supposed 'pay for' rule now in effect in Congress is the bastard father of the border-adjustment tax."[1] In other words, the "pay for" requirements were forcing Republicans to invent ways to make up for supposed static revenue loss that would surely have deleterious effects on the dynamic growth that would come from a tax cut. Larry was against it from the start, as he and our compadre Steve Forbes saw it as a hidden national sales tax that would massively increase the government's tax take of the economy.

There was some ingeniousness to the idea, and a strong economic justification for it. The BAT was designed to correct one of stupidest features of our corporate tax: the backward way we tax international transactions.

Consider this simple example: If you are an American company making cars in Michigan, you have to pay a 35 percent profits tax on the car made here. Then if the car is sold across the border to Mexico, the Mexican government slaps on a 16 percent value-added tax. So the car is taxed on both sides of the border. Almost all countries tax goods produced in the United States this way.

Now let us say that the auto factory is moved from Michigan to Mexico City. The car produced in the factory in Mexico is not taxed by the Mexican government if the car is sold in the United States. Even more amazing: the United States imposes no federal border tax on the imported car. To summarize, the car is taxed twice if it is built in America and then sold abroad and never taxed if it is built abroad and sold here in the United States. Little wonder why American companies are moving to China, India, Ireland, Mexico, and the like. We were stacking the deck against American producers and workers. Our federal tax was effectively a 35 percent tariff imposed on our own goods and services.

As we saw it, there were three economic arguments in favor of the BAT:

1. It could end all talk of tariffs and trade wars. At various times, Trump has suggested between 5 and 35 percent tariffs on foreign goods imported here. But tariffs violate our trade agreements and often lead to retaliatory measures by other countries. A better solution is to impose the Trump 15 percent corporate income tax on goods when they are brought into the United States and to exempt goods produced in the United States that are sold outside the country. This tax does not violate trade laws and only mirrors the valued-added tax systems other countries use to gain advantage over us.

2. A border-adjustment tax has a broader tax base, and thus the rate can be lower. The best tax system has a broad tax base and a low tax rate. To get the Trump tax rate down to 15 percent and still raise enough money

to fund the government, we need the broadest tax base possible.

3. A border-adjustment system taxes consumption, not production. Most economists agree that a good tax system taxes what people take out of the economy, not what they put into the economy. Many Keynesian economists have long argued that consumption is what drives the economy, but American consumers can't consume if they aren't producing something.

Steve argued that in exchange for a border-adjustment tax, the United States should eliminate all existing tariffs and duties, which now range from 2 percent on shoes to 25 percent on toys. This would eliminate all special-interest favoritism—the worst feature of trade protectionism.

These arguments may or may not have made sense as an economic matter, but as a political matter the BAT was a poison pill. Instead of focusing on the positive changes from tax reform, voters and conservative interest groups were focusing on this new Big Bad Tax. The business community was completely divided. As such, we all agreed very early on that the BAT had to go.

One of our contributions to the tax debate was to persuade the White House—which had been undecided on BAT—and, even more importantly, Paul Ryan and Kevin Brady, that the BAT had to be abandoned or tax reform would be stillborn. They finally threw in the towel, but not before Arthur personally went to Chairman Brady's office at the end of July to stick the nail in the BAT coffin. They still grouse to us whenever we see them that they were right on the BAT. Perhaps in a technical sense, they were.

But what we all agree on was that while the economics were debatable, the politics of the moment were not. Including the BAT would have killed any prospect of passing the tax bill in the Senate. It had to go.

THE LATE GREAT TRUMP TAX CUT

It should be noted that in the spring and summer, Larry, Steve, and Arthur were working together but separately. Larry and Steve were going around Capitol Hill as a dynamic duo, while Arthur was doing his own meetings with legislators and members of the administration. One time in July, Arthur met with seven members of Congress individually in a 24-hour period to talk about the merits of the proposed tax reform. Working all angles was absolutely necessary because by late spring of 2017, the signature Trump/GOP growth issue—tax reform—was secure in some undisclosed location . . . probably bleeding to death in a ditch.

Republicans were starting to openly whisper they might have to put tax reform off until 2018. Wall Streeters were starting to discount the higher probability that tax reform wasn't going to happen. Could it be that Republicans were going to blow a once-in-a-generation opportunity to rewrite and modernize tax law?

At this time, Arthur was working to spread his research on the corporate income tax rate to those in D.C. who would listen. In May, he met for an entire day with White House staffers to explain to the whole team the economic necessity of the 2017 tax reform. In June, he spoke in front of a roomful of members of Congress and delivered the same message. He came armed with an influential study which broke down the revenue-increasing behavioral effects of a reduction in the corporate income tax rate. This was crucial to get the deficit hawks on board.

On one of our various visits to Capitol Hill for high-level meetings with both chambers of Congress in the early summer, our message to GOP lawmakers contained some good news and some very bad news from recent private polling on the tax cut front.

The good news was that by a 62 to 30 percent margin, Americans believed that a tax cut would be good for the economy. We were solidly winning the case with voters that a big tax cut for businesses and families means jobs and growth.

The bad news was that when people are asked which party is better able to deliver a tax cut, 36 percent say Republicans and 38 percent say Democrats. That was certainly a wake-up call to Republicans, given that Democrats didn't even want to cut taxes at all. Voters witnessed the bungled GOP attempt to repeal and replace Obamacare and had lost confidence that a Republican Congress could get anything done.

The GOP was in danger of getting shut out in the first year of a new presidency. This would be a political and policy Hindenburg. But very few members of Congress or our friends in the White House and in the Treasury seemed alarmed or worried . . . no matter how many times we warned them that waiting until 2018 was a recipe for failure.

Every day on the calendar that was flipped over brought the probability of defeat closer. Near the end of the summer we were told that there were only about 25 legislative days left to get this mega-bill enacted. Uh-oh.

President Trump's tax cut was looking like legislative road kill.

THREE EASY PIECES

The three of us gathered in New York City in the spring to adopt a game plan to help resuscitate the tax plan. We were joined by our friend and cofounder of the Committee to Unleash Prosperity, Steve Forbes. We were all in passionate agreement that the delay in the tax debate was bleeding dry any presidential capital that Trump had left.

Our view was that tax reform should be kept as simple and understandable to voters as possible. This meant fewer moving pieces—scrap the Roadmap—and it meant getting back to the basics of what Trump had promised throughout his presidential campaign. We called our plan "Three Easy Pieces of Tax Reform," and used it to shake off the dust settling inside policy circles . . . and especially among the political team at the White House. Then–White House chief strategist Steve Bannon loved the idea.

We decided to jointly pen an op-ed for the *New York Times* to jump-start the debate. We were apprehensive because we didn't want to alienate our friends on Capitol Hill and in the White House. But we had run out of options.

We titled the article "Why Are Republicans Making Tax Reform So Hard?" It ran on April 19, 2017.[2] Here is what we wrote:

> In the aftermath of the healthcare blowup, President Trump and the Republicans need a legislative victory. Tax reform probably should have gone first, but now is the time to move it forward with urgency . . .
>
> One sure lesson from the healthcare setback is the old admonition "Keep it simple, stupid." The Republicans

tried to fix the trillion-dollar health insurance market instead of keeping the focus on repealing Obamacare.

They have a chance to make amends with a new tax bill and still hit the August deadline. We advised President Trump during his election campaign, and we believe the Republican Party's lesson for tax reform is this: Don't try to rewrite the entire tax code in one bill.

Instead, the primary goal of Mr. Trump's first tax bill should be to fix the federal corporate and small-business tax system, which has made America increasingly uncompetitive in global markets and has reduced jobs and wages here at home. The White House and the Treasury already have a tax plan that we were involved with last year. The three most important planks of that plan are:

First, cut the federal corporate and small-business highest tax rate to 15 percent from 35 percent, which is now one of the highest corporate tax rates in the world.

Second, allow businesses to immediately deduct the full cost of their capital purchases. Full expensing of new factories, equipment and machinery will jump-start business investment, which since 2000 has grown at only one-third the rate recorded from 1950 to 2000.

Third, impose a low tax on the repatriation of foreign profits brought back to the United States. This could attract more than $2 trillion to these shores, raising billions for the Treasury while creating new jobs and adding to the United States' gross domestic product.

To help win over Democratic votes in the House and Senate, we would also suggest another component: What many workers across the country want most from President Trump is infrastructure funding. As part of this bill, we should create a fund dedicated to rebuilding America's roads, highways, airports and pipelines, and modernizing the electric grid and broadband access—financed through the tax money raised from repatriation of foreign profits.

. . . For this strategy to work, Republicans need to take several steps. First, President Trump and Paul Ryan, the Speaker of the House, should stop insisting on "revenue neutrality." In the short term, the bill will add to the deficit. But President Trump's tax bill, like those of Presidents Ronald Reagan and John Kennedy, should be a tax cut, and it should be sold to the American people as such.

. . . The additional increase in real wages from the Trump plan could be nearly 10 percent over the next decade, which would reverse 15 years of income stagnation for the working class in America. And, if we are right that tax cuts will spur the economy, then the faster economic growth as a result of the bill will bring down the deficit.

Next, Republicans should abandon the so-called border-adjustment tax. A border tax is a poison pill for the tax plan: It divides the very business groups that the party needs to rally behind tax reform. Retailers like Walmart will never go along. A carbon tax would be even worse. The best way to bring jobs back to America is to simply lower tax rates now while rolling back anti-jobs regulations, such as rules that inhibit American energy production.

As for fixing the maddeningly complex individual income tax system—lowering tax rates and ending needless deductions—we are all for it, but that should wait until 2018. Jobs and the economy are the top priority to voters.

Republicans need to act with some degree of urgency. The financial markets and American businesses are starting to get jittery over the prospect that a tax cut won't get done this year. A failure here would be negative for the economy and the stock market and could stall out the "Trump bounce" we have seen since the president's election.

Mr. Trump should demand that Congress send him a jobs bill this summer that he can sign into law on Aug. 13, 2017. That is the day President Reagan signed his historic tax cut in 1981 at his beloved Ranch del Cielo in Santa Barbara, Calif.

That tax cut and President Kennedy's before it unleashed two of the longest periods of prosperity in American history, and that is a result Donald Trump should want to replicate.

The impact of the article was thunderous and immediate. Our friend Fred Barnes, the veteran political reporter and editor of the *Weekly Standard,* called it the "op-ed that changed the world."

Actually it would do greater justice to observe that this was "how Ivanka changed the world." When Ivanka Trump, a key friend and ally, saw the article in the newspaper that morning, she cut it out and put it at the top of a stack of must-read items for the president as he sat down behind his desk in the Oval Office.

President Trump read the piece, marked it up, and called a snap meeting with his legislative, political, and economic advisory teams in the Oval Office. He angrily pointed to the article and said, "This is the way we are going to get it done. They are right, let's get going on tax reform. No more delays."

Three days later, National Economic Council chairman Gary Cohn and Treasury Secretary Steve Mnuchin held a press conference and presented the latest version of the Trump tax plan, which looked an awful lot like what had been proposed in the *New York Times* op-ed. A few days later the president demanded that Congress get a tax bill on his desk before Christmas.

No one had thought that possible a week before. Now the odds of a bill had gone way up. In the following months, Arthur's own productive meetings with Cohn, Vice President Pence, and Secretary Mnuchin confirmed that there were indeed allies of supply-side economics in the White House once again, and they were serious about pushing reform through.

Rereading our statement nearly a year later, we readily admit there were many things we got wrong. Adding infrastructure spending seemed at the time a smart way to lure Democrats into the debate. That proved a nonstarter. Democrats were in such an intransigent "resistance" mode that they couldn't be budged to vote for any economic growth tax and spending bill even if it had things they and their constituent groups dearly wanted.

Second, our "Three Easy Pieces" plan was insufficiently ambitious. The final product that passed the House and Senate contained some very valuable changes to the individual income tax system, including a consolidation of the tax rates, a reduction in the top tax rate to 37 percent, and a small business exemption of 20 percent. We acknowledge that we were wrong on these points. Congress exceeded our expectations.

But most of the rest of the points helped focus GOP thinking. Tax cutting was back on the table. More than that, tax cutting was front and center in the policy debate for the next five months. *Politico* wrote that the "Three Easy Pieces" op-ed was one of the most influential pieces in many years.

But there were still many unresolved issues. The epic was just getting started.

RECONCILABLE DIFFERENCES

The next buzz saw we ran into was Charles Schumer, the Senate minority leader. Schumer had announced that the Democrats had zero interest in helping pass the Trump tax cut. He announced that he was confident that every Senate Democrat was a no.

This was a remarkable and depressing development. It also revealed just how far to the left the Democratic Party had slipped. This wholesale partisan "resistance"—as they called it—was unlike the Kennedy and Reagan years. In those golden years, some—even most—Democrats supported tax cuts. The famous JFK tax cut was supported by the vast majority of Democrats and actually was opposed by many Republicans, including that hero of the right Senator Barry Goldwater, who voted no because of the alleged impact on the federal deficit. In 1986 Democrats worked side by side with Reagan to pass the tax reform bill—which cleaned out the tax code of special-interest provisions and lowered the top personal tax rate to 28 percent.

The Senate vote was a remarkable 97–3. In 1986 nearly every Democrat in the Senate—including Ted Kennedy, Howard Metzenbaum, Al Gore, and Pat Moynihan—supported a top tax rate of 28 percent. In 2017 not a single Senate Democrat supported anything below a top tax rate of 40 percent. Cutting the top marginal rate was seen as a blasphemous giveaway to the rich, rather than a valuable and proven way to create jobs and generate powerful upward economic mobility for workers.

Alas, Democrats had officially put themselves on notice that they were now an anti–tax cut party. We say that with no joy. Equitable prosperity is not a partisan issue and should be a bipartisan crusade. President Trump has entered the ranks of John F. Kennedy, Ronald Reagan, and Bill Clinton in enacting smart tax cuts designed to get the economy out of the doldrums and back to growing at 3 percent or more per year.

United Democratic opposition presented a daunting challenge. Could we hold the 52 Republicans together?

The only vehicle to pass a bill with 51 votes rather than the normal 60 required in the Senate was "reconciliation," a process that allows the Congress to put a target tax cut inside the budget and pass the tax cut with a simple majority of the votes. Everyone understood from the start that reconciliation was vital to the bill's passage given the Democratic "resistance."

Reconciliation, in the budget context, is a procedure that dates back to 1974, when, in the aftermath of Watergate, the congressional rules required that the House and Senate budget committees pass a "budget resolution." The Senate procedures permitted it to pass a tax cut without a filibuster—with 51 votes—as long as the revenue loss was agreed to in advance in the House and Senate budget resolution—called the "reconciliation instructions."

The 51-vote rule would work as long as Congress passed a budget earlier in the fiscal year that allowed for a tax cut of predetermined size over a particular number of years—in Trump's case, ten years. Since the reconciliation process allowed deficits only within the ten-year window, technically the tax cuts would have to expire by 2027 if they increased red ink in the years thereafter.

It was clearly not an ideal way to pass a tax cut. But it was the only way. Just as Reagan and George W. Bush had used this process to pass their tax bills, we urged Trump to use this mechanism to pass as big a tax cut as possible. As it happens, Donald Trump does big very, very well.

There was one major drawback to using reconciliation. The law empowered the Congressional Budget Office and Joint Committee on Taxation's highly flawed economic models to serve as referees and "score" tax bills. History had proven time and again that their perverse rules of "scoring" make it more difficult to reduce marginal tax rates because they always overstate revenue losses. We had made the case showing the actual numbers that over the last 30 years almost every tax hike had overestimated revenues to be raised by the federal government. Almost every tax cut had overestimated the revenue loss from a tax rate cut. The 1997 capital gains tax rate cut had been "scored" to lose tens of billions in revenues. Once enacted, that rate cut led to massive gains in tax receipts because people were willing to sell shares and realize (pay tax on the gains) once the rate was no longer confiscatory.

As for the Trump tax cut, we argued for a "tactical nuclear option inside reconciliation" that would throw out the broken static models and replace them with dynamic scoring that recognizes the positive impact of lower tax rate incentives on growth. The CBO was estimating real economic growth over the next ten years that would continue to stagnate at a 1.8 percent annual pace. However, looking at history, we could see that growth would increase with more take-home pay and handsome rewards for business. Our advice was to plug 3 percent growth into the models. This was perfectly consistent with what Trump had been saying since day one on the campaign trail. (In fact, Trump was consistently pushing for policies that he hoped would bring the growth rate to 5 percent!)

So . . . let Trump be Trump. Instead of assuming that the Trump tax cut would fail, we told congressional Republicans to have courage in their convictions, which were well supported by history. The prosperity under JFK, Reagan, and Clinton predicts that a tax cut would succeed in generating powerful economic growth.

Why not 3 percent growth rate over the next ten years? Three percent is still below America's long-run average. But if you slash tax rates, particularly on large and small businesses, it is reasonable to assume more investment, new companies, profits, productivity, wages, and job creation. It is not just reasonable to project 3 percent real GDP growth. It is conservative.

FASTER GROWTH MEANS LOWER DEBT

To hammer home this point and to get the deficit hawks—such as Senator Jeff Flake of Arizona and Senator Bob Corker of Tennessee—in our corner, we published a piece in the *Wall Street Journal* that sparked a lot of attention. It pointed out that the long-term deficit forecasts showing an alarming surge of the national debt over the next two or three decades only underscored why the nation so direly needed faster growth. Here is what we wrote in our piece from April 25, titled "Growth Can Solve the Debt Dilemma":

> The Congressional Budget Office's latest report on the nation's fiscal future is full of doom and gloom. The national debt will double in the next 30 years to 150% of gross domestic product—which is Greece territory. Interest payments may become the largest budget line, eclipsing national defense. Federal spending is expected to soar

over 20 years from 22% of GDP to 28%. Never outside of wartime has Washington's burden been so heavy on the economy.

We pointed out, however, something that few of the budget hawks in either party had recognized. The reason the debt forecast was so grim was that its growth forecast was so slow. As we put it:

> The report's most troubling forecast, by far, is for decades of sluggish economic growth. The CBO projects that America will limp along at an average 1.9% annual growth over the next 30 years. This is a sharp downgrade from historical performance. Between 1974 and 2001, average growth was 3.3%. An extra percentage point makes a world of difference. If weak growth persists, there is almost no combination of plausible spending cuts and tax increases that will get Washington anywhere near a balanced budget.[3]

The article then explained the only conceivable way out of the debt trap: 3 percent growth. We showed policymakers the impact of compound interest when it comes to faster growth. By 2040, the economy would expand not to $29.9 trillion, but to $38.3 trillion, according to an analysis by Research Affiliates, a California investment firm. That's an additional output of $8.4 trillion—roughly the entire annual production today of every state west of the Mississippi River.

By 2047, the economy would grow to $47.1 trillion, almost $13 trillion more than the CBO's baseline estimate. That would spin off an additional $2.5 trillion each year in tax revenues—enough money to pay all the bills and cover most of the unfunded costs of Social Security and Medicare. The only time we balanced the budget in 50 years was in the late 1990s under Bill Clinton, and it was a result of very fast economic growth of 4 percent, a booming stock market, and a capital gains tax cut that opened the flood gates to added investment revenue. Now 3 percent growth was a precondition to making any progress on taming our $20 trillion national debt.

Growth of 3 percent would stop the debt-to-GDP ratio from skyrocketing with modest spending restraint. Instead it would start to fall almost immediately, eventually to about 50 percent, because the economy would be so much larger. Congress and the White House ought to understand that what matters most for heading off a fiscal crisis is making sure that the economy grows faster than the government. No other debt reduction policy—certainly not a tax increase—comes close to having the fiscal effect that sustained prosperity does.

For our strategy to work, of course, we needed to double the pace of growth from 1.5 percent under Obama's last year to over 3 percent from 2018 to 2027. Many blue-chip economists agreed with the CBO that a growth rate of about 2 percent is the best that America can achieve because of the retirement of the baby boomers. Our belief was that there were at least 10 million Americans who could and should be working if the job market improved and they were rewarded for working by higher after-tax returns.

We reiterated at the end of the *Wall Street Journal* op-ed, "There's simply no way to fix the long-term fiscal problems with 1.9% growth, no matter how sharp the budget knife. What America needs is real and sustained growth."

Larry spearheaded on this one almost single-handedly. His mantra was that an economy growing at 3.1 percent will generate $4.5 trillion more than an economy growing at 1.8 percent.

This became the rallying cry of the White House and the GOP Congress over the course of the tax fight.

GO BIG OR GO HOME

But how big would the tax cut be? The moderates in the Senate were still nervous about revenue losses. Senators Collins, Corker, McCain, and Flake wanted a relatively small tax cut. They wouldn't budget one dollar over a maximum revenue loss of $1.5 trillion over ten years. This sounds like a very big number, and indeed it is. But out of $45 trillion in expected revenues over this time, it meant that the tax relief would be about three cents of every dollar of taxes—even on a static basis.

This was an improvement over "revenue neutrality." But still, small ball. The deal with the deficit hawks came down to this: Congress would live within the $1.5 trillion debt ceiling, but we would use scoring on a "dynamic" basis, which assumes economic growth. This would give us about another $1.5 trillion of tax cuts. It was a crucial concession by the deficit hawks and a breakthrough in congressional tax scoring. We weren't entirely satisfied. We wanted an estimate of $3 trillion more revenue from the tax cut's dynamic effects, which we believed were fully supported by historic data. Instead we got a score of $1.5 trillion feedback. Yet this was a breakthrough. For the first time in decades, Congress would take into account the faster economic growth that tax rate reductions would generate.

We were now confronted with another challenge. Even with the dynamic scoring, we still had about $4 trillion of cuts that we needed to stuff into a $1.5 trillion box. If the score of the tax bill coming out of the CBO was one dollar over the cap, we were out of business. Finished. We had to pull off a Houdini escape-artist act to get the tax bill we wanted and still comply with the rules. Again we huddled up with congressional leaders to retain all the tax rate reductions and abide by the reconciliation rules.

In a meeting with House Ways and Means chairman Kevin Brady, we suggested a clear way out of the box. We knew that some of the provisions of the tax bill—mostly the corporate tax rate cuts and the income tax rate cuts for small business—were highly unpopular with the class warriors inside the Democratic Party. But the middle-income tax cuts—the child credit, the doubling of the standard deduction, and the cuts in the lower-income tax rates—were generally supported by Democrats. Our goal was to preserve as much of the tax bill as possible, even if Democrats were to win Congress and possibly the White House again someday.

Why not make all the tax cuts that the Democrats liked temporary, and the tax cuts that the Democrats hated permanent? We would have a five- or six-year life span for the child credits and deductions but a permanent life span for the business rate cuts.

We were fairly certain that the middle-income tax cuts would be extended in any case. What member of Congress or senator would dare let them lapse? So this was a way to preserve the heart and soul of the tax plan and create an accounting fiction that the $1.5 trillion was still being honored.

Were we being dishonest? No. Our view was that all these budget projections about what level revenue and spending would be in four, five, or ten years were complete hocus-pocus. Congress can't even predict what the tax revenues will be one or two years into the future, let alone five or six. The ten-year forecasts are typically off by hundreds of billions of dollars. The forecasters were a gang of blind men tossing darts against a wall. And their dreadful record showed that they weren't even hitting the wall, let alone the target!

So we had few misgivings in messing with a cracked crystal ball and no compunctions about doing so. We used the absurd static scoring of CBO and the Joint Tax Committee against them.

This was also about the time when Republicans decided to add the repeal of the Obamacare individual mandate tax penalty to the plan. This was good policy because it would free 10 million Americans from having to buy health insurance they couldn't afford and didn't want. But the CBO's bizarre model forecast that the cancellation of this tax would *raise* some $150 billion for the government. It was the dumbest thing we had ever heard, but if that was what the referees were going to call, we'd gladly take it. Thanks, CBO!

Congressional Democrats were livid when they realized that we were bending their own rules against them. They ran to their friends and complained that the "tax cuts for the rich" were permanent and the middle-class tax cuts "go away after five years." Our response to Schumer and Pelosi was, if you want to make the middle-class tax cuts permanent, let's pass a bipartisan tax bill in 2018 or 2019 to do just that. You could almost see the smoke coming out of their ears. They had been outwitted.

We want to again emphasize that our goal here wasn't to deceive the public or use phony numbers. We are well aware of the negative consequences of an ever-rising burden of deficit spending. We did find it highly ironic, however, that economists from the Obama administration—the people who doubled the national debt in just eight years—were lecturing *us* on fiscal responsibility. They doubled the debt . . . while raising taxes! The debt exploded under Obama for one major reason: the economy grew by about half its normal growth rate trend.

Our goal was to supercharge the economy so that the debt burden on future generations would shrink, at least in relative terms to the economy as a whole, and be much more manageable because they would inherit a more prosperous nation with more productive capacity and wealth. We also strongly favored spending reforms that would slow the stampeding growth of government, though neither party seemed much interested in that. Our point was that if government is going to keep expanding, we'd better make sure the real economy grows even faster, preventing Uncle Sam from turning into King Kong.

Now we had a big beautiful tax bill, to borrow a phrase from Trump, with almost all the pro-growth stimulants that would help make that future possible. We were ready to rock.

LAFFER'S TAX TUTORIAL

There were still plenty of nervous Nellies in Congress who were on the tax-cutting fence. The bill was unpopular with voters and had only about a 25 percent approval rating in the fall of 2017. Democrats and the media had persuaded Americans through their public relations blitz that the Trump tax cut would raise their taxes.

The left's propaganda machine told anyone who would listen that Republicans wanted to pass a middle-class tax *hike* and a giant wet kiss for the super-wealthy. And we still heard arguments from left-wing groups like the Tax Policy Center that Trump's tax cut would blow a $6 trillion hole in the budget. If that was true, even we would have been against the bill.

It was, of course, fake news. But it was being repeated so often in the elite media echo chamber that you couldn't really blame the voters for being misled. It was time for us to set the record straight.

It was Arthur who provided the most powerful—even devastating—technical rebuttal to the Tax Policy Center and other liberal academics and policy wonks on the budget deficit arguments. Arthur published a study in September 2017 distributed by the Committee to Unleash Prosperity that became the bible, of sorts, on Capitol Hill and inside the White House. Arthur walked through the logic of his argument in the paper and then later in a presentation to Senate Republicans during a Steering Committee lunch. His conclusion: the $6 trillion revenue loss forecast was a giant hoax that could not withstand even a moment's serious economic scrutiny.

Arthur's analysis showed that while some of the tax provisions, such as the doubling of the child credit, would lose money for the government for sure, the corporate tax rate of about 20 percent (which Congress was considering) would yield about the same revenue—and possibly more—than the current system with a 35 percent rate. No one could estimate precisely how much revenue feedback there would be, but we were certain that the government scoring agencies (CBO and the Joint Tax Committee) were ignoring major real-world effects of the tax cut that could add trillions of dollars of unaccounted-for revenues. Certainly the impact was not zero. When taking into account reduced tax evasion with lower tax rates, the increase in economic activity, the positive impact of state and local tax receipts, and the $1 trillion or more of repatriated capital that would return to these shores (and pay taxes), he showed that a 20 percent business tax rate could raise as much as the 35 percent rate.

The Laffer paper also cited the recent example of countries like Canada and Japan. Canada cut its highest corporate tax rate from 36 percent (2003) to 25 percent (2012), and Canada's corporate tax revenues as a share of GDP rose from 3.15 percent to 3.29 percent respectively. Canada then reversed its corporate tax rate policy and raised the highest corporate tax rate in 2015, and tax revenues fell. Ouch!

Meanwhile, Japan cut its highest corporate tax rate from 40.9 percent in 2003 (its rate in 2003 was tied for the highest in the OECD) to 32.1 percent in 2015, and corporate tax revenues as a share of Japan's GDP rose from 3.3 to 4.26 percent.

Arthur's study's conclusion is worth repeating:

> Looking exclusively at corporate tax revenues and the highest corporate tax rate, the evidence is not strong but it most definitely does not support the notion that a cut in corporate tax rates leads to a decline in tax revenue. In fact, if there is an effect, it's most likely that a drop in business tax rates increases tax revenues and a rise in such rates lowers tax revenues.

The international and historical evidence was firmly on our side that a corporate tax cut would lose far less revenue— and perhaps gain some—than critics claimed.

One convert to this way of thinking was Treasury Secretary Steven Mnuchin. We had worked with Mnuchin almost from the very beginning of our involvement in the campaign and developed a great working relationship. He was a bit new to the policy game, having come from a finance and business background. But he proved a very quick study.

He was bombarded with a lot of the same criticism that we had been fighting since day one: "There is not a shred of evidence to support the secretary's pay-for-itself claim," Jared Bernstein, formerly Vice President Joe Biden's chief economist, griped. "Sure, significantly faster growth would spin off more revenues. But there's simply no empirical linkage between tax cuts and growth that's both a lot faster and sustained."[4]

However, Mnuchin swatted away the critics masterfully. He countered that an ambitious tax cut would unleash businesses that had felt constrained by the highest corporate tax rate in the industrialized world. Corporations, he said, would be freed to build plants and create jobs in the United States instead of in foreign countries and would bring home money that currently is sheltered overseas.

"Under static scoring, there will be short-term issues," he conceded to Congress. "Under dynamic scoring, this [the corporate tax cut] will pay for itself." We couldn't have said it better ourselves.

The $6 trillion revenue loss figure was officially down for the count.

Were we right? Only time will tell.

THE STUPID PARTY GETS SMART

But we still needed concrete revenue offsets to cover the cost of the rate reductions and the child credits, as well as small business tax cuts. We wanted to broaden the tax base as much as possible and find other revenue sources to make up the difference. The Republicans have long been affectionately known as the "Stupid Party." Waiting until mid-November to pass a must-pass tax cut would have seemed to confirm that label. But for once the pachyderms got smart.

Mitch McConnell was the first to see the opportunity that lay ahead. In the past, tax reform had been bipartisan—and in a more rational world, this bill would have been wildly bipartisan. But once Democrats declared they would be unified as obstructionists on tax reform, there was never a reason to throw even a bone to the "resistance" movement.

McConnell, one of the canniest legislative tacticians in living memory, understood that playing nice with Chuck Schumer wouldn't buy any votes. So why bother trying?

Instead, Republicans adopted several smart pay-fors that were grounded in good economic policy while simultaneously putting the hurt to left-wing groups dependent on government largesse.

The first pay-for was the cap on the state and local tax deduction. No longer could tax filers deduct their entire state and local tax bill from their federal taxes. This was a $1 trillion pay-for in the tax bill, by far the biggest.

Left-wingers argued that this meant that states and localities were going to be victims of the Trump tax cut. In fact, states and cities were in some ways the biggest beneficiaries of this federal tax cut. When the federal government doesn't take $2.5 trillion from the taxpayers of states, that's $2.5 trillion that stays in the local and state economies and never has to go to Washington in the first place, as we pointed out to a large number of governors and mayors. Uncle Sam's leaving money where it originated—and creating a climate of bottom-up economic growth—is the best thing he can do for states and cities.

The most important factor by far for state and local governments in terms of paying their bills is a strong national economy. Trump's tax cut would help us get there. This is why more than 100 state legislators signed a letter to Congress, urging them to pass the tax cut and not flinch from capping the state and local tax deduction.

But blue states—which are more heavily taxed—would get hit harder than low-tax red states. As a matter of vote counting, the states with the highest taxes—California, New York, New Jersey, Connecticut, Illinois, and Minnesota— were states with not one single Republican United States senator.

We were strongly in favor of this policy change no matter which color states would lose the most. (Larry lives and pays taxes in Connecticut; Arthur is a tax refugee from California; and Steve long ago fled his home state of Illinois—three of the highest-tax states.) But the federal government should not be an enabler for overtaxing state and local governments and shouldn't be bailing out bankrupt public employee pension programs. There is no possible justification for a person living in Tennessee or Utah or New Hampshire having to pay higher federal taxes to subsidize the overpriced public sectors in New Jersey and Connecticut.

That's particularly true when one considers that there is no evidence that higher taxes in these states lead to better schools or police protection.

New York spends $7,500 per person on state and local government. New Hampshire spends less than $4,000. Yet public services are better in New Hampshire than in New York.

Liberals instantly understood some of the repercussions of this policy shift. The big blue states either must cut their costs, and taxes, or the exodus of high-income residents from these states will accelerate. We have estimated that unless

New York, California, New Jersey, and Minnesota cut their state and local income tax rates—of 10 percent or more—they will lose about 3 million residents—most likely their biggest taxpayers—to other states in the next four years. This could put a big revenue hole in these state budgets. California and New York already lost a net 2.5 million residents to other states from 2007 to 2016.

This cap also ironically made the Trump tax cut *more* progressive. The $10,000 cap on the state and local deduction meant that about 90 percent of tax filers would be unaffected. The people who *would* be hurt by this provision were very wealthy tax filers in high-income-tax-rate states.

Here were left-leaners like Governor Andrew Cuomo of New York defending a $1.5 trillion tax loophole for the richest 1 percent whom they elsewhere rhetorically flog.

So this is what hypocrisy looks like.

Next was the gutsy decision by Republicans (and mentioned above) to offset the cost of the tax cut by eliminating the individual mandate tax imposed mostly on Americans who earn less than $50,000 a year. This was a tax primarily on poor people whom Democrats claim to want to protect. The purpose of the tax was to induce Americans to purchase health insurance. We found it amazing that Obamacare subsidizes people to buy health insurance, penalizes them if they don't, and yet at least 13 million Americans still refused to buy it. That would seem to be the sign of an inferior product.

Finally, an idea that didn't get much attention is the tax on college endowments. These are massive storehouses of wealth. Harvard and Yale combined sit on roughly $20 billion. This is enough to give every student free tuition at these schools from now until forever . . . and the colleges would never run out of money. Instead these university endowments are like giant tax-exempt hedge funds with very little largesse going to help students pay their exorbitant tuition and room and board.

The GOP plan placed a small 1.4% tax on endowment net investment income for schools with more than 500 students and at least $500,000 of investments per student. Our complaint here was that by our calculations, the tax rate was way too low. But, nevertheless, the first shot across the bow of the university-industrial complex was fired.

Will this hurt education? Professor Richard Vedder of Ohio University, an expert on higher education, has documented that university tuitions don't go down when these schools have bigger endowments. They go up.[5]

Perhaps our favorite bonus provision added to the tax bill was allowing drilling for oil in Alaska's Arctic National Wildlife Refuge. This was something that sensible people had advocated for since the mid-1980s. We agreed with Trump that this would create jobs, help resuscitate Alaska's economy, *and* make America more prosperous by adding 10 million barrels of oil production a year. Bonus: it will also bring in additional federal revenues, as the energy companies that will drill there will pay federal income and payroll taxes, as will their employees, plus corporate taxes and royalties.

It was a major win-win for the economy. The objections of environmental extremists were overstated and unpersuasive. The area of drilling would be equivalent to a medium pizza on a football field. We had learned from the building of the Alaska pipeline in the mid-1970s that the environmental effects were greatly exaggerated. Economic development and environmental protection can, and must, peacefully coexist.

Even better was that the Alaska drilling was the one demand that Senator Lisa Murkowski had made in exchange for her vote. Senator Murkowski had voted against the Obama-care repeal bill three months before. Thus, her vote on the tax cut that included repeal of the individual mandate was very much a concern for Republicans, who had to get 50 yeses out of 52 Republican senators to enact this legislation.

All these changes created a consortium of special-interest lobbies that hated the tax bill. These included health insurance companies, green groups, Obamacare supporters, public employee unions, state and local officials, the welfare lobby, municipal bond traders, sociology professors, corporate lobbyists, and, most of all, left-leaning politicians. In short, those who protested were those who are funded by the loopholes eliminated.

Bravo, Trump! It doesn't get any better than this. What better way to drain the swamp?

THE PROBLEM WITH DELAYING THE TAX CUTS

A pivotal moment in the tax cut battle came on November 9 when Senate Finance Committee chairman Orrin Hatch released the Senate markup of the bill. This was a very good bill. It was actually better than the House bill—an unexpected accomplishment. Usually the Senate waters down the House's bills, but in this case, Chairman Hatch and Senator Pat Toomey of Pennsylvania, his lieutenant on the tax bill, added more growth tonic.

The Hatch tax bill also had lower income tax rates and most of the other features of the House bill—and was superior in certain ways to the House bill.

One feature that gave Arthur heartburn, though, was a provision to delay the corporate tax cut for one year, so that it would begin in 2019, not 2018. This was to save money.

The Senate was up against the $1.5 trillion budget resolution hard cap on the ten-year size of the tax cut. Hatch couldn't get the rate down to 20 percent unless the tax cuts were delayed until 2019.

The proponents of this policy argued that the capital expensing provision (100 percent depreciation in one year that was scheduled to take effect on January 1, 2018, and last for five years) would offset the one-year delay in cutting the corporate tax rate. Here's Speaker Paul Ryan on the issue: "Phasing in [sic] the corporate reduction still is very good for economic growth. . . . You still get very fast economic growth and you actually are encouraging companies to spend on factories and plants and equipment and hiring people sooner with the phase in."

At a meeting with some 30 Senate Republicans, Arthur insisted that the logic here was completely wrong. If they delayed the tax cut, it would hurt the economy and harm the GOP in the 2018 midterm elections. "If the tax bill is proposed and signed into law," he explained, "then the current statutory maximum corporate tax rate and current depreciation schedule are no longer relevant. You would instead ask yourself the following question: which would I rather have, A) 100 percent expensing and a 35 percent corporate tax rate or B) 100 percent expensing and a 20 percent corporate tax rate? If B is your answer, which it should be, then you will postpone your actions until the second year, 2019. The choice between A and B is the correct choice businesses will face if Congress passes the bill with a delay of the corporate tax rate cut."

Then Arthur asked the senators: "What option would you choose?"

He also gave the senators a valuable economic history seminar.

In 1981 when President Reagan's tax bill passed, the president gave me a congratulatory call, yet he sensed early in the conversation that I was not as excited as he thought I should be. He was incredibly excited about getting the tax bill through—and I was too—yet I was concerned about the effect of phasing in the tax cuts. I asked him, "How much would you shop at a store a week before that store has its big discount sale?" He saw the point immediately.

History demonstrates that broadcasting a delay in a tax rate cut corresponds to a delay in economic activity until the new lower tax rates are fully phased in. Arthur had lived through the delaying of the 1981 income tax cuts, which were not fully phased in until 1983. He contends this made the 1982 recession much deeper than it might have been had the cuts been effective immediately. He said the phase-in mistake delayed the Reagan expansion by about 18 months. Don't repeat that mistake, he pleaded.

In the end, Arthur carried the day. None of the senators, especially the ones who were up for reelection in November 2018, said they would support the tax cut delay. That was the end of that.

The GOP senators compromised with a 21 percent corporate tax rate—one percentage point higher than the 20 percent reported out of the House—but effective immediately on January 1, 2018.

DON'T FORGET SMALL BUSINESSES

Throughout the debate, we never forgot the Trump demand that the tens of millions of small businesses needed to get a tax cut too. It turns out that as the plan got negotiated in the

House and Senate, small businesses were getting a tiny tax cut while corporations got a sizable rate cut.

That wasn't fair, and one senator who took a stand for this this was Senator Ron Johnson of Wisconsin. In early December, as the bill was headed for the Senate for a final vote, Johnson told the media he was a "no" on the tax bill. This news sent shock waves through the Capitol. "If Congress wants to pass a tax bill that doesn't help small businesses, they will have to do it without my vote," he announced.

Senator McConnell and his staff asked us to see what we could do to pull Johnson back into the fold. We had worked with him from the time he had first run for Senate in Wisconsin back in 2010. One thing was for sure. Without Ron Johnson's aye there would be no tax bill.

We visited Johnson the day after we visited two other last-minute dissenters, Steve Daines and Bob Corker. Johnson, one of the few actual small business owners in the United States Senate, was as angry as a Wisconsin badger when we came into his office. He growled at us that the tax bill as passed through the Senate was false advertising. "There is no tax cut for many of the millions of small businesses," he protested. He walked us through the reams of analysis he had done, and . . . his proof was irrefutable. The bill was offering crumbs for small businesses, and this was a bait and switch.

We vowed to work with Johnson to fix this. Johnson wanted two things. A lower top income tax rate of 37 percent, down from nearly 40 percent under the current code. Since about two-thirds of the folks in this income tax bracket are small businessmen and -women, this made sense. He also wanted a 20 percent exemption on small business income from federal tax. We liked that idea too. This would bring the top small business tax rate down to an effective rate of about

30 percent for most successful small businesses, down from nearly 40 percent under current law.

The White House was fully in support. We reminded President Trump that he had always told us from the start he wanted a low tax rate on the small businesses of America and that the Johnson amendment would deliver on that promise. It would also create a rough parity for large corporations and small businesses. When taking into account the double tax on corporate dividends and capital gains, all business profits would be subject to roughly a 30 percent tax rate.

We went back to Senator Johnson and laid it out for him. He was a happy camper. The Trump tax cut would be the biggest small business tax cut in at least 15 years.

Liberals uttered a primal scream about the 37 percent tax rate. Tax cuts for millionaires! they shrieked. But they seemed to forget that in the United States, small businesses pay their income tax on the individual income tax return of the owner, not through the corporate tax system. They couldn't seem to understand the basic truism that a very high top income tax rate of 39.6 percent was nearly the highest in the world on small businesses, and thus hurts small and medium-sized firms. Without these companies prospering and expanding, where were the new jobs going to come from? We liked to quote from the former House majority leader Dick Armey: "Liberals love jobs, but they hate employers. You can't have one without the other."

We were disappointed that professional-service small businesses such as accounting, financial, and communication firms were precluded from accessing the lower rate. While we agreed that the optics of a hedge fund paying a lower tax rate than a wage earner in the heartland would be bad, we wanted to see this lower rate extended to *all* small businesses that are also employers, regardless of industry classification, in order to do the most good for employees, job seekers, and the over-all economy.

We routinely talk to men and women who own and operate small businesses. Most of them told us that if Congress delivered on the Trump tax cut, they would invest most of their tax savings into growing their businesses so they could become medium and even large businesses over time. This is what happened in the immediate aftermath of the tax bill.

This is how President Trump will create the next generation of Home Depots, Costcos, and FedExes.

STOP THE STEALTH CAPITAL GAINS TAX HIKE

Another brushfire we helped snuff out could have burned down the bill. No one knows quite how it happened—which says a lot about how the sausage-making factory works on Capitol Hill—but someone, probably a committee staffer, slipped into the Senate bill a stealth capital gains tax *increase* on long-held assets. When we learned about this after reading through the bill, we rang the alarm bell and were surprised to discover most members of Congress had no idea that this booby trap was buried in the bill.

The provision turned the capital gains tax on its head by requiring shareholders to sell their oldest shares of stock in a company before their newest purchased shares. The older the share, typically, the larger the taxable capital gain. This is called the first-in, first-out (FIFO) accounting system.

Consider this example. Let us say you bought 100 shares of Apple stock in 1998 at $100 a share. And let's say you bought another 100 shares in 2008 at $300. If you sold 100 shares at

$500 a share, you would have to "sell" the oldest stock and pay a capital gains tax on the $400 difference between the price you bought it for and what you sold it for. Under the current law you could sell the shares you bought for $300, realizing a capital gain of only $200. Now, this accounting change to FIFO might make sense in some circumstances . . . except that the gains on stocks are not adjusted for inflation. On many sales of long-held stock, as much as half of the reported and taxable "gain" is due to the increase in price, but not value, attributable to inflation.

This sneaky booby trap would have meant that the actual capital gains tax incurred upon sale could more than double the tax due for many stock and asset sales.

So the Senate rules would have required millions of Americans to pay a stiff tax on phantom gains. That is patently unfair, and we told the congressional leadership this would discourage the very long-term investment the bill was intended to stimulate.

Under the Senate bill, there was also an exception for mutual funds, exchange-traded funds (ETFs), and other institutional funds. They would continue to apply the current law tax treatment.

So get this: the regular Joes and Jills who want to buy and sell stock on their own would have to pay the higher capital gains tax. The big investment funds were being provided a more generous set of rules with lower taxes. Good news for Fidelity and Vanguard. But what about Joe and Jill Lunch Bucket? Forced FIFO would have pressured small investors to purchase stock through the big fund managers—and pay their fees. This is, of course, antithetical to President Trump's populism, his commitment to having regular people—his base—get a fair shake. It was an alarming provision.

In addition to the fairness factor, the higher tax on capital gains would have discouraged people from buying stock, or investing, in small start-ups in the first place. This provision would have also exacerbated the lock-in effect of the capital gains tax. When the tax on gains is higher, Americans are much more reluctant to sell their shares and pay the higher tax.

This benefits old established companies like Boeing and Microsoft. It dries up capital for smaller and fast-growing firms that could become the next generation's Apple, Google, or Uber.

But Ways and Means Committee chairman Kevin Brady saved the day! We contacted the chairman, and he and Speaker Ryan sprang into action, alerting the Senate that no bill would be approved in the House booby-trapped with such an unintended capital gains tax hike. Were we lucky or smart to have tripped across this subtle booby trap? The offending provision was stricken from the bill.

FIFTY IS NIFTY

There are only 52 Republicans in the Senate. President Trump needed 50 + 1 votes to win. We lost a lot of sleep in those last few weeks over the possibility that we would come up one or two votes short. This is exactly what had tripped up Obamacare's repeal and replace. On the final vote, John McCain, who was undergoing treatment for brain cancer, opted to vote against Obamacare repeal. Obamacare, with all its egregious flaws, survived.

We just couldn't have it on our conscience that we allowed a defeat of the president's signature initiative—the tax cut. Too much was at stake. The importance of this legislation transcended that of mere politics.

One of the factors that helped get 50 + 1 votes in the Senate was the severe negative political consequences of losing. Nearly every Republican over the summer recess had been pilloried by conservative voters for failing to deliver on repealing and replacing Obamacare. This reinforced the sense that failure was not an option on the signature GOP issue—the big tax cut. The Congress, both House and Senate, was looking at an electoral wipeout in November 2018 if Capitol Hill failed to deliver a major, historic tax cut.

The three of us made the case—over and over—that the powerful economic burst of adrenaline since Trump's election, and the surge in business and consumer confidence, would reverse course if the Congress failed to deliver the promised tax cut. The main thing the GOP had going for it at this stage was the good feelings voters had about jobs and growth prospects. Optimism abounded.

We reminded Congress at every turn that passing the tax cut would support a big stock market rally, promoting the happiness of their voters, and that stalling out on the tax cut would certainly prompt a bearish market sell-off, to their detriment. The likelihood of a market panic—and an economic contraction—buttressed wavering Republicans to support the tax cut.

Finally, we made the case that the tax cut *had* to be passed before Christmas. If the bill was unfinished heading into 2018, there was a good chance it would not happen. Republicans had lost the special election in Alabama—of all states—when voters ruled Judge Roy Moore unfit for office. The GOP would have a Senate majority of only one vote in 2018.

The window in which to pass the Trump tax cut was slamming shut fast. We felt like Harrison Ford as Indiana Jones trying to outrace that massive boulder rolling toward him down the hill. Hurry!

This created a mad scramble to get the tax cut passed, in December, and in less than three weeks. It was a daunting challenge, but not impossible.

We worked closely in the final weeks with Brendan Dunn—McConnell's policy director, who was in charge of counting the votes and making sure Republican support didn't falter on the eve of President Trump's historic tax cut.

One of the darkest days was in early December. Leader McConnell updated us on the status of the pending Trump tax cut. "We have big problems on our side of the aisle," he wrote. "We don't have the votes right now."

Leader McConnell gave us the names of the key Senate stragglers. Our mission now was clear. The list included John McCain, Bob Corker, Ron Johnson, Steve Daines, Jeff Flake, and Susan Collins.

Each had different reservations about the bill. Some thought it cut taxes too much. Others said it cut taxes too little. The week before Christmas Larry, Steve, and Arthur met separately with each of these senators, in some cases several times.

Larry flew to D.C. on December 18 and spent the entire day scrambling with Steve from one office to the next in a last-ditch effort to make the case, cajole, and, as a last resort, twist off arms if necessary.

Larry was recovering from dental surgery the day before, but he still rose to the occasion. When Steve met up with him in front of the Hart Senate Office Building that morning, Larry looked like he had been clocked with a Joe Frazier left hook. His jaw was the pink color of watermelon and he was moaning and slightly slurring his words.

We wondered whether he would make it through the day . . . stacked as it was with one-on-one meetings with United States senators. Talk about taking one for the team! But we really felt this was about changing the direction of the American economy for a decade. That's how big the stakes were.

Larry and Steve sat with the undecided senators. (Arthur had been on Capitol Hill a few days before . . . doing the same rounds and making the economic case to turn around the no votes.) Larry and Steve were the ninth-inning relievers. We didn't do the hard sell. We patiently walked through the virtues of the Trump tax cut with many wavering senators.

All the senators—so it seemed to us—wanted to vote for the Trump tax cut. None of them wanted to go down in history as casting the vote to kill Trump's tax cut.

That said, getting all of them to vote yes was a heavy lift.

The bill had been pummeled by the media and their enablers, the plethora of left-wing special-interest groups. Before the vote, fewer than one in four voters supported the bill. Millions of Americans thought it was a tax increase, because that was the fake news delivered through much of the elite media.

Fortunately, we knew the features of the tax plan intimately. We had the facts on our side. We knew also that about 90 percent of middle-income voters would pay less, not more, in federal income taxes.

Our line to the senators was that once the public sees the tax cut—and extra take-home pay in their fatter paychecks—they would figure out that the media, Chuck Schumer, and Nancy Pelosi had been lying to them. They would see the proof in their paychecks.

That was our calculus.

The two Republicans we were worried most about were Bob Corker and Susan Collins. We knew that if we could earn their votes, the Trump tax cut would pass.

Both had principled objections to the bill, and we respected that. They were both worried about the deficit impact, and Collins worried about the impact of Medicaid payments to her state of Maine. Corker was the senator who insisted that the price of the tax bill not exceed $1.5 trillion over a decade—out of about $45 trillion in expected revenue collections. He demanded assurances that we weren't violating that promise. He was skeptical that the growth dynamic we were predicting would happen.

We explained that the additional growth from passage of the bill would significantly reduce the fear of a budget deficit. What we repeated, over and over, was that we could expect $3 trillion more revenue from 1 percent faster growth. The CBO confirmed this relationship. We needed to "grow the denominator" (and shrink the numerator) of the debt-to-GDP ratio or else our fiscal future would get worse, not better. That was the only way out.

Some of these Republicans had bought into the "limits to growth" narrative of the left—that the economy has a ceiling of 2 percent annual real growth. This is America. Don't buy the pessimism, Senator.

And as a purely political matter, we reminded these crucial U.S. senators that Trump and the Republicans won the election by promising jobs and prosperity. A majority of voters agreed with Trump that a tax cut would be good for the economy. Failure to get a pro-growth tax cut done would imperil nearly every GOP seat. Conservative voters weren't

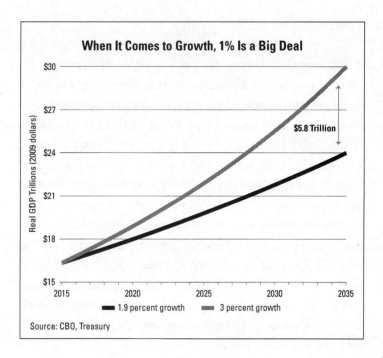

When It Comes to Growth, 1% Is a Big Deal

$5.8 Trillion

1.9 percent growth   3 percent growth

Source: CBO, Treasury

going to buy into the lame excuse that "the CBO wouldn't let us do it."

At the end of those meetings, both Senator Corker and Senator Collins sat back and almost sighed in relief, half whispering, "OK, I'm a yes on the president's tax cut." We knew at that magical moment we had it.

On December 18 the two senators on the fence made their public declarations that they would vote for the Trump tax cut the next day. It was one of the happiest days of our professional lives. This bill would be the most pro-growth tax bill since Reagan. It would change the country.

President Trump would make history.

POSTSCRIPT

A few months after the tax cut passed, Steve met up with President Trump at his winter retreat, Mar-a-Lago in Palm Beach, Florida. Trump was eating dinner, and Steve had been invited as one of the guests for a reception there that night. At dinner, Steve ambled over to the table where Trump and first lady Melania were seated. Steve walked past the Secret Service agent and tapped the president on the shoulder when he wasn't in conversation. He turned around, jumped out of his chair, and jubilantly spurted out: "Steve, isn't this the greatest tax cut ever? Can you believe the impact this is having? All the jobs. All the bonuses." He was referring to the 5-million-plus workers—mostly low- and middle-income Americans—who had already received bonuses and pay raises in the aftermath of the new tax law. The unemployment rate had neared a 30-year low just weeks before.

Steve replied, "Mr. President, it's working out better than when we drew it up on the chalkboard two years ago in your office in Manhattan." Trump nodded his head yes and replied with a big smile: "It really is, isn't it?"

7

Deregulator in Chief

"I was born to regulate. . . . So long as I'm regulating, I'm happy."

—MARTHE KENT, an Obama OSHA regulator[1]

In May 2016 Trump held the first meeting of the Economic and Business Policy Council. This was a highly impressive group of respected CEOs of highly profitable companies. They were leaders of banks, manufacturing companies, technology firms, retailers, construction companies, and energy companies—to name a few. The meeting took place in the master conference room a few floors down from Donald Trump's office in Trump Tower. Steve and Arthur were the economists invited to the session.

One of the major conveners of that meeting was Harold Hamm, the billionaire founder and chief executive of Continental Resources. Harold was the epitome of the American dream. He grew up in rural Oklahoma with eight brothers and sisters in a home without plumbing. He left home at 17, got involved at the lowest rungs of the oil and gas business, and built up the drilling business at a swift and steady pace. His major breakthrough was to be the first wildcatter to drill wells in North Dakota using the new techniques known as horizontal drilling and hydraulic fracturing. He owned many of the most productive wells in the center of the Bakken Shale and made a fortune drilling the seemingly endless pool of shale oil and shale gas.

Trump loved Harold and his rags-to-riches story from the start. The two could not have been more different, one a suave New York real estate developer who loved to hear himself talk and the other an unsophisticated, taciturn Okie whose favorite pastime wasn't golf but quail hunting in the remotest areas of southern Texas. Hamm wrote one of the first big checks for Trump and his allied PACs, and he stood by Trump during the mountains and the valleys of the campaign. Almost immediately he became a valued confidant.

The two of us attended the meeting as Trump's economic gang, and let's just say we were easily the poorest people in the room by a few zeroes on our tax returns. At this meeting Trump boasted that he was going to "win on the economy because for eight years Obama hasn't known what he is doing and knows nothing about business." He pledged that he would be "the greatest pro-business president ever," which was like hearing a Pavarotti aria to these assembled businessmen and -women.

Then after a five-minute greeting along these lines, Trump said to the 25 or so CEOs, "I want to hear from you. How can we help your businesses grow and prosper and create jobs?"

He sat back and listened intently, then queried these executives for almost an hour and a half. We had originally suspected that he would stick his head in, say hello, and then politely leave and have the campaign staff—that is, us—listen to their stories and advice. It turns out that Trump can be a very good listener when he wants to be.

Everyone was asked to pinpoint the one thing the feds could do to make their lives easier. We thought that they would mostly say cut taxes. Some did, but not most. The number one concern of the bankers, builders, techies, energy suppliers, coal producers, manufacturers, hospital administrators, and media magnates was simply this: please get the government off our backs. As one coal executive put it: "We are being strangled by regulation and red tape. If you want to make America great again, please put a muzzle on the regulators."

They complained about everything from the Dodd-Frank bank regulations to the EPA's Clean Power Plan rules, to OSHA, the FDA, and the Labor Department stifling their growth and profitability. It wasn't just the laws themselves, but the Obama regulatory zealots who were universally hostile to business—especially the fossil fuel industry—and seemed intent on shutting down companies, not helping them comply with the thicket of often-contradictory rules.

All this had a big impact on Trump's thinking as he devised his economic game plan. We had told him in our briefings that the regulatory burden had the economic impact of a second income tax. Our friends at the Mercatus Center had crunched the economic impact numbers of the deadweight loss of regulation, and they estimated just shy of $2 trillion of lost output per year due to compliance costs—which was a little more than the federal income tax raised each year. Those costs had exploded under Obama. As one of the CEOs said at the meeting, "The Obama regulators treat us like enemy combatants." But hearing this directly from the nation's major job creators seemed to hit Trump in the forehead with the force of a sledgehammer.

It was not long after this revelation that Trump began to deliver a new and memorable line on the campaign trail. "For every new regulation my agencies create, we will have them repeal two. The number and cost of regulations will go down in my administration," he pledged.

Now, a skeptic might reasonably say: Of course a bunch of rich business owners are against regulation, for the same reason cats don't like bells put on their collars. We *have* health, safety, and environmental regulations precisely because we can't trust business to act responsibly. And in many cases that's absolutely true.

In many conversations we had with Trump, he would get a stern, no-nonsense look on his face and say, "We're going to make sure we have the cleanest air and the cleanest and safest water ever. I want beautiful water." No argument here from us.

What we were talking about was cutting regulations whose costs far exceeded their public benefits, and finding ways to protect the health and safety of the public and the planet but at lesser cost to everyone. As economists, we wanted to find ways to make sure that the benefits of regulation exceeded the costs, and we had hundreds of examples where that wasn't the case.

KILLING COAL

The three of us had spent a lot of our careers assessing the costs of regulation, so we knew what the economic models and theories were telling us. Regulations hurt jobs, incomes, and American competitiveness. But it wasn't until we traveled with and for Trump to beleaguered areas of the country where people were hurting and their livelihoods had been lost that we really observed firsthand how the iron fist of the regulatory state could crush whole towns and communities.

The most heartbreaking example was when we traveled to coal country: mining towns in West Virginia, Ohio, Virginia, and Pennsylvania, to name a few. On one memorable visit to Charleston, West Virginia, the annihilation of small coal communities was a depressing sight to behold. Where mining was once in full swing with second- or third-generation miners, truckers, and construction crews that worked hard and long hours for an honest day's paycheck, the mines were now mostly shut down and people stood in unemployment lines. Many had become addicted to methamphetamine and opioids, and they sat on the porches of their tiny homes in the mountains with nothing to do. In work there is dignity, personal gratification—a raison d'être. In idleness and layoffs there are depression and feelings of worthlessness. Suicide rates soared, schools and playgrounds and malls were shuttered, half of the homes (many of them were trailer homes) were abandoned. The scene in these towns looked like what you would see in a third-world country, and it brought back the imagery of despair from *The Grapes of Wrath*. No one smiled. The main places of commerce seemed to be the liquor stores and the pawnshops. People's life savings were in their homes, as low in value as they might be, so the logical choice of moving to where the jobs were was a money-losing last resort.

Now, we believe in the free market idea of creative destruction. There is a life cycle in businesses and industries that is conducive to growth and higher living standards over time. Old industries—from horse-and-buggy producers, to rotary phones, to DVD players, to typewriters—are replaced with better, cheaper, faster devices. This is called progress.

But what we were witnessing wasn't creative destruction. This was a planned governmental purge. Yes, the surge in output of cheap natural gas put a huge dent in the rival coal industry. But coal has been on a long track of becoming much cleaner and much cheaper. Coal can compete with natural gas on a level playing field. (We laughed at liberals whose cavalier response to the dying coal industry was that we must let market forces play out. But they were willing to spend tens of billions of dollars a year on green energy subsidies to wind and solar power—which in most markets are about three to four times more expensive than coal.) But Obama and his green allies were on a crusade to crush the coal industry as part of their grandiose plan to save the planet. They had no reservations about sticking a knife into the back of an industry that even at its low point employed hundreds of thousands of workers and supplied one-third of America's electric power.

They were willing to allow these communities to die. We often observed that it is highly doubtful that the university professors, the journalists, and the billionaire donors to Greenpeace and the Sierra Club would have been nearly so committed to combating global warming if it were their own jobs, their families, their communities, and their life savings that were going to be destroyed. Global warming alarmists were so committed to their cause that there was no limit to how many of *other* people's jobs would have to be sacrificed at the green altar. If they ever cared to leave their homes in Beverly Hills and Harvard Square and visit the human misery their jackbooted regulatory policies were causing, would it have changed their minds? Killing coal squashed the spirit and savings of hundreds of thousands of families—needlessly.

Trump stood with these workers and promised to rebuild American coal.

Hillary, meanwhile, promised more government welfare benefits, retraining funds, and education dollars for the victims of the war on coal. But when she was with her donors, she promised to kill every coal job in America, which elicited howls of approval. What humanitarians!

This story is a microcosm of the effect of a heavy-handed, destructive regulatory state. Those who are most victimized by regulatory tyranny are the lowest-income Americans who face higher prices, more unemployment pink slips, and destruction of their communities, whether in rural America or inner cities like the war zones of Detroit, Baltimore, and Newark. Regulation is not an evenly distributed tax on America, it is a highly regressive tax that punishes the poorest Americans the most. More and more working-class voters recognized this high cost to their families. Trump got it. Hillary and the liberals continued to pretend that regulators are your friends.

IF IT MOVES, REGULATE IT

One of the men on Capitol Hill who played a lead role for Trump on the deregulation front, responsible for the legislation to roll back Dodd-Frank, was Jeb Hensarling of Texas. We had worked for years with Hensarling and at one point had supported him to be elevated to Speaker of the House, after Denny Hastert of Illinois left that post. Hensarling is one of the most talented and sharp-witted congressmen we have ever met, and he understands economics, having served many years earlier as an aide to Senator Phil Gramm of Texas—who in an earlier life was a distinguished economics professor. (Yes, people who understand that demand curves slope downward and that if you tax something, you get less of it are sometimes elected to Congress.)

In the fall of 2017, Hensarling wanted to meet with us for some help on the financial deregulation bill he had authored.

We asked him why he thought the economy and stock market had boomed so rapidly since Trump's election. Hensarling quipped: "The answer to that is easy: on November 7, 2016, the beatings stopped." We laughed, but there was so much truth to this.

Obama and his regulatory SWAT team had for eight years intimidated and beaten down business with an avalanche of regulations and hyper-enforcement that was likened to the Brooklyn Mafia. This blanket of fear that hung over manufacturers, drug companies, energy and chemical producers, tech firms, insurance companies, banks, and small businesses stunted growth. If you see the guy down the street getting mugged, you're not likely to travel down that avenue. At least the Mafia took only 10 or 15 percent and didn't shut you down. The intimidation game, as our friend Kim Strassel of the *Wall Street Journal* described it, was as much a growth killer as the laws and regulations themselves. In *The Wizard of Oz*, the Munchkins come out of hiding to dance and sing only when they are absolutely certain the Wicked Witch of the West is dead. For many businesses, the feeling after the election of Trump and the ouster of the Obama regulators was "Ding Dong the Witch Is Dead."

Consider first the raw numbers. By the end of Obama's presidency, there were 2.1 million civilian employees of the federal executive branch—mostly regulators and other busybodies—people who are most assuredly not "here to help." That's about 235,000 (13 percent) more full-time employees than there were in 2007. The boost in executive branch employment was undoubtedly spurred by the growth of the federal regulatory burden over that same period.

We see this in the overall number of regulations, which is an imperfect but highly instructive measure of federal red tape for businesses to get tangled up in. If we look at pages in the Federal Register, we see a steady rise in the pace of rule-making. Thankfully, the level still hasn't exceeded the number under the worst regulator of all time—Jimmy Carter—but the regulatory switch was definitely turned on in the Obama administration. George W. Bush was no great shakes on the rule-making front either. His 2007 energy bill regulated everything from fuel-efficiency standards to lightbulbs to air conditioners and refrigerators.

Even more telling was the enactment of major regulatory rules with a cost to the economy of more than $100 million. These aren't nuisance regulations, they are the major job and prosperity killers. At the top of the list was the aforementioned Obama Clean Power Plan law that crippled the coal industry and added huge costs to utilities.

An influential 2017 analysis by Jason Pye of Freedom Works, a grassroots conservative watchdog group, found that under Barack Obama there were well over 500 new regulations with costs to the economy of more than $100 million each![2] Altogether these regulations added a minimum of $50–100 billion in costs to the U.S. economy. Pye checked to find out how many of these expensive regulations were approved by Congress—which under our Constitution is the branch that's supposed to make the laws. The answer was exactly *zero*. Trump is pushing a reform called the REINS Act, which would require a positive vote by Congress before any regulation with a price tag of more than $100 million goes into effect.

TWENTY-TWO TO ONE

One of Trump's first actions as president was to honor his promise to repeal two existing regulations for every new one. He signed Executive Order 13771 within his first few weeks in office.

This order also mandated that there could be no increases in net regulatory costs for fiscal year 2017 and was extended for 2018.

The results are in, and the deregulation effort has been an over-the-top success. Thus far, instead of two repeals for every new rule, the ratio has been closer to "twenty-two for one."[3] According to the same report, these combined actions saved $8.15 billion in government spending—which doesn't include the billions saved by consumers and companies.

The administration also successfully eliminated, delayed, or streamlined 1,579 regulatory actions that were left "in the pipeline" by Obama regulators for future implementation. They were tossed into the trash cans.

Trump recently announced that he has upped the ante and now wants three regulations repealed for every new regulation. Our friend Mick Mulvaney of the Office of Management and Budget (OMB) tells us this alone will save businesses and consumers and workers just short of $10 billion.

Below we highlight several priority areas where Trump has made a difference in getting government snoops off our backs.

KILLING COMMUNITY BANKS

Washington operates under the principle of the law of unintended consequences. Laws and edicts often have precisely the opposite effect of what the politicians hoped for.

Exhibit A was the Dodd-Frank law, which was supposed to reduce the risk of another financial meltdown as we saw in 2008 and 2009. Yes, we all want to prevent that kind of financial trauma from ever happening again. But one of our most persistent pieces of advice to Trump was to repeal most, if not all, of the 2,300-page Dodd-Frank.

One of the cruelest ironies of the financial regulation bill of 2009 signed into law by Obama was that the two principle authors of the bill—Barney Frank of Massachusetts and Chris Dodd of Connecticut—were in no small part the arsonists who started the fire in the first place.

Obama and the Democratic Congress said they were taking aim at the big banks in order to prevent such a catastrophe from happening in the future. But instead the bill has made big banks bigger, and their ammunition wiped out small community banks throughout the country—even though small banks posed no "systemic risk" to the financial system and had nothing to do with the 2008 crisis.

The same banks that were described as "too big to fail" are now bigger than ever before. The top five largest banks now control 44 percent of U.S. banking assets. The consolidation of major banking institutions (funded in part by taxpayer dollars) comes with added risk to our economy, and at the expense of smaller banks nationwide.

Meanwhile, the number of banks in the United States continues to fall precipitously. The days of the Building and Loan that was run by Jimmy Stewart in *It's a Wonderful Life* are over.

Why has Dodd-Frank contributed to consolidation and empowered the "too big to fail" banks? Rescinding this law would make life a lot easier for smaller community banks, which do not have the economies of scale to keep up with intense regulations.

Arthur summed it up well in a study he authored on the excessive regulation of the automobile industry in the late 1970s. It's amazing how some things don't change:

> All regulations create a wedge between prices paid by consumers and the prices received by producers. When compliance with a regulatory wedge involves a common or fixed cost, it is equivalent to a lump sum tax. As a result, there is a differential impact on the profitability of large versus small firms. This differential increases for industries characterized by economies-of-scale production.[4]

To give you an idea of the cost, the six largest banks in the United States spent a combined $70.2 billion on regulatory compliance in 2013. As many as one in five people on Wall Street's job is to make sure nobody is violating the 20,000-plus pages of bank regulations. Just imagine the burden on community banks that do not have the funds to hire compliance analysts. It is clear that community banks have been on the decline, and fresh regulatory burdens over the last eight years have not helped.

While big banks have the money to hire scores of experts and compliance officers who can deal with new regulatory red tape, many small community banks lack the resources to comply with additional government regulations. As one would expect, this legislation has caused the big banks to get bigger and forced small banks to close up shop. A study from Harvard University found that since "around the time of the Dodd-Frank Act's passage," the "community banks' share of assets has shrunk drastically—over 12 percent."[5] While small banks should be the backbone of personal and small business loans in our communities, they are bearing the brunt of the damage caused by the Dodd-Frank bill. Many small businesses have complained of a credit squeeze that is inhibiting business start-ups and expansions—which means fewer jobs. The demise of community banks is one explanation for this lending freeze in small towns across the country.

Dodd-Frank was also a classic catch-22—the kind that only government could think up. Under the 1970s-era Community Reinvestment Act, Congress hoped to radically discourage bank "redlining"—a practice in which banks simply would avoid approving mortgages in communities with certain zip codes that have high percentages of minority residents. So Congress forced banks to make loans in these low-income communities. They were called Community Reinvestment Act (CRA) loans, and they were intended to reduce discriminatory lending practices by banks. In some cases banks had to lower their underwriting standards to ensure that the minority applicants were eligible for the loans. What is also clear is that the CRA created a culture in bank lending offices to issue loans with very relaxed underwriting standards to fill "quotas."

But then when the mortgage industry blew up in 2007 and 2008, Messrs. Dodd and Frank and many other liberal activists accused the banks of "predatory lending"—which was a practice by mortgage writers to make loans that low-income and often minority home purchasers could not afford to pay over time. To be sure, there were exotic and misleading "balloon loans" with low interest rates at the beginning of the loan period that rose over time—thus putting huge unexpected costs onto the backs of unassuming home buyers. Millions of those loans went into default, in part because of unsavory lenders. The lenders didn't care, because Fannie Mae and Freddie Mac provided 100 percent repayment guarantees.[6]

This left bank loan officers hanging from the horn of a dilemma. If a minority couple came in for a loan and the officer denied the loan, the bank could be accused of discriminatory lending policies and face severe penalties. But if the officer decided to approve the loan to comply with the CRA, the bank could now be accused of predatory lending practices. For several years after the housing recession, banks swung the pendulum back in the direction of making it very difficult for even qualified borrowers to get loans. The locks on the barn door were secured long after all the animals had fled.

At the time of this writing, Trump is pushing for the repeal of Dodd-Frank's lending requirements, and he and Hensarling have already won some reforms. In its place and to prevent the need for more bailouts, Washington should concentrate on breaking up Fannie Mae and Freddie Mac, which were at the epicenter of the crisis and required the biggest bailout in American history. A new replacement law for Dodd-Frank would limit Fannie and Freddie mortgage guarantees to the median home price in each metropolitan area, so that the program would help low-income and first-time home buyers, make mortgage lenders responsible for the first 20 percent of losses on a mortgage default (to ensure good underwriting practices), and, most importantly, require a minimum down payment of 10 percent on all federally guaranteed mortgages.

Audits of the mortgages that failed indicate that almost 90 percent of the defaults were of loans with down payments of less than 5 percent. With little skin in the game, homeowners whose homes fell in value by more than the down payment had a financial incentive to default rather than pay their monthly mortgage payments—and that's what millions did.

These simple measures could do more to prevent another real estate meltdown than all the Dodd-Frank rules—times ten. But Trump's housing department should be paying close attention. The feds are back to providing 100 percent taxpayer guarantees on 3 and 4 percent down payment loans again. Washington has learned nothing from the housing crisis.

REAL AFFORDABLE HEALTHCARE

On healthcare, Trump's major regulation reform so far was ending the Obamacare individual mandate penalty on those who can't afford Obamacare plans. This has liberated an estimated 10 million Americans—mostly young workers—from paying a tax of up to $1,000 a year for failing to purchase insurance they can't afford. The average income of those hit by the tax was less than $40,000 a year, so this was a highly regressive Obama-era tax. We thought Obamacare was supposed to help, not burden, these families.

Trump has also made it a regulatory priority to allow Americans to reduce their insurance costs by allowing for the sale and purchase of health plans across state lines. In some states an insurance package for a family of four can be twice as expensive as one that could be purchased in a nearby state—mostly because of onerous regulations. Trump also will allow Americans to buy short-term health plans outside Obamacare. This will make affordable health insurance available to lower-income Americans.

KEEP YOUR HANDS OFF THE INTERNET

Another big pro-consumer act was ending the Obama-era internet rule called "net neutrality," which was likely one of the most controversial and publicly debated regulations in the history of the Federal Register. When it was finally rescinded in late 2017, FCC chairman Ajit Pai received numerous death threats, and many across the United States were furious. The regulation reclassified broadband as a utility, thus mandating that internet providers (Verizon, Comcast, etc.) could not charge content creators (Facebook, Google, Netflix, etc.) for their use of bandwidth in order to eliminate paid prioritization, and they also could not favor one content creator over another in their internet and cable packages.

However well intentioned, the regulation was far from a victory for internet users and instead represented another example of government deciding that it is a better judge of efficient action than the market.

Thanks to the new rules, internet providers will now be able to charge content producers for their use of bandwidth, and this has launched a new influx of cash investment to prevent internet traffic jams by creating better, faster, and cheaper internet. Verizon and AT&T have announced plans to spend billions of dollars to expand broadband access to millions more Americans thanks to this deregulation.

Our view, shared by Trump, is that if there is any area that is thriving without government interference, it is the internet. The innovation and proliferation of low-cost competitors have brought the internet and broadband connections to virtually every home, school, and business in less than two decades. That happened largely because the internet remained tax and regulation free.

A GROUNDBREAKING POLICY

Trump was always highly supportive of developing America's abundant resources. He expressed frustration with bans on using our timber, our energy, our coal, and our mineral resources. We were with him solidly on this. We can create jobs, increase our national output, raise money for the government, and become less reliant on foreign nations for valuable and strategic resources, we told him in a memo during the campaign. He loved this idea. It fit nicely with the theme of "Putting America First" and would bring development to areas of the country that were economically depressed.

While most Americans are familiar with America's vast energy resources, less well known is that we are also number one in the world in strategic mineral resources. But under Obama regulators, those resources remained in the ground and America became dependent on other nations for rare earth minerals.

As a matter of national security and economic development, it never made any sense for the United States to be highly reliant on China and Russia for strategic minerals. Our dependence on foreigners for these resources has had nothing to do with geological impediments. It is all politics.

A little history here is instructive. As recently as 1990, the United States was number one in the world in mining output. But by 2016, according to the U.S. Geological Survey, the United States was nearly 100 percent import dependent for at least 20 critical and strategic minerals (not including each of the "rare earths") and other key minerals. We have grown totally dependent on imports for strategic metals necessary for everything from military weapon systems to cellphones, solar panels, and scores of new-age high-technology products.

Thanks to years of an inane anti-mining policy dictated by Washington, it takes seven to ten years to get mining permits here, versus two or three years in Australia and Canada. This has discouraged the kind of mapping and exploring that was done in the Old West when mining for gold, copper, coal, and other resources was common.

In December 2017 the Trump administration issued a long-overdue policy directive, called "A Federal Strategy to Secure Reliable Supplies of Critical Minerals." The goal is to open up federal lands and streamline the permitting process so America can mine again.

This should immediately open up mining for a suite of 15 primary minerals that have been referred to as "the vitamins of chemistry." They exhibit unique attributes like magnetism, stability at extreme temperatures, and resistance to corrosion—properties that are key to today's manufacturing. These rare earth elements are essential for military and civilian use for the production of high-performance permanent magnets, GPS guidance systems, satellite imaging and night-vision equipment, cellphones, iPads, flat screens, sunglasses, and a myriad of other technology products.

We worked with Ned Mamula, a brilliant geoscientist and adjunct scholar at the Center for Science at the Cato Institute and one of the world's experts on mineral resources. "Our mineral situation today is similar to our vulnerability to OPEC nations for oil and gas in the 1970s," Mamula says. He showed us statistics from the government's own assessments, which documented, as Mamula put it, that "No nation on the planet is more richly endowed with an underground treasure chest of these resources than the United States. We have hundreds of years of supply with existing mining technology."

How much is it all worth? The U.S. Mining Association estimates more than $6 trillion in resources. We could be easily adding $50 billion of GDP every year through a smart mining policy. Trump wants to do for strategic domestic mineral production what his pro-drilling energy policy has done to vastly expand domestic supplies of oil, gas, and coal.

Environmentalists haven't reacted positively to Trump's executive actions here. They have threatened lawsuits and other legal obstacles to this pro–economic development mineral policy—just as they oppose more open drilling in places like Alaska and offshore.

Do we want Vladimir Putin or an increasingly militaristic China to hold the commanding heights on strategic minerals that could be the oil of the twenty-first century?

China's leaders have been known to boast that the Middle East has the oil and China has the rare earth minerals. Wrong. America does—and Trump's America-first resource policies are, for the first time in decades, letting companies go out and mine for them. In the end, this could be one of Trump's most valuable deregulatory policies. The economic benefit could be in the trillions of dollars.

THE BEATINGS HAVE STOPPED

A secret to Trump's economic success—and more significant than any single one of these regulatory rollbacks—is the message that the Trump administration is sending to businesses nationwide. The government isn't here to slit your throat. This has created a new era of business optimism, and it started literally the day after the election.

The research foundation at the National Federation of Independent Business (NFIB) has a vast body of historical data on small businesses, and one item they attempt to quantify through their survey is optimism. In 2017 this survey recorded the highest annual average for optimism since 1983, the year that Reagan's first round of tax cuts phased in. In 2018 the profitability of small businesses hit an all-time high as well.

We submit that much of this increase in economic optimism in the United States is directly tied to Trump's aggressive federal deregulation effort. Small businesses (those with 50 or so employees) benefit the most here. That is because small and start-up firms experience disproportionately higher regulatory costs per employee compared to medium and large firms.

Of course, we can't pretend that the upturn in optimism is entirely due to deregulation. After all, President Trump did sign a massive tax cut for small businesses into law. We'd say that made more than a bit of difference as well.

THE WRECKING BALL

Here's one final indication that all this regulatory reversal is working as planned. In October 2017, *Time* magazine published a cover story with a cartoon picture of Trump as wrecking balls decimating whatever comes into his path. The title blared: "The Wrecking Crew: How Trump's Cabinet Is Dismantling Government."[7] The story warned that "while Trump is busy tweeting, these three people are undoing American government as we know it," referring to Housing Secretary Ben Carson, Department of Education Secretary Betsy DeVos, and EPA director Scott Pruitt.

"If you look at these Cabinet appointees," White House advisor Steve Bannon is quoted as saying, "they were all selected for a reason. And that is the deconstruction." That's for sure. We worked on the transition. We recommended many Cabinet and regulatory agency personnel to Trump. They were all people, with a few exceptions, dedicated to making government less costly, less intrusive, and more business and consumer friendly.

That same week, the *New York Times* ran a lead editorial complaining that Team Trump is shrinking the regulatory state at an "unprecedented" pace. The editorial praised Obama for erecting regulatory walls to new heights.[8] These and other media reports have had all the subtlety of a primal scream. Pruitt is excoriated for allowing a deterioration of clean air and clean water rules.

At precisely the time these articles hit the newsstands, the stock market raced to new all-time highs of over 24,000 on the Dow, we had another blockbuster jobs report with another drop in the unemployment rate, and housing sales soared to their highest level in a decade.

Are liberal anti-Trumpers so ideologically blindfolded that they are incapable of connecting these dots? The Trump deregulation policy has smashed the regulatory state at a dizzying speed—and continues to do so. The same people who say that Trump doesn't deserve credit for the economic revival because he hasn't done anything significant yet are the ones complaining of Trump cutting down regulations at the speed of a sawmill.

After all this time, the media and the left-wing agitators still don't get Trump. Loosening the noose of burdensome regulation is a way to resuscitate American jobs and prosperity. The two go hand in hand. Like taxes, the power to regulate is the power to destroy. One person we worked with closely during the campaign was Donald Trump Jr., and his response to the *Time* article was brilliant. He tweeted: "I consider it a compliment to what my father is trying to accomplish as president."

8

Saudi America

"Anyone who tells you we can drill our way out of this energy problem doesn't know what they're talking about—or isn't telling you the truth."

—Barack Obama, 2012[1]

"The United States of America cannot afford to bet our long-term prosperity, our long-term security on a resource [oil] that will eventually run out."

—Barack Obama, 2011[2]

No one in America was more flabbergasted by the shale oil and gas revolution than President Barack Obama. No one was more thrilled by it than Donald J. Trump.

Trump has always loved the amazing and improbable pro-America energy comeback story. Just loved it. So much so that it would be hard to find an issue that he and Barack Obama disagreed on more thoroughly and fundamentally than energy policy. The contradictory stances reflected their conflicting worldview. Obama's energy policy was Jimmy

Carter redux. We are running out of fossil fuels. They are destroying the planet. We have to shift right now to "green" energy no matter what the cost or risk to the economy and American workers. Obama governed as a true climate change fanatic who genuinely believed that the planet would soon be under water because of the melting of the ice caps—if we didn't decarbonize immediately and atone for our past sins of burning fossil fuels for the past century.

Trump is more like Reagan: use America's abundant natural resources. Trump saw instantly the game-changing significance of the American shale oil and gas revolution. He believed in the potential for a big coal comeback. The whole story fit perfectly with his Make America Great Again narrative and its Reaganesque sense of can-do optimism. He saw the potential for millions of high-paying middle-class jobs and massive increases in American production that would leave the Saudis in the dust and crush OPEC once and for all. He saw the shale revolution as a way to bring back to life economically depressed areas that had been left for dead by Obama and the global warming alarmists of the left. Trump viewed the climate change agenda—and the Paris climate accord—with contempt.

For our part, we were in complete agreement with Trump on this agenda from day one. The country desperately needed a new all-in pro-America energy policy. We told Trump at the first meeting of his campaign Economic Policy Council that if his goal was 3 to 4 percent growth, one large step toward getting there would be mining and drilling for America's vast and nearly inexhaustible energy supplies. We had been early-on enthusiasts for the shale oil and gas revolution that had begun a decade earlier and had changed the entire world energy picture overnight. The United States, we confirmed to him, could become a major energy exporter within five years of his presidency.

We walked him through the program that would for the first time in 50 years liberate America and the rest of the Western world from reliance on OPEC oil forevermore. No more sending tens of billions of dollars a year to Saudi sheikhs.

For Trump, in his usual Trumpian fashion, oil independence wasn't nearly good enough. "Let's make America energy dominant," he practically shouted, and this became a major and recurring theme for the campaign. Now he is on his way to achieving that goal within the first two years of his presidency.

Trump couldn't understand the logic of why Obama was prohibiting more drilling and exploring for resources on federal lands. It seemed to him—and we agreed—a no-brainer. "If we have these valuable resources," he reasoned, "we should be using them. Why would we send our dollars to places in the world that are financing terrorists that are trying to kill us?" He also loved the idea of raising billions of dollars of federal revenues from royalties and leases paid by private companies. We suggested that the money could be used for any of three of his other policy priorities: reducing federal borrowing, financing a tax cut, or paying for an infrastructure program.

Stephen Miller, then the president's policy director for the campaign, was fully on board too. Miller was familiar with the new frontiers that had opened up for American energy due to hydraulic fracturing and horizontal drilling technologies. As a former aide to Senator Jeff Sessions on the Budget Committee, he knew of the growing evidence that oil and gas development could help solve many of the budget problems by raising money for the Treasury at a time when we were running trillion-dollar deficits and the feds could use every penny they could get.

"I want you guys to know," Miller told us on the campaign plane after one meeting with Trump in June 2016, "Trump is all in on the American energy production issue." He told us that Trump would be giving a major energy speech and asked if we could prepare a strategy memo that would help define the new energy revolution and also specify the fiscal and economic benefits from Trump's drill, drill, drill strategy.

This wasn't a difficult task. Steve had just recently written a book on the topic called *Fueling Freedom: Exposing the Mad War on Energy.* The coauthor was Kathleen Hartnett White, one of the nation's foremost experts on energy policy—and a consultant for Trump on energy policy during the campaign and transition. The premise of the book was that the twenty-first century could easily be the century of North American energy supremacy—which would give the United States great economic and geopolitical advantage in the decades to come. Most of the Trump policy team was familiar with the message that America had this new opportunity to increase American fossil fuel production at a fantastic rate.

What Trump wanted to know was the precise steps the federal government needed to take to get us there and open up America's treasure chest of natural resources.

THE ENERGY DOMINATION MEMO

A few days later we sent Miller a memorandum that we called "How Trump Can Capitalize on America's Energy Opportunity." We suggested that Trump highlight the following themes in the speech and as the pillars of his America First energy strategy:

1. The best estimate is $50 trillion of oil and gas resources under federal lands. This $50 trillion treasure chest beneath us could be recovered by mining and drilling on non–environmentally sensitive lands and in federal waters.

2. Leasing and royalty payments and income tax revenues could raise $3–10 trillion in federal revenues, depending on what happened with the world price.

3. Shale gas is a wonder fuel: abundant, cheap, reliable, made in America, and clean-burning. Natural gas *reduces* carbon emissions, as even the Obama administration Energy Department admits.

4. Clean coal is here and it is real. The United States has reduced emissions from coal plants by more than 50 percent and in some cases 90 percent over the last 40 years.

5. We are *not* running out of fossil fuels. We have more coal—500 years' worth—than any other nation. We are the Saudi Arabia of coal. We also have 200 years of oil and gas.

6. Within five years the U.S. can be energy independent for the first time in half a century if we allow drilling (it turns out Trump pro-drilling policies will get us there sooner than that).

7. China and India are building hundreds of coal-fired plants. They have no intention of reducing their carbon emissions. The Paris accord is an unfair hoax on American workers.

8. Voters care more about jobs and their family finances than "global warming." Trump should say that he will never ratify *any* climate change treaty that costs America jobs.

9. A pro-America energy policy means millions more high-paying union jobs—welders, truckers, pipefitters, construction workers, engineers, etc.

10. We estimate a pro-America energy policy could raise economic growth by almost 1 percentage point per year—or about $180 billion extra American output annually.

11. The left's push to "keep it in the ground" is an economic suicide pact that will make America less prosperous, less safe and secure, and more reliant on foreign oil. Imagine if 40 years ago Saudi Arabia had decided to "keep it in the ground."

Some of these points may seem fairly obvious today. But in early 2016 these new realities of the energy industry were still not widely known or accepted—and some still aren't to this day. Our major argument to Trump was that this issue was the missing third leg of the stool to get to 3 to 4 percent economic growth.

1. Cut taxes
2. Slash regulations
3. Produce American energy

Trump articulated these America First energy themes throughout the campaign. It became one of his favorite issues. And the Trump voters—especially in the heretofore-blue midwestern states—loved it too. This was a common-sense issue the campaign used to crash through the blue wall in the Midwest and bring Reagan Democrats into the Trump camp.

HAROLD HAMM AND THE NORTH DAKOTA MIRACLE

We would like to report that we were the primary campaign advisors who turned Trump on to the economic power of the shale oil and gas revolution. But truth be told, that distinction goes to Harold Hamm—the man who turned Trump on to fracking and the boundless potential of domestic shale oil and gas. Harold was the voice on this issue. We were the echo chamber.

It's appropriate that Trump learned of this amazing and transformational story from Harold because he is the man who is perhaps most responsible for the shale oil and gas revolution. Harold is the CEO of Continental Energy. He is a soft-spoken, mild-mannered, and modest Okie. He is also brilliant and stands beside such American business icons as John D. Rockefeller and Bill Gates for changing the direction of the U.S. economy and bringing massive benefits to American consumers.

Hamm and Floyd Farris of the Stanolind Oil and Gas Corporation and the inventors of modern fracking technologies are the two men most responsible for pulling America out of the wreckage of the financial crisis in 2008–09. These two did far more than Barack Obama or Nancy Pelosi or any politician or economic guru in Washington to bring about the 2009–15 recovery. The real economic stimulus during that time was not the government's $830 billion spending and borrowing barrage. It was the shale revolution.

Hamm was convinced that the oil deposits stored inside the vast Bakken Shale formation were almost five times more endowed with recoverable energy than the government experts had estimated. He calculated that the entire energy deposit in Bakken was 24 billion barrels—which would make

North Dakota one of the three largest oil and gas production states. He proved to be mostly right, which means this single oil development almost overnight doubled America's proven reserves. When adding this to the Permian Basin in Texas and the Marcellus Shale in Ohio, Pennsylvania, and New York, we have tripled our reserves. "The Bakken is almost twice as big as the oil reserve in Prudhoe Bay, Alaska," Hamm told us when we first met him in 2012. It is the geological gift that just keeps giving. The massive Bakken oil fields stretch for hundreds of miles from Montana into North Dakota. The pool is bigger than the state of Delaware. Yet amazingly, many Americans don't even know about this natural resource bonanza right in our own backyard. Through Obama's eight years in office, his federal regulators acted as if they wished it had never been discovered at all.

The technology that made the Bakken reserve so instantly bountiful is an innovation called "horizontal drilling," which allows drilling not just two miles deep, a monumental achievement in and of itself, but also then tens of thousands of feet horizontally. Harold Hamm was one of the pioneers of this drilling innovation in the 1990s. It makes oil wells much more productive and long-lived. These drilling innovations were first put to the test in Oklahoma, North Dakota, Texas, Pennsylvania, and Ohio in the early years of the twenty-first century.

Geologists have known the oil was there—though they vastly underestimated how much of it there really was—but it was never considered "technologically recoverable" because there was no known method to extract the energy products at anywhere near affordable costs. Now, thanks to American ingenuity and know-how, we have pioneered those methods to give Americans access to vastly more oil and gas, and it's becoming cheaper every year.

Hamm almost single-handedly put the lie to the concept of peak oil and the popular Malthusian idea that our energy natural resources are running dry. Hamm scoffs at "these experts [who] have been saying we are running out of oil since the mid-1860s when our oil came from Pennsylvania."

Hamm's message to Trump was one of sheer optimism: with the right set of national energy policies, the United States is well on its way to being "completely energy independent by the end of the decade." No one in the Obama White House was listening—or wanted to listen.

But that's not all there is to Harold Hamm's upbeat vision of America's energy potential. He calculates that if Washington would simply allow drilling permits for oil and natural gas on federal lands and federal waters, "I believe the federal government could over time raise more than $10 trillion in royalties." That's $10 trillion with a *t,* enough to pay off almost half of the national debt! Our fiscal impact numbers were slightly lower than this, but even if Harold's numbers were off by 50 percent, it was still a staggering sum that made it plain for Americans to see the enormous opportunity from a rejuvenated American energy industry. Trump's attitude when he listened to Harold was: Why aren't we doing this all over the country? "Every action the Obama administration has taken on energy policy has been designed to slow down the domestic oil and gas industry," he would tell Trump.

Before meeting Trump and persuading him of the great potential here to do great things, Harold tried to get Obama behind the initiative. It never went well. Back in 2010, Hamm was invited to a White House dinner and when it was his turn to talk briefly with President Obama, "I told him of the revolution in the oil and gas industry and how we have the capacity to produce enough oil to enable America to replace

OPEC as the largest producer. I just wanted to make sure that he was aware of the increasing supply, and what could be done." So what was Obama's reaction to that? "He said, 'Oil and gas will be important for the next few years. But we need to go onto green and alternative energy.'" Hamm's reaction was "Even if you believed that, why would you want to stop oil and gas development?"

One thing that we have always found refreshing about Harold Hamm is that—unlike most leaders running big oil and gas companies—he is thoroughly unapologetic about his industry and the value of the energy power that he supplies in making American households and industry run. If you listen to the pronouncements from the big oil companies like Chevron and BP, they seem almost embarrassed about what they produce, and in order to be seen as "good corporate citizens," they fund green groups that use the money to try to drive them out of business.

In 2015, in an editorial in *Investor's Business Daily*, Steve suggested that Hamm should receive a Nobel Peace Prize. He argued that "Overnight, thanks to Harold Hamm, we have solved the Malthusian world problem of scarcity and rising prices of natural resources. The world is not running out of cheap and abundant energy, we are running into it.

"Some will counter that fossil fuels and fracking hurt the environment," the editorial continued. "Wrong. Shale gas has been by far the most important development over the last decade at reducing carbon emissions into the atmosphere."[3]

Harold may have received an icy reception at the Obama White House, but Candidate and now President Trump eagerly embraced his message that now was the time to unleash a much bigger energy boom for the years to come.

HOW SHALE ENERGY CHANGED THE WORLD

In 2005 *National Geographic* magazine published a remarkable cover story titled "The End of Cheap Oil." This is supposed to be one of the world's most respected science magazines. What was remarkable about the story was that it was remarkably wrong—every last word of it. Yet this reflected the conventional wisdom of the time—and even that of some today.

This foolish article was written, we now know, right on the eve of the energy equivalent of the "green revolution" that created massive increases in food output due to modern farming techniques in the second half of the twentieth century in the United States and across the planet. The shale industry too emerged unexpectedly and almost overnight. The surge in domestic fossil fuel production and the hundreds of billions of dollars of added national output was unpredicted even by experts in the industry as recently as 2008–09.

You can't understand what happened to the American economy since 2008 if you don't understand the shale oil and gas revolution, which Hamm and other drillers created. What they created was the most spectacular oil and gas boom in American history. U.S. oil and gas production from 2007 to 2014 expanded by almost 75 percent.

It didn't happen because God suddenly endowed America with oceans of new reserves. The oil and gas have been there for hundreds of thousands of years—or more. The spectacular revival of U.S. energy development is a result of America's technological prowess, entrepreneurial spirit, and a commitment in the industry to expanding domestic output. Humanity cracked the code of how to get at unlimited energy resources.

This drilling revolution saved the American economy. From the beginning of 2008 through the end of 2013, the oil and gas extraction industry created more than 100,000 jobs while the overall job market shrank by 970,000. In other words, for at least the first four years of the "recovery" from the Great Recession of 2008–09, the oil and gas sector of the economy was adding jobs while most industries were shutting down.

Oil and natural gas producers and suppliers added $1.2 trillion to the GDP in 2011 alone. That was 7.8 percent of the nation's GDP. Oil and gas producers directly contributed over $470 billion[4] to the U.S. economy in spending, wages, and dividends—more than half the size of the 2009 federal stimulus package ($787 billion)—only this stimulus didn't require an act of Congress or massive deficit spending. About one-third of the energy spending investment—or about $266 billion—was for opening and developing new energy projects and enhancing refinery capacity and other downstream operations.

According to Mark Mills, an energy analyst at the Manhattan Institute, "About 10 million Americans are employed directly and indirectly in a broad range of businesses associated with hydrocarbons."[5] He notes that prior to the shale revolution, energy jobs had been falling for 30 years in America. Now energy is one of the major employers in the nation.

There are two types of people in the world: those who get the national significance of this game-changing energy development, and those who don't. Thankfully, Donald Trump always has.

Most in Washington remained oblivious for a long time. While the shale revolution was getting off the ground, the federal government in Washington, D.C., was pouring money into green energy. Many European governments did the same. But almost all the rise in output of energy over the last decade came from the relatively unsubsidized fossil fuel industry, while almost none of it has come from green energy. This is despite $150 billion in taxpayer financing being pipelined to green energy under George W. Bush and Barack Obama. Amazingly, it was the unsubsidized sector that boomed. The subsidized sector gave us Solyndra, Fisker Automotive, and other bankruptcies.

Progressives contend that oil and other fossil fuels get subsidies too. That is true, and in our opinion they are unwarranted. But for comparison purposes, the Institute for Energy Research has found that for every dollar of subsidy per unit of energy produced by oil and gas and coal, wind and solar get more than $100. There is simply no rational comparison. It would be like comparing the guy who takes dollar bills out of the petty cash drawer with Bernie Madoff.

MADE IN AMERICA ENERGY

The collateral job growth and community development from this revolution in drilling have been phenomenal. In Youngstown, Ohio, steel plants have been rebuilt. In places like Wheeling, West Virginia, fracking has brought an enormous revitalization to an area that was once left for dead with closed-down steel mills, coal mines, and factories. Now it is a city with BMW dealerships in the heart of town. Farmers in places from Pennsylvania to North Dakota have gotten rich leasing their land for drilling. Meanwhile, thanks to the Marcellus Shale, Pittsburgh is back as an oil and steel town. It has become the capital of the Marcellus natural gas production. Towns like Buffalo are coming back because the workers and families from the Marcellus Shale operations in small-town Pennsylvania spend their earnings in the large cities in upstate New York.

American manufacturing has started to make a comeback in recent years, especially since Trump's election. Low energy prices due to shale energy have been a major springboard for this recovery. In 2014 the energy group called Energy In Depth documented the impact on manufacturing in the United States from cheap oil.[6] It counted over 100 new major manufacturing facilities, with $80 billion in capital investment and 500,000 jobs.

The United States now has just about the lowest electricity prices of any of our major industrial competitors. The differential is gigantic compared to Europe. Our power costs for industry are anywhere from one-half to one-fifth that of producers in Euroland.

Shale gas drilling technologies have lowered the cost of natural gas from approximately $12 per 1,000 cubic feet in 2008 to around $4 in 2015. Natural gas at these low prices has become the second-largest generator of electricity (just slightly behind coal; 1 percent comes from solar power, which is a spit in the ocean), which explains how the United States reduced its carbon emissions more than any other nation over the ten-year period ending in 2015.

The part of this story that appeals to the Trump administration is that as horizontal drilling has triggered this explosion of new natural gas and oil, American reliance on foreign oil has fallen drastically. Monthly oil imports are down by almost 20 percent from what they were eight years ago,[7] and by 2019 net imports could be down to zero. This means the elusive goal of energy independence is easily within our grasp in the near term. The math here isn't complicated. Every time we drill for a barrel of additional oil in the United States, it is a barrel we *don't* have to get from OPEC, Russia, or other hostile nations.

Those like Barack Obama who once pronounced that the United States was running out of fossil fuels and that we would soon drill our last barrel of oil have been proven dead wrong. Thanks to the giant shale oil and gas plays in North Dakota, Texas, Oklahoma, Wyoming, West Virginia, Pennsylvania, and Ohio, America isn't running out of oil and gas; we are running into it.

Of course, the profoundest of ironies here is that the industry that Barack Obama and his regulators despised the most—oil and gas—was the industry that saved his presidency. Now, some might say that Obama made all this happen—and he even took credit for the drilling boom despite the fact that he did everything he could to stop it.

One other economic windfall from America's fossil fuels renaissance is worth mentioning given the developments of recent years: lower prices for electric power and gasoline at the pump. Before the shale revolution, oil prices were near $100 a barrel and predicted to go higher. For the last three years the oil price, which still fluctuates due to world supply and demand, has averaged about $60 a barrel. The price of gasoline would be at least $1 a gallon more without the shale factor. A rule of thumb is that every penny reduction in gas prices represents more than $1 billion in annual savings to American consumers.

So American families are saving about $100 billion a year due to shale drilling. This is a *real* and durable stimulus, because this extra money injected into the economy never has to be paid back. The typical household in America spends about \$6,000 a year on energy.[8] Cutting these costs by 40 percent means nearly \$2,400 in savings for each family.

But Trump's adversaries in the Democratic Party continue to resist the administration's new pro-drilling policies. Ironically, Democrats are obsessed with reducing "income inequality," but they seem to miss the point that lowering energy costs *reduces* the income gap between rich and poor. Census Bureau data reveal that the poor spend twice as large a share of their family budget on energy costs as do rich people. So any restrictive policy—such as cap-and-trade, severe EPA emissions regulations, environmental treaties—would hurt the poor far more than the rich. Any measure to slow down domestic fossil fuel production is nothing more than a regressive tax on those with low incomes.

One study cited in the *Wall Street Journal* found that the savings to the poor from the reduction in natural gas prices were two to three times bigger than the benefits from the Low Income Home Energy Assistance program.[9] And yet shale gas and oil cost taxpayers nothing.

Since energy is a basic input into everything we produce and consume, lower oil prices make *everything* cheaper—from a candy bar to a computer to an airline ticket. Low domestic energy costs—especially from shale gas—are helping revitalize American manufacturing across the country.

TRUMP'S DECLARATION OF ENERGY INDEPENDENCE

Whenever we (led by Harold Hamm) talked to Trump about America's energy revolution and explained the fantastic growth of the shale industry, we would say: "Sir, imagine how big this could be if Washington were governed by a president in the Oval Office—ahem—who wanted this revolution to happen and expand." He would nod—he got it and didn't need prodding.

We explained to him that this shale phenomenon was no flash in the pan or a fad technology that would burn itself out. Just the opposite. The really good news we reported was that the shale oil and gas boom is merely in its infancy.

To date, more than 90 percent of the oil and gas drilling boom has been on private lands. Only about 6 percent has been on public lands. An all-out drilling strategy by Trump could potentially double American production, we have estimated.

Add to this that the technology keeps getting better and better, meaning that the industry can make money even as the price of oil gets lower. At the start, the frackers needed $100-a-barrel oil. Now they can make money at $60 a barrel. Soon it will be $40–50 a barrel.

The key here is for the United States to maintain its unrivaled technological prowess. Just as in medical innovation, where almost all new wonder drugs, vaccines, and medical devices were invented on these shores; and just as in the tech sectors, where almost all new giant digital-age computing breakthroughs were invented in an incubator known as Silicon Valley, so it is with energy innovation. The rest of the world is 10–15 years behind the United States in drilling innovation.

We always stressed one other point. To us as free marketeers, what is most exciting about the potential expanded growth of this industry is that it requires no government subsidies whatsoever. And though some at the Department of Energy under Obama tried to take credit for inventing fracking—even while they disparaged it as an evil technology—this was all driven by the private sector.

Shortly after the election, the transition team asked us to prepare a memo on what steps the new administration should take to vastly increase American energy production and achieve Trump's goal of American energy dominance. We worked with several experts to put this guidance memo together. One was Harold Hamm. Another was the invaluable energy team at the Institute for Energy Research. And we also relied heavily on the work of Jack Coleman, one of the nation's premier authorities on America's storehouse of energy resources. He had been working as a point man on energy policy in the Reagan White House and the Congress for more than two decades and was our energy expert at the Committee to Unleash Prosperity.

We called the memo "How Do We Make America Energy Independent?" and we're honored to report that many of the ideas have been adopted by the Trump administration and others are in the works. Here is what we advised the Trump team:

> The upside from producing American energy—both from an economic and national security standpoint—is almost incalculable. Yet, the American people have not seen a results-oriented national energy program determined to achieve American energy self-sufficiency, and then large volumes to export to the world.
>
> . . . Like every other nation, we should be developing our own oil and natural gas resources. This is a simple matter of economics. Would we rather have the hundreds of thousands of new high-paying oil and gas production jobs in the United States where the investment will turn over in our economy and build it on a broad base, or would we rather send the production investment and oil purchase

dollars to other countries to build the economy and create jobs there? There's nothing wrong with purchasing and importing foreign oil, but there's a big problem when we're forced to do so because we're prevented from producing our own.

So what are the steps that are necessary to create this prosperous and energy-rich future for America?

1. Continue to clear barriers to the exporting of American oil and natural gas. In 2015 Congress strong-armed the Obama administration to lift the legal restrictions, and all remaining regulatory barriers should be eliminated immediately.

2. Allow drilling on federal lands. More than 90 percent of all drilling over the last seven years has been on private lands. There are tens of billions of recoverable oil under federal lands that could be drilled.

3. Build a national network of pipelines across the country by allowing the permitting for projects like Keystone XL and many others.

4. Allow the building of refineries in the United States. The Energy Information Agency says: "The newest complex refinery with significant downstream unit capacity began operating in 1977 in Garyville, Louisiana."[10] So it has been almost forty years since a major new refinery has been opened in the United States even though the U.S. population has nearly doubled since the mid 1970s and our energy production has doubled as well. This is largely due to environmental laws that make refineries in the United States prohibitively expensive if they can be built at all.

5. Put a leash on the EPA to allow our energy resources to be harnessed and used in an environmentally responsible way. The EPA has an agenda to put the coal industry

out of business and to destroy the natural gas and oil industries as well and they are succeeding. Environmental rules have to be shown to be cost-effective, meaning that the cost to the economy of complying with the rules is justified on the basis of the environmental benefits—and measured honestly. Very few if any of Obama's anti–fossil fuels regulations come close to meeting this test. Start by repealing the Clean Power Plan regulations that were meant to decapitate our coal industry.

6. Eliminate regulatory barriers to building nuclear power plants and allow micro-nuclear to be used for energy production.

7. . . . End all subsidies for all forms of energy. The left complains about taxpayer subsidies for oil and gas. To the extent they exist they should be ended. But the cost of wind and solar energy grants, loans, loan guarantees, and so on cost in the tens of billions of dollars.

. . . If we get this right, America—not Saudi Arabia or Russia or OPEC—will be the future energy capital of the world.[11]

The strategy we proposed was a radical departure from the philosophy of the Obama administration, most congressional Democrats, and virtually all of the green lobby, which, like modern-day Luddites, wanted America to "keep it in the ground" because they worry about man-made "climate change." This explains why in January 2016 the Obama administration suspended leases on federal lands for coal. It also explains why the Obama administration issued fewer federal land leases than its four predecessors—even as the demand for leases due to fracking soared. Even worse, the amount of time it took to process a permit to utilize land for energy production increased from 205 days under George W. Bush's final term to 242 days under Obama.[12]

We estimated that the United States could create at least 1 million new jobs. Residents of North Dakota could vouch for this, as their energy production continues to power the state to the lowest unemployment rate in the country. It is now a place where even McDonald's workers make $15 an hour and sometimes get signing bonuses. The added production from a nationwide pro-drilling and pro-mining offensive could be worth one percentage point increase in GDP.

THE ENERGY PRESIDENT

Since the day Trump took office, he and his energy secretary Rick Perry and his EPA director Scott Pruitt have been clearing away the multitude of Obama-era hurdles blocking the road to American energy dominance. On no issue did Trump jump out of the gates more quickly than energy policy.

In early 2017 Trump called for a new American renaissance, and not just in renewable energy—but in pursuing the nearly inexhaustible supplies of oil, natural gas, and coal in this country. In June 2017 Trump gave a nationally televised speech calling for "U.S. dominance in global energy production." He explained that after decades of relying on foreign energy supplies, the United States is on the brink of becoming a net exporter of oil, gas, coal, and other energy resources. In that speech and the subsequent policy direction of his new administration, Trump began to implement many of the strategies we had emphasized in our memo a year earlier. He said correctly that more domestic energy production and expanding opportunities for oil and natural gas exports would strengthen the country's influence globally, increase America's economic might, and help stabilize global markets. Energy Secretary Perry has consistently echoed these themes.

Trump also pronounced himself a non-Malthusian—and that he was instead someone who believes that we are not running out of oil and gas. Trump believes that "[o]ur country is blessed with extraordinary energy abundance . . ."[13]—which gives the United States an enormous strategic and economic benefit. He declared himself all in on ending permanently the 1970s-era ban on exporting oil and gas. (With U.S. oil production booming, former president Barack Obama reluctantly signed a law lifting a decades-long ban on exports as part of an energy deal with the Republican Congress.) Trump is working to ensure this foolish ban never comes back.

The Trump administration reversed a slate of regulations and policies that have limited energy development or made it more expensive, such as the Obama moratorium on new coal leases on federal land mentioned above and regulations that effectively banned coal mining near streams.

The Interior Department has begun to repeal or soften Obama-era mandates that acted as de facto abolitions of hydraulic fracturing. Most important of all, the White House suspended the so-called Clean Power Plan, the Obama administration rule designed to shutter coal production by imposing nearly impossible standards to slash greenhouse gas emissions from electricity production.

Another big Trump energy victory was the lifting of the nearly half-century-long ban on drilling in the oil-rich Arctic National Wildlife Refuge. This could unleash billions of barrels of additional American energy production.

Finally, Trump has issued an Executive Order to require utility companies to take into account the resilience and reliability of our electric power generated from coal and nuclear plants.

FORGET PARIS

Trump's biggest boost to the American fossil fuel industry was pulling the United States out of the unworkable and unsustainable Paris climate accord. We were never prouder than when he made this pronouncement in the spring of his first year in office. We have no doubt that many other Republican presidential candidates would have lacked the courage of their convictions and tenacity to take the heat from the left and stick to this pledge. Trump's decision met with universal hostility in the media, and one CNN reporter even said that it could mean that sea levels would rise dramatically and that parts of America would be fully submerged under water in a few years. European and Chinese leaders blasted Trump and America for "surrendering its world leadership" role. The sanctimonious leaders in Asian and European nations pledged to move full speed ahead on clean energy with or without the United States.

But of course this was always an obvious lie in every way. The Europeans were all in on the Kyoto climate change deal back in 2001—an international treaty the United States rightly rejected. Euroland promised a massive shift to green energy and to abandon fossil fuels to dramatically reduce their greenhouse gas emissions. But guess what? The "green" energy revolution was a bust. None of these countries came close to meeting those targets. Now they, especially Germany, are moving away from the sanctimoniously "clean" (and horrendously expensive) energy sources. So why would we believe them when they say they are now solemnly committed to a new treaty when they violated the last one?

Even more amazing is that the United States—even though we did not make a pledge to reduce our greenhouse gases in accord with that treaty—has reduced our carbon emissions more than almost all of the Paris signatories have. The shale revolution is responsible for *reducing* greenhouse gases. The conversion of U.S. utilities from coal to natural gas has meant cleaner air. Coal has also become cleaner, which is reducing U.S. emissions.

In other words, the green protesters have it all wrong on fracking and horizontal drilling. These technologies greatly reduce greenhouse gas emissions and make climate change less probable in the future.

Contrary to the flood of insults directed at the Trump administration, the United States is not the bad actor on the world stage on environmental protection; we are the world leader in environmental stewardship.

The even more preposterous claim by the global warming–industrial complex is that China and India—the two largest polluters by far—are moving away from fossil fuels and transitioning to wind and solar power.

Nonsense. Here is what the *Wall Street Journal* reported in a November 2016 story about China and India "doubling down" on fossil fuel use: "China's government said it would raise coal power capacity by as much as 20% by 2020, ensuring a continuing strong role for the commodity in the country's energy sector despite a pledge to bring down pollution levels. In a new five-year plan for electricity released Monday, the National Energy Administration said it would raise coal-fired power capacity from around 900 gigawatts last year to as high as 1,100 gigawatts by 2020."[14]

An energy industry newsletter headlined its report in March 2017 with this eye-popper: "Japan, India, and China

Still Turning to More Coal throughout 2020s, Which Means More CO2 and Air Pollution." The *Wall Street Journal* found that just the *increase* in China's coal production will be more than the entire energy use of Canada each year. Has anyone been to Beijing or Shanghai lately? The air is filthy as factories belch out black smoke and clouds of smog that hang over the cities.[15]

It wasn't just China that was addicted to coal. At almost exactly the same time that the Paris accord was being finalized in 2015, news reports indicated: "Nearly 2,200 New Coal Power Plants in Planning Worldwide."[16]

One study by the prestigious scientific journal *Proceedings of the National Academy of Sciences* found that the nations of the world were in the midst of a global "renaissance of coal," not confined to just a few countries like China and India. It found that coal had become the energy of choice for developing nations across the globe. The report indicated, "This renaissance of coal has even accelerated in the last decade."[17]

The *PNAS* study also concluded that coal was popular because "it is often the cheapest energy option in many parts of the world, relative to other sources like oil, gas, nuclear, or renewables." This meant that those wealthy environmentalists on the left were trying to force poor people to stop using cheap energy and start using expensive energy.

The Paris accord was expensive and ineffectual wishful thinking, with America as usual getting stuck paying the costs. Liberals had stashed a multibillion-dollar slush fund in the bill to bribe other countries to cut their emissions. We were going to take lectures from these nations about saving the planet? This was like taking a lesson in personal hygiene from the *Peanuts* character Pigpen.

We should have learned by now that with foreign nations, you always have to watch what they do, not listen to what they say. China wasn't interested in reducing pollution levels. It was hyperfocused on one goal: gaining global industrial dominance and using the cheapest and most reliable energy sources possible to get there. China and Europe wanted the United States to transition to more expensive energy sources in no small part so they could regain competitiveness in manufacturing, transportation, steel, and high-tech products. Europeans had shown they couldn't compete with the low price of coal and natural gas in the United States, so they wanted us to stop using them.

Trump argued correctly that the United States doesn't need a massive international bureaucracy at the United Nations to promote clean energy. We had for a decade reduced our carbon emissions more than other nations that had been sanctimoniously attacking the United States as a planetary polluter. The Paris accord would have crippled efforts to tap into our 200-year supply of clean-burning and efficient shale gas, our 250 years of oil, and our 500 years of coal, which, as EPA director Scott Pruitt has noted, had achieved more than a 50 percent reduction in pollution in recent decades. Clean coal is here, and rather than shut down this industry, we should allow technology and innovation to make it cleaner still through gasification and other methods.

The combination of the Obama Clean Power Plan rule and the Paris accord threatened tens of thousands of jobs. For example, EPA rules aim to reduce carbon dioxide (CO_2) emissions from U.S. power plants by 30 percent. That's an enormous and costly burden on our power-generating utilities. According to Energy Ventures Analysis, an energy research firm, the annual costs for residential, commercial, and industrial energy customers in America would be about $173 billion higher in 2020—a 37 percent increase. Average annual household gas and power bills would increase by $680, or 35 percent.[18] The poor would take a pounding and gas prices would rise.

For months afterward, the media and green groups groused that Trump's decision to withdraw from Paris would give China a global lead on the renewable energy technologies of the future. In reality, Beijing has always had only one quest, and that is to replace America as the globe's economic superpower. Raising energy prices and transitioning to highly inefficient forms of electricity production in China are wholly inconsistent with that goal.

Does any of this sound like the agenda of a planet that is ready to swear off fossil fuels?

How is any of this going to save the planet? It isn't. We would simply be shifting jobs out of the United States to nations like China and Mexico that use much dirtier energy. Liberals were twisted into a pretzel in defending the Paris agreement. On the one hand, they said that it was needed to save the planet from environmental catastrophe. On the other hand, they argued that the emission targets in the accord were "voluntary," so they couldn't cause too much pain and suffering. Our advice to Trump was that Paris was a fraud; the accord meant that the United States would abide by the targets, but the rest of the world would evade them—thus imposing all the burden on America.

Trump has already been proven right. In 2018, Germany acknowledged it will not meet its climate targets. Neither will Australia, Brazil, Japan, and others. Those were false and sanctimonious promises.

Many of the Trump advisors we worked with were genuinely concerned about climate change and wanted action as an insurance policy against an environmental crisis of epic proportions. One point that we, Steve Miller, and Energy Secretary Perry made was that even if you do believe in the apocalyptic predictions, it was naive to believe that any United Nations agreement would save the planet. Governments that can't balance their budgets, can't deliver the mail, and can't keep criminals off the street aren't capable of changing global weather patterns.

The only effective way to address climate change is through economic growth and technological progress. The richer and more technologically advanced the world will be 50 years from now, the better our grandchildren will be equipped to solve environmental challenges.

While pulling out of the Paris accord, Trump made very clear his doctrine on energy: Americans want a clean environment. We demand clean air and clean water to keep our society healthy. The reductions in pollutants over the last 50 years have been little short of miraculous. But environmental rules need to be made in ways that won't cripple our economy. The top priority now must be to accelerate economic growth, create more jobs, and expand incomes for workers. No industry is helping achieve that goal more today than our domestic energy producers. End of argument.

VOTERS TAKE DOWN THE GREEN ENERGY LOBBY

Early in the campaign, we sat in on a meeting that Trump convened with energy experts—including CEOs of energy companies and utilities. He asked one prominent CEO what he thought was the proper mix of energy sources to power our $20 trillion economy in the years to come. This executive said: "About 30 percent from natural gas, 30 percent from coal, 30 percent from nuclear power, and about 10 percent from renewable energy." Trump thought about it for a minute and said: "That sounds about right, except for the 10 percent from renewable energy." His point was that wind and solar power were so preposterously oversubsidized and inefficient, they should serve only small niche markets in America's energy future. We happened to agree with that assessment. We had explained to him many times that absent gigantic and unsustainable government subsidies, "green" energy could not possibly compete with cheap coal and natural gas.

The way we put it to Trump was this: Could one think of a more foolish national energy strategy than pumping hundreds of billions more tax dollars into this "green" energy sinkhole? He couldn't. This would be like buying the stock of rotary telephones on the eve of the release of the iPhone. Cheap and abundant shale oil and gas are here to stay. Yet all Hillary Clinton, Bernie Sanders, the Sierra Club, and the United Nations wanted to talk about was "green" energy.

It's important to understand that much of the solar and wind industries wouldn't even exist today—by their own admission—were it not for the exorbitant taxpayer dollars and corporate welfare funding to Big Green through refundable tax credits, research and development loopholes, renewable energy mandates, loan guarantees, consumer incentives, and layer upon layer of other subsidies, many hidden. Solar Energy Industries Association executive director Rhone Resch admitted to Congress: "The reality is that we will lose 100,000 jobs if we lose the investment tax credit—and these are conservative numbers. Ninety percent of solar companies will go out of business."

If you were to ask what lobby was the biggest loser after the 2016 ballots were counted, it would have to be the "green" energy industry. The day after the presidential election, the

Sierra Club sent out a high-alert email to its donors that moaned: "We can't believe this is happening." The executive director of the green group called the election "deeply disturbing for the nation and the planet." Well, yes, if you're a climate change alarmist who hates fossil fuels, you're in for a bad four and maybe eight years.

Greenpeace executive director Annie Leonard was even more apocalyptic, saying: "I never thought I'd have to write this. The election of Donald Trump as President has been devastating.... There's no question, Donald Trump's climate denial is staggering. He wants to shut down the EPA, cancel the Paris Climate Agreement, stop funding clean energy research and drill baby drill."[19]

Well, yes, that was exactly what Trump wanted to do. If this was such a crazy and planet-threatening agenda, why did he win?

Americans liked what Trump was saying on energy, and they went to the polls and rejected environmental extremism, among other leftist priorities. That is why the biggest loser on election night was the Big Green movement in America, who were dedicated to the anti-prosperity proposition that to save the planet from extinction we must deindustrialize the United States and throw millions and millions of our fellow citizens out of their jobs. And by the way, the left is caught in its own internal contradictions. If it truly believed that we were facing an extinction-level event, obviously it would be promoting, not resisting, safe nuclear power—which emits zero greenhouse gases.

Voters, smelling hypocrisy, turned their thumbs down on the climate change lobby. Rightfully so.

These groups were openly rooting against American industry and American workers. The Sierra Club actually declared "victory" in 2016 in the war on coal-fired power even though it helped push several of America's leading coal production companies into bankruptcy. Sierra Club spokeswoman Lena Moffitt took credit for helping to reduce coal use in America, but she neglected to mention the tens of thousands of miners, truckers, construction workers, and other blue-collar workers who lost their jobs due to the Sierra Club campaign. What humanitarians these people are!

They also hate natural gas, even though it is a clean-burning fuel. Moffitt promised that the Sierra Club would "bring the same expertise that we brought to taking down the coal industry and coal-fired power in this country to taking on gas in the same way . . . to ensure that we're moving to a 100% clean energy future."[20]

There are an estimated 10 million Americans who are directly or indirectly employed by the oil and gas and coal industries. And leftist "green" groups were openly boasting to their donors that they hoped to put every one of these people out of a job? The voters whom we had met in states like Ohio, Pennsylvania, Wisconsin, Indiana, and Michigan weren't so excited about losing their jobs at the hands of climate change fanatics. They viewed this as another ploy by Washington to ruin their lives and completely ignore their economic plight in favor of grandiose dreams of the government somehow changing the weather.

In so many ways, climate change was one of the primary issues that allowed Donald Trump to crash through the blue wall of the industrial Midwest. The Democrats' witless opposition to building the Keystone XL pipeline, which could create as many as 10,000 high-paying construction, welding, pipe-fitting, and electrician jobs, is emblematic of how the party that was supposed to represent union workers turned its back on its own members and their families.

In the Trump campaign, we weren't at all surprised that at the end of the day, voters massively rejected the radical environmental agenda predicated on making America poorer. Why was the left so surprised by this result? We always told Trump that nearly every poll for at least the last five years had shown that climate change barely registers as a leading concern of American voters. Jobs and the economy were always issues number one and two, and global warming was usually close to last on the list. A 2015 Fox News poll found that only 3 percent of Americans believed that climate change was "the most important issue facing America today." That meant 97 percent disagreed with Barack Obama, Hillary Clinton, Bernie Sanders, and Tom Steyer that global warming was the greatest threat to America.

This didn't stop Hillary Clinton from telling West Virginians that she would put every coal miner out of a job. Then she wondered why she got crushed in this unionized, historically reliably Democratic state.

COAL'S COLOSSAL COMEBACK

One theme of this book is that Donald Trump has a talent for proving his critics wrong. His victory was, of course, the prime example, but consider also the coal industry comeback.

During the campaign, we would debate liberal energy experts associated with Obama or Hillary Clinton who were contemptuous of the Trump claim that he would rebuild the coal industry and save jobs in rural coal towns across the country. In short, Trump's critics were certain that there was *no way* Donald Trump could or would ever revive the coal industry.

He was called a liar and a charlatan for going to West Virginia and Pennsylvania and other parts of economically depressed Appalachia promising that he would bring back coal jobs. "Coal is dead," the Sierra Club declared triumphantly to its donors in 2016. "Coal Isn't Coming Back," a *New York Times* piece assured us a few weeks after the election. "Saving coal is one promise he [Trump] won't be able to keep," the author predicted.[21]

Jason Bordoff, a policy advisor in the Obama White House and now the director of Columbia University's Center on Global Energy Policy, insisted when Trump rolled back Obama's anti-coal executive orders: "Scrapping the Clean Power Plan may slow the decline of coal—but it's not bringing coal back."[22]

Well, coal and mining are back. In the year since Trump's election, America *added* 50,000 more mining jobs after years of steady decline. Hillary Clinton, by contrast, promised her left-wing millionaire and billionaire environmental friends that she would put every remaining coal worker out of a job.

She wanted to finish the job started by Obama in their war against fossil fuels. A 2015 report by the American Action Forum found that coal-fired power plants shed about 40,000 jobs under Obama, and at least 10,000 coal mining jobs were lost through 2015.[23]

It should be noted that, after the election, despite Trump's pro-coal campaign, coal's role in U.S. energy production still declined. According to the Energy Information Administration (EIA), which tracks energy use in production on a monthly basis, about 1.2 billion megawatt hours of electricity came from coal in 2017—the lowest year for coal in the last decade.[24] Meanwhile, the EIA is forecasting that natural gas is going to remain the primary energy source for electricity generation.[25] Natural gas passed coal in electricity production for the first time in 2016 and, as of the most recent rolling 12-month totals, is still well ahead.

That's not all. The Department of Commerce's Bureau of Economic Analysis reported on July 21, 2017, that "mining increased 21.6 percent . . . The first quarter growth primarily reflected increases in oil and gas extraction, as well as support activities for mining. This was the largest increase since the fourth quarter of 2014."[26]

As for the drilling and mining industries, they have gained more than 50,000 jobs since Trump's election. Many of these were in the oil and gas industry, but some were in coal, whose output increased 12 percent in 2017.

Liberals complain that coal activity isn't a major producer of jobs because the industry is producing a lot more coal with a lot fewer workers. That is absolutely true. That is called productivity. A study by the Institute for Energy Research points out that it takes wind and solar at least 30 times more man-hours to produce a kilowatt of electricity than are required to produce that same energy from coal or oil. If you don't think this productivity advantage of fossil fuels is a good thing, then you probably think we should bring farm jobs back by abolishing tractors and modern farm equipment.

But coal jobs are not just tied to the actual mining of coal. Coal is tied to steel jobs, trucking jobs, and manufacturing jobs. Using cheap and efficient energy makes every other American industry more productive, and thus makes

American employers far more competitive in global markets. Productivity creates higher-paying jobs in America, it doesn't destroy them.

We are not the only country that is using a lot more coal. Of all places, the *New York Times* reports that "Chinese companies are building or planning to build more than 700 new coal plants at home and around the world, some in countries that burn little or no coal. . . ." India is building hundreds more.

Will the coal industry survive as we proceed into the twenty-first century? Who knows? Trump has shown, though, that if government gets off the coal industry's back, it can have a significant and beneficial effect on miners, manufacturers, and consumers. The reason so many nations are turning back to coal and natural gas is very simple: price and reliability. On both measures, fossil fuels are much more efficient than wind and solar power generation.

No one knows what the next big thing will be in energy. What is certain is that Washington bureaucrats certainly don't know—as the Obama administration proved when caught by surprise by the shale revolution.

Perhaps the next big thing in energy will be micronuclear reactors that could be safe, affordable, and green (with no carbon emissions) sources of electric power production. Perhaps solar can finally emerge as an economically viable alternative, at least where there is a lot of sunshine. Wind turbines, due to intermittency, seem an unreliable source of energy for a modern world until storage technology dramatically improves. The best strategy going forward, and the one we see Trump adopting, is to let the market, not bureaucrats, dictate our energy future.

KEEPING THE LIGHTS ON

Two headlines from 2018 pay tribute to the success of Trump's pro-America energy policies.

The first comes from the *Wall Street Journal*'s front page on January 18, 2018:

> U.S. Oil Output Expected to Surpass Saudi Arabia, Rivaling Russia for Top Spot: Boosted by shale industry, rising U.S. production could undermine OPEC's efforts to shore up oil prices[27]

According to the story:

> U.S. oil production is expected this year to surpass Saudi Arabia's output, upending a global pecking order that has been a basis for U.S.-Middle Eastern policy for decades.
>
> Crude output in the United States will likely climb above 10 million barrels a day in 2018, which would top the high set in 1970, the International Energy Agency said Friday.

The second story appeared in Reuters in April 2018, and we couldn't have written a better headline: "Trump's revenge: U.S. oil floods Europe, hurting OPEC and Russia."[28]

The story began:

> As OPEC's efforts to balance the oil market bear fruit, U.S. producers are reaping the benefits—and flooding Europe with a record amount of crude. . . . "U.S. oil is on offer

everywhere," said a trader with a Mediterranean refiner, who regularly buys Russian and Caspian Sea crude and has recently started purchasing U.S. oil. U.S. oil output is expected to hit 10.7 million bpd this year, rivaling that of top producers Russia and Saudi Arabia.

This is the energy renaissance that Trump envisioned from the first time we met with him. Trump understood from the start that the American shale oil and gas revolution is only in its infancy. It will continue to be an economic and geopolitical game changer of epic proportions for decades to come.

Why is this so critically important to America's economic future? Energy is the lifeblood of a nation's economy. When it is abundant and reasonably priced, the economy prospers. According to the U.S. Energy Information Administration, the U.S. Geological Survey, and private think tanks like RAND, the resources in states like Alaska, California, Colorado, Texas, Utah, and many others, as well as under the outer Continental Shelf, are so bountiful that we could extract more than 1.5 trillion barrels of oil and approximately 3 quadrillion cubic feet of natural gas. This is at least 50 times the annual U.S. consumption.

Just to be clear: we are not talking about drilling in Yosemite or Yellowstone or, as President Obama once joked, on the National Mall next to the Washington Monument. The drilling would happen in not especially delicate areas.

According to one estimate from energy expert Jack Coleman, the output from drilling on federal lands could bring into the Treasury $1.5 trillion from oil and gas royalties charged to oil drillers and another $1.7 trillion in direct federal income taxes by the energy producers and their workers.

Lease payments should raise nearly $40 billion, bringing the total revenues to above $3 trillion over 25 years and $10 trillion over 50 years. This estimate is very similar to an analysis performed in 2015 by experts at the Institute for Energy Research, who found that over the next 37 years, the oil and gas on federal lands could generate $4 trillion in federal revenues. And, of course, it would generate vastly more abundance, including many good-paying jobs, in the real economy.

This drilling strategy has just begun under Trump because the Obama administration's anti–fossil fuel obsession created roadblocks to drilling permits and valuable energy infrastructure projects like new pipelines. It would make sense to dedicate a share of the trillions of dollars of revenue gains from drilling on federal lands to discovering ways to reduce the impact of carbon in the atmosphere through, for example, carbon-recapture innovations.

All this means that a pro-America energy policy can be designed in a way that helps pay for tax cuts, expands high-paying American jobs and growth, and is fully consistent with the imperative of environmental conservation.

As Trump once asked us: "What are the possible arguments *against* this?" It turns out that there aren't really any.

9

The Art of the Trump Trade Deal

*"[Other nations] have been taking advantage of the
United States for a long time. I am not happy with
their requests. But I will tell you, in the end, we
win. We will win, and we'll win big."*

—DONALD TRUMP, April 2018[1]

Readers might be surprised to learn that Trump—who rails
against trade deals, complains that foreign countries are
"eating our lunch," and has insisted many times that "NAFTA
is the worst trade deal in the history of the United States"—
does not consider himself to be a trade protectionist. He gets
visibly agitated when anyone makes that accusation and
rebels at the suggestion that he's another Herbert Hoover (the
president who signed into law the disastrous Smoot-Hawley
tariff in 1930).

During one pivotal moment during the campaign,
Trump asked us for help on his major address on the economy at the Detroit Economic Club. This was July 2016, and
Trump had finally sewn up the nomination. Almost everyone
in the media and the Republican Party wanted to know what

the agenda would be for this untested outsider who would take on Hillary for the presidency. The event was so closely watched by the media and voters that the club had to move the venue from the normal auditorium into a massive convention center ballroom.

On the campaign plane from New York to Detroit, Larry and Steve joined in a line-by-line review of the speech to get the precise economic language right. We were joined by Steve Mnuchin, Steve Miller, Jared Kushner, and, of course, Trump. After the lengthy discussion and myriad edits, when the speech was ready to be put in the teleprompter, Trump strolled over to us and asked, "What do you guys think of the speech?"

We looked at each other apprehensively and Larry spoke up for us. "We like it, Donald, but we are concerned that there is nothing in here about the benefits of international trade. You need to reassure people that you understand that trade is good, and you don't want to sound like a protectionist." Steve cringed and half thought Trump might toss us out the window.

He thought about it for a moment and then blurted out to everyone in the cabin: "They're right. We need to make the point that I'm not an isolationist or a protectionist." He added: "I'm a businessman. Of course I understand the value of international trade." Then he turned to Steve Miller and said: "Steve, we need to add a sentence that says free trade is good, but it needs to be fair trade. I don't want to come across as a protectionist." Trump then recited a line about the benefits of "free and fair trade," which was added to the speech. That one sentence got widely picked up by the media and has been Trump's riff ever since.

A few days earlier, Arthur had had a phone conversation with Trump on the economic speech. Arthur, after praising the contours of the tax plan, pressed Trump on the trade issue. He politely but firmly warned Trump, then and later in the Oval Office, that "trade protectionism is one of the four prosperity killers: along with taxes, inflation, and excessive regulation." Arthur warned Trump that if he raised tariffs, this could undo some of the benefits of the tax cuts. The three of us said it over and over to the campaign team: "Tariffs are taxes."

To say the least, Donald Trump is a work in progress on trade. We viewed our role as economic advisors was to nudge him in the more pro–free trade direction while being respectful of the promises he made on the campaign trail of taking a tougher stance on trade deals than previous presidents. Throughout the campaign, we were excoriated for supporting Trump and "selling out our free trade principles." Far from it. We always said from day one to everyone—including most importantly Trump himself—that we did not agree with his philosophy on trade, but we wanted to give him the best advice we could along the way. Larry is now taking on that task on a daily basis—and who better to do so?—at the White House.

One thing Trump always intimated to us was that he was using the threat of tariffs against China, Canada, Mexico, and the Eropean Union, among others, "as leverage to get them to lower their tariffs on American products." His view was that persistent trade deficits with other nations were prima facie evidence that they were getting the better of us and that by threatening trade sanctions, he could force foreigners to buy more American steel, soybeans, pork, blue jeans, bourbon, and the like.

After spending much time with Donald Trump, we think we've developed a pretty good understanding of his philosophy on trade and his trade negotiation tactics and goals. The good news is that Trump, we believe, is a president who firmly supports and recognizes the advantages of trade across national borders. But he also believes the way to get there is to use America's prized multitrillion-dollar consumer market as the bargaining chip to force our competitors to open up their markets to us. The crux of the Trump trade agenda is to "negotiate much better deals for American companies and American workers." He says that in the end what he is after is the *reduction* in global tariffs and trade barriers in ways that create more jobs in the United States. Because Trump is a master negotiator, he likes the idea of negotiating one-on-one bilateral trade deals, rather than complicated multilateral trade deals that don't always give the United States a strategic benefit. This view runs against the tide of trade negotiations for at least the last several decades.

The peril of his outside-the-box approach to trade is twofold. First, he is overly concerned and at times obsessed with the "trade deficit" between the United States and other countries. As discussed below, we believe the trade deficit is a nonproblem and a false metric to measure trade progress. And second, the risk of a full-throttled trade war, with rising, not falling, trade barriers is a clear and present danger that could undo much of the amazing economic, job, and stock market progress Trump has achieved so far in his presidency. He is playing a high-stakes game of poker here with a big upside. But if it doesn't work, the ramifications scare us to death.

TRUMP, TRADE, AND VOTERS

Critics of Trump's trade policies complain that Trump is trying to overturn the three-decades-long free trade orthodoxy that has reigned in Washington and other capitals around the globe—the so-called new world order. The charge is that he ignores the benefits of multilateral trade deals like NAFTA, the Asia trade deal, and our bilateral relationships with nations like China and Japan. Perhaps that is true. But it is also inarguably true that free trade advocates have dismissed the costs of trade deals to some segments of the American population. For better or worse, Trump's trade position was not a turnoff, but a turn-on, to many millions of voters, especially in the Rust Belt states of the Midwest. The elites told these folks that they are beneficiaries of trade deals. Many millions of voters went to the polls and told the elites: we beg to differ. These voters declared: we agree with Trump's skepticism on trade deals.

We saw it on the campaign trail firsthand. When Trump said American workers are being "played like suckers" on trade deals, the crowds erupted. Trump clearly struck a nerve with hard-hat voters by promising a reversal of many of these trade pacts and even to slap tariffs on bad actors, most notably China. In his 14-point campaign manifesto on trade, he pledged to "modify or cancel any business or trade agreement that hinders American business development, or is shown to create an unfair trading relationship with a foreign entity." While some of our friends on the right berate Trump for what they ridicule as a "know-nothing" approach to trade and immigration, these issues helped carry him to the Oval Office.

As such, Trump's ever-evolving trade strategy is complicated: it doesn't fit neatly into one of the two boxes—free trade or protectionist. He is seeking a new America First trade policy that allows international trade to continue, but on terms that are more advantageous to the United States.

The fact that Trump was more persuasive with voters on trade than the think tank pundits and the double-breasted

Ivory Tower academic economists suggests they weren't doing a very good job making their case. The fact that the populist on the left in 2016, Bernie Sanders, was making many of the same arguments that Trump was suggests that the free trade consensus that many politicians and academics thought had filtered down to voters hasn't happened.

Too many elites have responded to Trumpism by thumbing their noses at anti-trade blue-collar workers as uninformed and even ignorant. Our point was that if voters weren't for free trade, the problem was us—the free trade advocates—not them. If people don't buy New Coke, Coca-Cola doesn't respond: What's wrong with those stupid consumers, don't they understand New Coke is better than old Coke? Any company that blames consumers for failing to buy their product doesn't stay in business for long. Trade is the future, and we need to get to a point where voters view trade as a force for good, not evil.

Our purpose in this chapter is not to make the case for free trade. Readers can go back to books by Adam Smith and Milton Friedman for that tutorial. Rather, our job is to briefly explain the Trump doctrine on trade. We agree with some of it and disagree strongly with other parts—and we will explain our disagreements—but our main objective is to uncritically lay out Trump's vision and strategy.

THE TRUMP TRADE DOCTRINE

To understand the Trump strategy on international trade, as we have said before, one has to first read his best-selling book *The Art of the Deal*. One thing we have discovered about this president is that with Trump—whether it is dealing with Congress or foreign governments—it *always* comes down to cutting the best deal possible. We have been continually impressed with how good a negotiator he is.

His opening bids on trade have been very tough. He pulled the United States out of the Pacific trade deal, as promised. He has insisted on the renegotiation of the North America Free Trade Agreement, or NAFTA—and has threatened to pull out of the deal altogether unless Mexico and Canada make concessions that would better protect American jobs and intellectual property. In early 2018, Trump called for a blanket tariff on imported steel (25 percent) and aluminum (10 percent), and then in May 2018 he threatened a 25 percent tariff on imported autos.

We strongly disagreed with these tariffs and predicted, as happened, that the market would react negatively to these trade restraints. Steel, aluminum, and auto stocks rose, but most other stocks fell decisively. It was highly doubtful that the steel and auto tariffs would help save manufacturing jobs, because for every one of the 150,000 or so steel and aluminum workers who would benefit, there were about 50 American manufacturing workers who use steel—producers of cars, trucks, vans, heavy equipment, oil and gas, etc.—whose jobs would be hurt by the higher-priced metals.

These American manufacturing firms tend to be competing in hypercompetitive global markets. If they must use steel that is 25 percent more expensive than steel bought by the Chinese, Japanese, Mexican, or European manufacturers, at the margin our Made in America products will be more expensive. Some of those 5 million manufacturing jobs will be put in harm's way. Moreover, since so many of the things American consumers buy today are made of steel or aluminum, a 25 percent tariff would likely get passed on to consumers at the cash register. This is a regressive tax.

Similarly, many foreign autos—Mercedes, Toyota, Honda, BMW, and others—are built in the United States. Such is the integration of global supply chains in this twenty-first-century global economy. The stock market hated the auto tariffs, and the Dow lost several hundred points at just the suggestion of them.

The question we want to answer is, why is Trump taking such a hard line on trade even with our allies? Part of the answer is that Trump was out to grab the entire world's attention. He wanted to alert international leaders that there was a new sheriff in town enforcing trade laws and that foreign nations like China that have benefited tremendously from near-unfettered access to America's consumer markets would have to start opening their own markets in a more reciprocal fashion.

Trump has made three major complaints about the current array of trade deals; on two of these he has a point, and on the third, we think he is off base.

First, many if not most of our major trading partners—most notably, China—are violating trade agreement rules left and right and stealing American patents and intellectual property (IP). And they have been doing so for years and years with impunity.

American pharmaceutical companies, for example, are the runaway global leaders in developing new prescription drugs. This requires massive outlays of capital. A 2014 Tufts study estimated the cost of developing and bringing a prescription drug to market at $2.6 billion.[2]

Making those huge outlays of shareholders' money becomes harder to justify when foreign companies reap the benefits. Under U.S. law, biological patents are protected for 12 years. In Canada, those same drugs are protected for only eight years, and in some cases Mexico provides no protection at all unless drug manufacturers are willing to go through an expensive legal process.

Trump's trade negotiators need assurances from our trading partners that these drugs and vaccines will not be stolen and that American companies will be paid a fair price for the lifesaving drugs they have worked to bring to market. Holding Mexico, Canada, and China to the same legal standards we abide by in the United States could save billions of dollars that can be reinvested in research to produce even more innovative treatments.

When other nations impose tariffs, steal, or impose price controls on American-produced prescription drugs, it means that American consumers pay higher prices here at home to cover the research and development costs. This is unfair to American consumers. It is one reason our healthcare costs are more expensive than in other nations.

Trump often points to a 2017 analysis by the Office of the United States Trade Representative, which estimates that IP thievery perpetrated by China alone costs us between $225 billion and $600 billion each year. China also accounts for a major share of stolen U.S. trade secrets. That costs us another $180–540 billion annually. Millions of U.S. jobs are put in jeopardy because of the unfair trade practices routinely employed by China and other countries.

The Trump doctrine on trade regards this theft as something that cannot stand. Trump believes that Washington has tolerated these abuses out of a misguided fear that to stand up to these nations would risk overturning the apple cart of free trade. There has also been a sense of resignation in previous administrations on this issue—a conviction that there wasn't much America could do about it.

Trump's response to this is: nonsense. America has been played as a sucker. The United States shouldn't absorb all the production and innovation costs of developing a new technology, or drug, or vaccine, and let the rest of the world copycat the invention or the patent with impunity. His solution is to impose punitive tariffs on nations that steal our technology.

Trump's second beef on international trade deals is also legitimate. Other nations are imposing very high trade restrictions on American products, even though we have lowered our tariffs against them. The Council of Economic Advisers points out that the average tariff rate in the United States today is about 3.5 percent. In Canada the rate is 4.1 percent, in the European Union it's 5 percent, in South Korea it is 13.9 percent, in China it is 10 percent, in India it's 13 percent, and in Mexico it stands at 7 percent. The rest of the world imposes tariffs almost triple what we charge on imports. This doesn't include non-tariff barriers—quotas, domestic content rules, domestic ownership rules (prevalent in China), value-added taxes and others—that can effectively block American companies from penetrating a foreign market.

"How is this free trade?" Trump would ask us many times. His view was "It isn't free and it certainly isn't fair trade, when we lower our trade barriers but other nations don't lower theirs."

We've heard Trump say many times that we don't have "free trade" arrangements with other nations because many if not most countries—especially China and Japan and to a lesser extent the European Union—have much higher trade barriers on our goods than we have on theirs. To borrow a phrase that trade advisors Robert Lighthizer and

Peter Navarro use often, the trade deals we've struck are not "reciprocal."

Trump's goal is to tear down these protectionist walls against American agriculture, autos, trucks, technology, and agricultural products. He has used national security concerns as the rationale for retaliatory tariffs. He says that steel imports threaten the "long-term viability" of our domestic industry. "Core industries such as automobiles and automotive parts are critical to our strength as a nation," Trump said in April 2018. These imports totaled almost $200 billion in 2017, with Canada, Germany, and Japan the major export nations. Section 232 of the Trade Expansion Act of 1962 empowers the president with the ability to "determine the effects on the national security of imports."

One major component of Trump's trade philosophy is his belief that we can impose our will on other nations, because major trading partners like China, Russia, Japan, and Mexico need America far more than we need them. We both benefit from our trading transactions, but they benefit more than we do. China's economy is highly dependent on access to American markets. The U.S. economy is only incidentally dependent on Chinese imports—though clearly U.S. consumers benefit greatly. The Trump administration believes we should strategically exploit that commanding position in the world to the benefit of our own businesses and workers. He is betting that the threat and perhaps implementation of tariffs will drive other nations to the negotiating table and lead to concessions and better deals than we now have. Some have criticized this strategy as the "weaponization" of trade. It is designed to put the interests of American companies and workers first.

This, we believe, is what Trump meant when he said controversially in early 2018 that "trade wars are winnable."

Trump's view is that any tit-for-tat retaliation by our trading partners will hurt them far more than us.

Trump's major ambition is to strike a deal with China that increases American exports and stops the stealing of IP. For decades, the Bushes, Clinton, and then Obama ignored the cheating and stealing that were the routine trading practice of Beijing. Its GDP in 1990 was about 5 percent of ours. Now its GDP is closer to 65 percent of ours. China is not just a major player, it will soon contest America for economic superpower status. It is also rapidly building its military and makes no bones about its imperialistic empire-building designs all over Asia. China facilitated the North Korean nuclear missile program. These are not the actions of a friendly nation but of an adversary.

Trump's thinking on trade, and especially with regard to China, was highly influenced by a 2011 book by now White House economist Peter Navarro titled *Death by China*. It made the case that the rise of China as an economic and military power has been blindly enabled by naive federal policies over the last several decades. Beijing's recent announcement of its "Made in China 2025" program makes clear its ambition to overtake the United States as the world's dominant player in technology, military weapons, artificial intelligence, and robotics. The Chinese want to be the host country for the next generation of Googles, Apples, Amazons, and Microsofts. We doubt that is likely to happen because a huge and growing percentage of Chinese investment is state-led, and if we know anything from history, it is that such central planning will ultimately fail.

Trump is also confident that he can use American economic might to leverage a better deal with Canada and Mexico on NAFTA. The goal is to negotiate a NAFTA 2.0 deal that modernizes a pact that is now nearly 25 years old. Since NAFTA's enactment two decades ago, trade across the borders of our three countries is up almost 60 percent—a good thing. Trump is right to insist on greater intellectual property rights as a part of the new agreement. But jeopardizing NAFTA could interfere with his broader ambitions on the global scene. NAFTA is vital to ensuring that North America remains the economically supreme continent over Asia and Europe. North America, for example, can easily be the Middle East of oil and gas production within the next few years and maintain that status for decades to come. The integration of the United States, Canadian, and Mexican economies is a positive for our joint economic and national security as we confront growing threats and aggression from the rest of the world.

DO TRADE DEFICITS MATTER?

The third area of the Trump trade doctrine is the view that U.S. trade deficits are a major problem for the American economy going forward. A trade deficit occurs when the value of the products we sell to a foreign country is less than the value of what they sell us. We have discovered from personal experience that Trump views the trade deficit with nations like China, Japan, and Korea, and with the European Union as a major brake on economic growth. One of the conditions he has established with these trading partners is that they must work to lower their annual surpluses with the United States. By far our biggest trade deficit is with China, at roughly $500 billion a year. The reported trade deficit, as we have often reminded the Trump administration, often does not include financial, computer, accounting, consulting, and other service areas that the United States often dominates.

Our view is that Trump is far too concerned with the trade deficit—which is offset almost dollar for dollar by our capital import surplus. Nations run trade surpluses with the United States because they *want* to invest here and need surplus dollars to do so. We have tried to persuade the Trump trade negotiators (and obviously we have a key ally in Larry, as National Economic Council director) that the trade deficit is not a meaningful indicator of economic conditions here at home. We prepared a study for the Trump administration in early 2018 that economic prosperity in America has been strongly and positively correlated with trade deficits, not trade surpluses. Yes, you read that right, and do not wipe your glasses or adjust your computer screen. This finding surprised President Trump and some of his trade representatives, but the evidence is powerful:

- Start with the birth of our nation. Arthur has compiled the data going back to colonial times and through the end of the Civil War. From 1747 until 1854—more than 100 years of American history—we ran a trade deficit virtually every year. To be exact, the United States had 95 years of trade deficits and only 13 years of trade surpluses, including 1775 and 1776 (the revolution), 1811 and 1813 (also a war), 1842, 1843, and 1844. The world's greatest economy was effectively created by importing foreign capital net, that is, by running trade deficits. By importing capital net, the United States grew enormously, employed workers at high wages, and created a job and wealth creation machine rarely seen before. America was built on trade deficits.
- During the Great Depression, the volume of international trade plummeted after the passage of the infamous Smoot-Hawley tariff, which put taxes on the imports

of thousands of products. As a consequence, there was not much of a trade deficit or surplus in the 1930s as the economy and living standards continued to contract. The lesson of the Great Depression is that what matters for an economy to grow is the volume of trade, not whether one country is running a trade surplus with another.

- President John F. Kennedy reduced global tariffs by some 35 percent early in his presidency. From the first quarter of 1963 through the first quarter of 1966, generally viewed as the Kennedy era, six of 13 quarters had growth above a 6 percent annual rate, five quarters above 8 percent, and only three quarters slightly below 3 percent. That's amazing.

- The 1970s was the last period when the United States ran persistent—though small—trade surpluses. The presidencies of Nixon, Ford, and Carter gave America the worst decade for real family incomes, the stock market, and national wealth accumulation since the Great Depression.

- In the 1980s the United States cut tax rates, regulations, and inflation (by strengthening and stabilizing the dollar). Reagan was a free trade advocate. As the American economy exploded with growth, foreigners poured trillions of dollars of capital into the United States. The faster the growth, the more the trade deficit exploded as a consequence.

- President Clinton signed into law NAFTA during his first term in office. The economy started off slower than under the other pro-growth, free trade presidents, even though President Clinton was an early adamant champion of NAFTA. During his tenure, there were two quarters where growth bested 6 percent and nine quarters where growth exceeded 3 percent. While not quite up to the standards of Reagan and Kennedy, still Clinton ranks as one of America's best presidents when it comes to free trade. The more the American economy soared to new heights, the higher the trade deficit grew.

- During the height of the Great Recession, from 2008 to 2009, the U.S. trade deficit decreased significantly, even as the unemployment rate *increased* from 5.8 percent to 9.3 percent. From 2009 to 2014, imports to the United States and the trade deficit increased significantly, but the U.S. unemployment rate *decreased* from 9.3 percent to 6.2 percent.

That's American history on trade in a nutshell: The U.S. trade deficit widens during U.S. booms (Reagan, Kennedy, and Clinton) and narrows during U.S. recessions (Nixon, Carter). During booms, investments in the United States are more attractive, and during contractions, U.S. investments are less attractive.

But what about all those high-paying manufacturing jobs that are fleeing overseas? It turns out that the unemployment rate is negatively associated with the trade deficit. When the trade deficit is high, the unemployment rate tends to be low. When the trade deficit is low or turns into surplus, the unemployment rate tends to be rising. We have also told Trump only half jokingly: "Sir, if you want a lower trade deficit, that can be achieved with a good long recession."

Our point was that his pro-growth policies were likely to create more prosperity and higher incomes, thus increasing American demand for imports and possibly and inadvertently widening the trade deficit.

Trump's goal with trade was primarily one of protecting and creating high-paying jobs here at home and making

America more competitive in global markets. We advised Trump that the surest way to gain an upper hand with China, Japan, Russia, and other rising nations was to change our domestic policies in Washington to make American businesses and products the most innovative and competitive in the world. This meant passing the tax cut and making our corporate tax rate more competitive in the global market. It meant reducing the cost of regulations that send jobs overseas. It meant making America energy dominant by expanding U.S. production of oil, gas, and coal—which would *reduce* our trade deficit.

We have urged Trump as he thinks about trade to heed the advice of President Ronald Reagan, who urged that we avoid the temptation of copycatting bad trade policies from other countries. As Reagan advised: "If one partner shoots a hole in the boat, does it make sense for the other one to shoot another hole in the boat?"[3]

Our constant advice, and we believe Trump instinctively got this, was that by making America more competitive by fixing our own self-inflicted wounds, we could raise wages and lower the unemployment rate (which hit a nearly 50-year low in April 2018). All that has happened. A report in May 2018 by the IMD Competitiveness Center in Switzerland examines 256 variables in more than 100 nations and found that the United States "jumped to the top spot in international competitiveness."[4] It all seems to be working.

IS TRUMP RISKING A TRADE WAR?

We are frequently asked: Does the Trump trade doctrine risk a trade war? Our answer is always the same: hopefully not, but it could happen, to everyone's detriment, if other nations don't stand down and play by the rules they agreed to. Trump's response (in a tweet, of course) to his critics is that "we've already been in a trade war for decades and we're losing." Other nations are clearly shirking on the trade laws, but it's hard to see how "we're losing" given that today our economy is the envy of the world.

When the U.S. economy started to pick up steam in 2017, economists said this just reflected stronger growth world-wide. As Trump threatened trade tariffs, we were told the rest of the world would "decouple" from America. Well, now the United States' economy is soaring and Europe's economic growth is at less than one-half percent and Japan's is stag-nant. So it is the United States that appears to be decoupling from the rest of the world, not vice versa.

We are of the view that getting very tough with China now, and forcing Beijing to back down, is critically important to American economic and national security. The short-term costs of a China stare-down now are trivial compared to a potential hot war with the Chinese a decade or two down the line. Trump seems to have made this doctrine conventional wisdom even among many of the elite who oppose most of his other policies.

We question whether it makes sense to pick a trade fight with Canada, Britain, Germany, Japan, and other allies when we need to be isolating China as the bad actor. This may weaken Trump's negotiation position with China.

What is undeniable is that the expansion of international trade from 1980 to 2005 launched the greatest period of pov-erty reduction in world history, with a billion people moved out of abject poverty. Trade has done more to reduce human deprivation, hunger, and inequality than all the trillions of dollars of charitable and foreign aid ever donated to poor nations. Meanwhile, nations with free trade policies that are connected to the global economy have per capita incomes that are about six times larger than nations closed off from the world trading system. Building walls of protectionism is no way to make your citizens prosperous.

Trump gets this, and so do most on his economic team. President Trump's Economic Report of the President in 2018 includes this wonderful assessment of the advantages of trade:

> Expanding the United States' trade abroad can offer the advantages of competition: increased productivity, greater economic growth, increased innovation, lower prices, and more variety. New markets may not only provide domestic firms with more potential customers than are available in the local market and a chance to build economies of scale; they also offer the opportunity to purchase lower-cost inputs. Consumers—and disproportionately low-income consumers—may benefit as import competition fosters innovation and product differentiation, and drives down the prices of goods and services.[5]

Hold that thought, Mr. President.

In the end, Trump believes that he can bring about a new world trading regime with strategic trade rules that give America a bigger share of the global winnings, making us richer and safer. Certainly our farmers, our technology and pharmaceutical companies, and our industrial blue-collar workers would applaud that.

We started this book by noting that we are optimists—just as Trump is. We are also persuaded that despite the threats of tariffs and the rejection of prior trade deals, Trump wants to get to genuine freer trade as his final goal. It didn't get much attention, but at the end of the G-7 meeting of major world leaders in Canada in June 2018, Larry, who had just been appointed National Economic Council director, pushed Trump to put on the table the option of a "zero tariff solution." This came in the wake of Trump being roundly criticized by Canada's prime minister Justin Trudeau and the European leaders for threatening a break from the "new world order" consensus on reducing trade barriers. Trump took Larry's advice and suggested to his counterparts: "No tariffs, no barriers. That's the way it should be. And no subsidies." Then he continued: "You want tariff free, no barriers. And you want no subsidies."

That doesn't sound like the declaration of a trade protectionist. It was illuminating that the defenders of the "new world order" in Canada rejected Trump's offer and then denounced him after he left town. This suggested that Trump might be right: the rest of the world wants American open borders for their trade but shrinks at the idea of opening up their own to American goods.

If Trump succeeds and gets the pro-America outcome at the negotiating table he seeks, other nations will start reducing trade barriers and open up their borders to the United States. If all this comes to pass, Donald J. Trump may be the president who scores the biggest victory for freer and fairer trade practices in American history.

Postscript

A Light Switch Is Flicked from Off to On

"Under Trump, I would expect a protracted recession to begin within 18 months. The damage would be felt far beyond the United States."

—Former Clinton and Obama chief economist
LARRY SUMMERS, June 2016[1]

"It really does now look like President Donald J. Trump, and markets are plunging. When might we expect them to recover? A first-pass answer is never . . . so we are very probably looking at a global recession, with no end in sight."

—PAUL KRUGMAN of the *New York Times*,
the day after the 2016 election[2]

"A President Trump Could Destroy the World Economy"

—Title of a *Washington Post* editorial, October 2016[3]

In early 2018, Donald Trump did something highly unexpected. With the U.S. economy now booming again, he flew to Switzerland and spoke at the Davos World Economic Forum, a conference of elite world leaders, CEOs, and self-important government bureaucrats. This was not a friendly crowd of well-wishers donning Make America Great Again hats. Trump had shunned this group in 2017—most everyone in the audience had been brutally against him—but now he had a story to tout to the buttoned-down policy audience. His message was brief and crisp: "Ladies and gentlemen . . . America is open for business again."

This world-class salesman was selling America to the gathered CEOs. Bring your business and your jobs to our shores. We will make you a deal you can't refuse. One commentator summarized his speech aptly by saying that "Donald Trump is a one-man Chamber of Commerce for America."

Whatever criticisms might be directed at Donald Trump eighteen months into his presidency—and there are admittedly plenty of missteps and misstatements—what we can say with certainty is that the NeverTrumpers were fantastically wrong about him and Trumponomics.

No, he hasn't "destroyed the world economy."

No, the stock market hasn't crashed.

No, there is no recession.

Those who foolishly believed these predictions by the deep thinkers of the left, and then foolishly acted on them, lost a whole lot of money. One person who was a big-time loser was that economic sage, documentary producer Michael Moore (no relation to Steve), who announced to the world that when Donald Trump was elected: "I sold all my stocks." Whoops! He sold with the Dow Jones at 18,000 and a year and a half later it was near 25,000—up a mere 39 percent. You're supposed to buy low and sell high, Michael.

Our point here is not to be triumphalist. At the time of this writing, July 2018, the economy is firing on all cylinders and is as healthy as it has been in 20 years. But we know from decades of experience that the economy is fickle and can turn on a dime, due to a multitude of factors, not least of which would be a trade war. Even more topsy-turvy is the stock market. So it is premature less than two years into his presidency to declare Donald Trump an economic savior. Ask us at the end of his second term about that.

But from our standpoint, having served as economic advisors to Trump and as part of a team of people who helped devise the strategy, so far Trumponomics is working. It is working so well that even *we* are amazed at the American economic transformation—both at the speed and the heights of the rebound.

Trump was elected to reverse a generation of economic stagnation and middle-class anxiety. He has already nearly doubled America's growth rate from 1.5 percent to just under 3 percent in the last quarter of 2017. And unlike Reagan, who rescued the economy from a deep and dreary recession, Trump is confronting a massive resistance movement from the other party. Reagan could at least count on some Democrats and the labor unions to support his fight against Moscow and his reengineering of the economy through tax cuts, sound money, and deregulations.

Trump is a more politically isolated figure, and yet his list of policy victories is impressive:

- The biggest pro-growth tax cut since the 1980s.
- Elimination of many of Obama's anti-growth EPA regulations.
- A slate of judges—first and foremost Supreme Court Justice Neil Gorsuch—who are, as our friend Leonard Leo, a constitutional expert, calls them, "the best group of federal judges ever nominated to the federal courts."

- Pro-American energy policies that will soon make America the top oil and gas producer in the world, while providing fresh hope for a fair shake for a coal industry to which Barack Obama and Hillary Clinton had proved hostile.
- Pulling the United States out of the anti-American, anti-prosperity Paris climate accord.
- Repeal of some of Obamacare's worst features, such as the individual mandate tax.

One point of this book is that quite apart from the discrete policy victories—and perhaps even more important—is the X factor at the heart of the Trumponomics agenda. Donald Trump is unequivocally pro-business. In so many ways for the employers, investors, and workers of America, that has made all the difference.

Consider, for example, the explosion of consumer confidence, the stock market climb, and the small business optimism rebound in the days following Trump's unexpected election. The election was like an injection of performance-enhancing drugs into the veins of the economy, and the results were instantaneous and felt coast to coast.

One of Steve's favorite reminiscences from Trump's first year in office was meeting the owner of a car repair shop outside Cleveland, Ohio. "How is business, Jimmy?" Steve asked. "Steve, to be honest, it was like a light switch was flicked from off to on the day after the election, and since then I've had more customers than my business can handle."

Jimmy is not alone in his bright-eyed assessment. The month before the 2016 election, the rating of the economy and jobs market was about 30 percent positive. In 2018 that number had soared to its highest level in 20 years, with 70 percent rating the American economy as "good or great."[4]

The key to appreciating Trump's economic accomplishments is to put aside for a moment your personal opinion of Donald Trump's words and actions in office. Forty percent of voters have consistently disapproved of Trump's behavior. Just judge Trump on his objective results.

The Dow's stock market rally since Election Day means over a $6 trillion rise in wealth. That has benefited the rich, yes, but also every one of the 100 million Americans who own stocks in 401(k) plans, IRAs, and pension plans. Investors are capitalizing the lower business tax rates and lower toll of regulation into higher stock valuations.

The job market impressively improved under Barack Obama's presidency following the Great Recession, when more than 8 million jobs vanished overnight. But the 2017 and 2018 decline in joblessness has been impressive as well. In April 2018 the unemployment rate hit its lowest level in nearly 50 years, and the black and Hispanic unemployment rates hit their lowest levels in almost 40 years. There are some 6 million more jobs in America than skilled workers to fill them.

All this was punctuated by the cascade of corporate announcements of more jobs, higher pay, and a torrent of new investment in America within one month of the Trump tax cut. Apple's glorious announcement of $300 billion coming back to America, with 20,000 jobs, a new business "campus," and $38 billion of tax payments to the Treasury, is just the kind of response we hoped for from the lower corporate tax rate and low repatriation tax.

Fiat Chrysler is moving an auto factory *to* Michigan with 2,500 jobs. After decades of outsourcing jobs from America, we are now seeing firms *insource* jobs. Walmart and Costco have both raised their starting hourly wages, which could affect more than 1 million workers. (Does Nancy Pelosi want to take back her charge that the Trump tax cut would cause Armageddon?)

In 2018 small business profits hit their highest level—ever. The *Washington Post* reported that in some areas of the country, blue-collar workers are earning $25,000 bonuses. Who do they think they are? Kevin Durant?

We loved the front-page headline in the *Wall Street Journal* in June 2018, "Economic Growth in the U.S. Leaves World Behind."[5] As the rest of the world's economies, including Europe, Japan, and China, lose steam, America is again the driver of global growth.

Something is going radically right here.

Trump's critics assured us that all of this was impossible; Paul Krugman dismissively snuffed that Trump's projection of 3-plus-percent growth was as likely as "driverless flying cars arriving en masse." Then when the speed-up in growth actually occurred, the Trump critics shifted to say that the growth rate they thought was impossible—even though they had predicted it would surely happen under Obama, but it never did—was now presumably a delayed reaction to Obama policies. It was a deeply convoluted logic, and especially unpersuasive given that so much of what Trump has done policy-wise on the economy has been to undo what Obama had put in place.

For those who want a full account of the Trump economic successes, we recommend the book *The Capitalist Comeback: The Trump Boom and the Left's Plot to Stop It* by our friend and colleague Andy Puzder.

In the end, we think the *Wall Street Journal,* which has hardly been kind to Trump since the day he announced for president, put it pretty well: "The only good thing about Donald Trump is all his policies."[6]

Acknowledgments

We wish to acknowledge the following people for their invaluable help in completing this book. First, we would like to thank our publisher Adam Bellow of St. Martin's Press for his encouragement and first-rate editing. Our agent Alex Hoyt played a big role in finding a home for the book.

Several people helped with the research, including Andrew Wofford, Nick Drinkwater, Luke Daigneault, Kristen Moser, Randi Butler, Samuel Bellet, Jeremy Benner, Erwin Antoni, Christian Andzel, Ralph Benko, Anne Moore, and Tim Doescher.

We are grateful to Corey Lewandowski, Steve Bannon, Sam Clovis, Rick Dearborn, Representative Mark Meadows, Ivanka Trump, Alexandra Preate, and Stephen Miller, who helped us recall the details of the key moments of the campaign and the first year of Trump's presidency. They each, of course, played a critical role in the formulation of the economic policies that became Trumponomics.

No one played a larger role in shaping and selling Trumponomics than our partner and friend Larry Kudlow, who was appointed director of Donald Trump's National Economic Council in April of 2018.

Thanks, finally, to Donald Trump for allowing us to play a small part in the making of this history.

Notes

CHAPTER 1: MEETING TRUMP

1. Thomas de Monchaux, "Seeing Trump Tower," *The New Yorker,* October 6, 2016, https://www.newyorker.com/culture/cultural-comment /seeing-trump-in-trump-tower.
2. Paul Krugman, "Realistic Growth Prospects," *The New York Times,* February 23, 2016, https://krugman.blogs.nytimes.com/2016/02/23 /realistic-growth-prospects/.
3. Stephen Moore and Larry Kudlow, "Is Donald Trump a 21st-Century Protectionist Herbert Hoover?" *National Review,* August 27, 2015, https://www.nationalreview.com/2015/08/donald-trumps-protection ism-is-worrisome-stephen-moore-larry-kudlow/.
4. Ashley Killough, "Jeb Bush: 'I Can Guarantee' Donald Trump Won't Be the Nominee," CNN, December 9, 2015, https://www.cnn .com/2015/12/09/politics/jeb-bush-donald-trump-nominee/index .html.
5. Buck Sexton, "Trump, Carson, Fiorina—Rise of the Outsiders," CNN, September 1, 2015, https://www.cnn.com/2015/09/01/opinions/sexton -trump-carson-fiorina-outsiders/index.html.

6. Betsy McCaughey, "Obamacare Is Making the Middle Class the New Uninsured," *New York Post,* September 6, 2017, https://nypost .com/2017/09/06/obamacare-is-making-the-middle-class-the-new -uninsured/.

7. "The Budget and Economic Outlook: 2015 to 2025," Congressional Budget Office, January 2015, https://www.cbo.gov/sites/default /files/114th-congress-2015-2016/reports/49892-Outlook2015.pdf.

8. Gallup, "Direction of the Country," Polling Report, June 1–13, 2018, http://www.pollingreport.com/right.htm.

9. Steve Benen, "Jeb Bush Urges Audience, 'Please Clap,'" MSNBC, February 3, 2016, http://www.msnbc.com/rachel-maddow-show/jeb-bush -urges-audience-please-clap.

10. Peggy Noonan, "Noonan: America and the Aggressive Left," *The Wall Street Journal,* February 28, 2014, https://www.wsj.com/articles /america-and-the-aggressive-left-1393544611.

11. Ted Lieu (@tedlieu), "Trump tax plan is Voodoo . . . ," Twitter, April 26, 2017, https://twitter.com/tedlieu/status/857288970341888000?lan g=en.

CHAPTER 2: BATTLE SCARS FROM THE BIGGEST POLITICAL UPSET IN AMERICAN HISTORY

1. Bret Stephens, "2016's Big Reveal," *The Wall Street Journal,* November 8, 2016, https://www.wsj.com/articles/2016s-big-reveal-1478564830.

2. Jonah Goldberg, "Conservative Purists Are Capitulating with Support of Trump," *National Review,* March 9, 2016, https://www.national review.com/2016/03/donald-trump-conservative-supporters-have -sold-out/.

3. Jonah Goldberg, "The Impossible Weirdness of 2016," *National Review,* October 29, 2016, https://www.nationalreview.com/g-file/2016 -election-weirdness-bill-clinton-hillary-clinton-attack-old-rules/.

4. CNN Staff, "Here's the Full Text of Donald Trump's Victory Speech," CNN, November 9, 2016, https://www.cnn.com/2016/11/09/politics /donald-trump-victory-speech/index.html.

5. Michael Gerson, "Republicans Deserve Their Fate," *The Washington Post,* October 10, 2016, https://www.washingtonpost.com/opinions

/republicans-deserve-their-sad-fate/2016/10/10/f6761bc0-8ef9-11e6
-9c52-0b10449e33c4_story.html?noredirect=on&utm_term=.ed21
ad3bc4f6.

6. "Transcript of Mitt Romney's Speech on Trump," *The New York Times*,
March 3, 2016, https://www.nytimes.com/2016/03/04/us/politics/mitt
-romney-speech.html.

7. The five counties are Loudoun County, VA; Falls Church City, VA;
Fairfax County, VA; Howard County, MD; and Arlington County, VA.
"Commuting Times, Median Rents and Language Other Than English
Use in the Home on the Rise," U.S. Census Bureau, December 7, 2017,
https://www.census.gov/newsroom/press-releases/2017/acs-5yr.html.

8. Arthur B. Laffer, "Game On," Laffer Associates, May 19, 2016.

9. The points in this memo originated in Andy Puzder and Stephen
Moore, "A Trump Economy Beats Clinton's," *The Wall Street Journal*, July 14, 2016, https://www.wsj.com/articles/a-trump-economy
-beats-clintons-1468537348.

10. Jonathan Swain, "Trump Adviser Tells House Republicans: You're No
Longer Reagan's Party," *The Hill*, November 23, 2016, http://thehill
.com/homenews/campaign/307462-trump-adviser-tells-house-repu
blicans-youre-no-longer-reagans-party.

11. Jeffrey Lord, "Ford Versus Reagan: The Sequel," *The American Spec-
tator*, May 24, 2011, https://spectator.org/37561_ford-versus-reagan
-sequel/.

12. Frank Rich, "What the Donald Shares with the Ronald," *New York*
magazine, June 1, 2016, http://nymag.com/daily/intelligencer/2016/05
/ronald-reagan-was-once-donald-trump.html.

CHAPTER 3: OBAMANOMICS AND THE ASSAULT ON GROWTH

1. David Freddoso, "Pelosi: Unemployment Benefits Create More Jobs
Than Any Other Initiative," *Washington Examiner*, June 30, 2010,
https://www.washingtonexaminer.com/pelosi-unemployment-bene
fits-create-more-jobs-than-any-other-initiative.

2. Arthur Laffer, Stephen Moore, and Peter Tanous, *The End of Prosperity: How Higher Taxes Will Doom the Economy—If We Let It Happen*
(New York: Threshold Editions, 2008), p. 9.

3. "Transcript: Obama and Clinton Debate," ABC News, April 16, 2008, https://abcnews.go.com/Politics/DemocraticDebate/story?id=467 0271&page=1.

4. Kyle-Anne Shiver, "Obama, the Closer," *National Review,* May 27, 2008, https://www.nationalreview.com/2008/05/obama-closer-kyle-an ne-shiver/.

5. Paul Krugman, "On the Inadequacy of the Stimulus," *The New York Times,* September 5, 2011, https://krugman.blogs.nytimes.com/2011 /09/05/on-the-inadequacy-of-the-stimulus/.

6. Robert Barro, "Robert Barro: Stimulus Spending Keeps Failing," *The Wall Street Journal,* May 9, 2012, https://www.wsj.com/articles/SB100 01424052702304451104577390482019129156.

7. Casey B. Mulligan, "How ObamaCare Wrecks the Work Ethic," *The Wall Street Journal,* October 2, 2013, https://www.wsj.com/articles /how-obamacare-wrecks-the-work-ethichow-obamacare-wrecks-the -work-ethic-1380750208?tesla=y.

8. Michael D. Tanner, "Welfare: A Better Deal Than Work," Cato Institute, August 21, 2013, https://www.cato.org/publications/commentary /welfare-better-deal-work.

9. "Trends in the Joblessness and Incarceration of Young Men," Congressional Budget Office, May 2016, https://www.cbo.gov/sites/default /files/114th-congress-2015-2016/reports/51495-youngmenreport.pdf.

10. "Press Release: Household Income Down by 3.1 Percent Overall Post Recession, but Many Groups Have Started to Recover Following 2011 Low Point," Sentier Research, 2014. http://sentierresearch.com/press releases/SentierPressRelease_PostRecessionaryHouseholdIncome Change_June09toJune14.pdf.

11. Larry Summers, "Why Stagnation Could Prove to Be the New Normal," LarrySummers.com, December 15, 2013, http://larrysummers .com/2013/12/15/why-stagnation-might-prove-to-be-the-new -normal/.

12. The Bureau of Labor Statistics defines "U-6 unemployment" as total unemployed plus all marginally attached workers and all employed part-time for economic reasons as a percent of the civilian labor force plus all marginally attached workers. "Marginally attached workers" are defined as persons who are not in the labor force, want and

are available for work, have looked for a job sometime in the prior 12 months, but are no longer looking. Marginally attached workers include discouraged workers who did not search for work because they believed no jobs were available to them. "Alternative Measures of Labor Underutilization for States, Second Quarter of 2017 Through First Quarter of 2018 Averages," Bureau of Labor Statistics, April 27, 2018, https://www.bls.gov/lau/stalt.htm.

13. "Remarks by Sen. Barack Obama," *Congressional Record,* March 16, 2006, https://www.congress.gov/crec/2006/03/16/CREC-2006-03-16 -pt1-PgS2236.pdf.

14. "Individual Market Premium Changes: 2013–2017," Assistant Secretary for Planning and Evaluation, Office of Health Policy, U.S. Department of Health and Human Services, May 23, 2017, p. 4, https:// aspe.hhs.gov/system/files/pdf/256751/IndividualMarketPremium Changes.pdf.

15. "Federal Subsidies for Health Insurance Coverage for People Under Age 65: 2017 to 2027," Congressional Budget Office, September 2017, https://www.cbo.gov/system/files/115th-congress-2017-2018/reports /53091-fshic.pdf.

16. "Updated Estimates for the Insurance Coverage Provisions of the Affordable Care Act," Congressional Budget Office, March 2012, https://www.cbo.gov/sites/default/files/112th-congress-2011-2012 /reports/03-13-Coverage%20Estimates.pdf.

17. Anne Case and Angus Deaton, "Rising Morbidity and Mortality in Midlife Among White Non-Hispanic Americans in the 21st Century," Proceedings of the National Academy of Sciences of the United States of America, December 8, 2015, http://www.pnas.org /content/112/49/15078.

18. W. Mark Crain and Nicole V. Crain, "The Cost of Federal Regulation to the U.S. Economy, Manufacturing and Small Business," National Association of Manufacturers, September 10, 2014, http://www.nam .org/Data-and-Reports/Cost-of-Federal-Regulations/Federal-Regula tion-Full-Study.pdf.

19. Stanley Druckenmiller, "Where's the Invisible Hand When You Need It?" *The Wall Street Journal,* May 2, 2018, https://www.wsj.com /articles/wheres-the-invisible-hand-when-you-need-it-1525311642.

CHAPTER 4: WHAT IS TRUMPONOMICS?

1. Mick Mulvaney, "Introducing MAGAnomics," The White House, July 13, 2017, https://www.whitehouse.gov/briefings-statements/mulvaney-introducing-maganomics/.
2. "Benefits and Costs of the Clean Air Act 1990–2020, the Second Prospective Study," U.S. Environmental Protection Agency, April 2011, https://www.epa.gov/clean-air-act-overview/benefits-and-costs-clean-air-act-1990-2020-second-prospective-study.
3. Mick Mulvaney, "Introducing MAGAnomics," The Wall Street Journal, July 12, 2017, https://www.wsj.com/articles/introducing-maganomics-1499899298.
4. Michael Tanner and Charles Hughes, "The Work Versus Welfare Trade-Off: 2013," Cato Institute, August 19, 2013, http://object.cato.org/sites/cato.org/files/pubs/pdf/the_work_versus_welfare_trade-off_2013_wp.pdf.
5. Simon Evenett and Johannes Fritz, "The 21st Global Trade Alert Report: Will Awe Trump Rules?" Global Trade Alert, July 4, 2017, https://www.globaltradealert.org/reports/42.

CHAPTER 5: DESIGNING THE TRUMP TAX PLAN

1. Nolan McCaskill, "Clinton's Camp Attacks Trump as Heartless Tycoon," Politico, May 9, 2016, https://www.politico.com/story/2016/05/hillary-clinton-donald-trump-heartless-tycoon-222972.
2. Shane Goldmacher, "Trump Launches Tax Plan Rewrite," Politico, May 11, 2016, https://www.politico.com/story/2016/05/donald-trump-taxes-tax-reform-223041.
3. Ibid.
4. Scott A. Hodge, "The U.S. Has More Individually Owned Businesses Than Corporations," Tax Foundation, January 13, 2014, https://taxfoundation.org/us-has-more-individually-owned-businesses-corporations/.
5. "'This Week' Transcript: Donald Trump," ABC News, May 8, 2016, https://abcnews.go.com/Politics/week-transcript-donald-trump/story?id=38951757.

6. John F. Kennedy, "Address and Question and Answer Period at the Economic Club of New York," December 14, 1962, The American Presidency Project, http://www.presidency.ucsb.edu/ws/?pid=9057.

7. Tim Hains, "WSJ's Henninger: Trump Delivered 'Excellent Speech' About Economy; Now His Task Is to Stay on Message," *RealClearPolitics,* August 8, 2016, https://www.realclearpolitics.com/video/2016 /08/08/wsjs_henninger_trump_delivered_excellent_speech_about _economy_taxes.html.

8. William Randolph, "International Burdens of the Corporate Income Tax," Congressional Budget Office, August 2006, https://cbo.gov /sites/default/files/cbofiles/ftpdocs/75xx/doc7503/2006-09.pdf.

9. "Real Stimulus for a Caving Economy? Corporate Tax Cuts," *Investor's Business Daily,* January 20, 2016, https://www.investors.com/politics /editorials/to-keep-the-economy-from-falling-into-recession-cut -corporate-tax-rates/.

10. Andrew Lundeen, "A Cut in the Corporate Tax Rate Would Provide a Significant Boost to the Economy," Tax Foundation, February 19, 2015, https://taxfoundation.org/cut-corporate-tax-rate-would -provide-significant-boost-economy/.

CHAPTER 6: THE TAX CUT HEARD ROUND THE WORLD

1. Arthur Laffer, "Border Adjustment Tax," Laffer Associates, March 21, 2017.

2. Steve Forbes, Larry Kudlow, Arthur B. Laffer, and Stephen Moore, "Why Are Republicans Making Tax Reform So Hard?" *The New York Times,* April 19, 2017, https://www.nytimes.com/2017/04/19/opinion /why-are-republicans-making-tax-reform-so-hard.html.

3. Stephen Moore, "Growth Can Solve the Debt Dilemma," *The Wall Street Journal,* April 25, 2017, https://www.wsj.com/articles/growth -can-solve-the-debt-dilemma-1493160796.

4. Peter Baker, "Arthur Laffer's Theory on Tax Cuts Comes to Life Once More," *The New York Times,* April 25, 2017, https://www.nytimes .com/2017/04/25/us/politics/white-house-economic-policy-arthur -laffer.html.

5. Allysia Finley, "Richard Vedder: The Real Reason College Costs So Much," *The Wall Street Journal,* August 26, 2013, https://www.wsj.com

/articles/richard-vedder-the-real-reason-college-costs-so-much-137
7299322.

CHAPTER 7: DEREGULATOR IN CHIEF

1. OSHA Director of Safety Standards Program Marthe Kent in the *National Review*'s Internet Update, June 26, 2000.
2. Jason Pye, "Regulator-in-Chief: Obama Administration Has Issued 600 Regulations with Costs of $100 Million or More," Freedom Works, August 8, 2016, http://www.freedomworks.org/content/regulator-chief-obama-administration-has-issued-600-regulations-costs-100-million-or-more.
3. "President Donald J. Trump Is Delivering on Deregulation," The White House, December 14, 2017, https://www.whitehouse.gov/briefings-statements/president-donald-j-trump-delivering-deregulation/.
4. Kenneth Clarkson, Charles Kadlec, and Arthur Laffer, "The Impact of Government Regulations on Competition in the U.S. Automobile Industry," H.C. Wainwright & Co. Economics, May 4, 1979.
5. Peter Fricke, "Study: Dodd-Frank Crushes Small Banks," *Daily Caller*, February 17, 2015, http://dailycaller.com/2015/02/17/dodd-frank-crushing-small-banks.
6. Fannie Mae was first chartered by the U.S. government in 1938 to help ensure a reliable and affordable supply of mortgage funds throughout the country. Today it is a shareholder-owned company that operates under a congressional charter. Freddie Mac was chartered by Congress in 1970 as a private company to likewise help ensure a reliable and affordable supply of mortgage funds throughout the country. Today is a shareholder-owned company that operates under a congressional charter. https://www.fhfa.gov/SupervisionRegulation/FannieMae andFreddieMac/Pages/About-Fannie-Mae---Freddie-Mac.aspx"
7. Massimo Calabresi, "While Trump Is Tweeting, These 3 People Are Undoing American Government as We Know It," *Time* magazine, October 26, 2017, http://time.com/4998276/demolition-crew/.
8. Eric Lipton and Danielle Ivory, "Under Trump, E.P.A. Has Slowed Actions Against Polluters, and Put Limits on Enforcement Officers," *The New York Times*, December 10, 2017, https://www.nytimes.com/2017/12/10/us/politics/pollution-epa-regulations.html.

CHAPTER 8: SAUDI AMERICA

1. Alister Bull, "Obama, Republicans Spar over Gasoline Prices," *Reuters,* March 1, 2012, https://www.reuters.com/article/us-usa-campaign-ene rgy/obama-republicans-spar-over-gasoline-prices-idUSTRE8201U A20120301.

2. Barack Obama, "Remarks by the President on America's Energy Security," The White House, Office of the Press Secretary, March 30, 2011, https://obamawhitehouse.archives.gov/the-press-office/2011/03/30 /remarks-president-americas-energy-security.

3. Stephen Moore, "Fracking Pioneer Deserves to Win Nobel Peace Prize," *Investor's Business Daily,* October 7, 2014, https://www.inves tors.com/politics/commentary/nobel-peace-prize-should-go-to -fracking-pioneer/.

4. Nick Snow, "Industry Officials Attack Latest Call to Raise Oil, Gas Taxes," *Oil and Gas Journal,* November 7, 2011, https://www.ogj .com/articles/2011/11/industry-officials-attack-latest-call-to-raise -oil-gas-taxes.html; "Economic Impacts of the Oil and Natural Gas Industry on the U.S. Economy in 2011," PricewaterhouseCoopers, July 2013, http://www.api.org/~/media/Files/Policy/Jobs/Economic_Impa cts_ONG_2011.pdf.

5. Mark Mills, "Where the Jobs Are: Small Business Unleash America's Energy Employment Boom," Manhattan Institute's Power & Growth Initiative, February 2014, https://www.manhattan-institute.org/sites /default/files/R-MM-0214.pdf.

6. IHS-CERA and American Chemistry Council, "Map: Shale Brings Manufacturing Back Home," Energy InDepth, January 2018, https:// www.energyindepth.org/wp-content/uploads/2018/01/Shale-Manu facturing-Map-1.pdf.

7. U.S. Imports of Crude, March 2010–March 2018, U.S. Energy Information Administration, https://www.eia.gov/dnav/pet/hist/LeafHand ler.ashx?n=pet&s=mcrimus1&f=m.

8. "Energy Cost Impacts on American Families, 2001–2013," American Coalition for Clean Coal Electricity, January 2013, http://www .americaspower.org/sites/default/files/Trisko2013.pdf.

9. John Harpole, Mercator Energy, "Hydraulic Fracturing: What Informs Me," presentation, 2013 National Energy and Utilities Afford-

ability Conference, June 11, 2013, http://www.mercatorenergy.com/wp
-content/uploads/2013/07/NEUAC-presentation.pdf; "Fracking and
the Poor," *The Wall Street Journal,* September 6, 2013, http://online
.wsj.com/articles/SB1000142412788732373430457854361329239
4192.

10. "When Was the Last Refinery Built in the United States?" U.S. Energy
Information Administration, July 24, 2017, http://www.eia.gov/tools
/faqs/faq.cfm?id=29&t=6.

11. The points from this memo originated in Stephen Moore and Kathleen
White, *Fueling Freedom: Exposing the Mad War on Energy* (Washington, D.C.: Regenery, 2016), pp. 246–47.

12. "Oil and Gas Production on Federal Lands Still a Disappointment," Institute for Energy Research, April 24, 2014, http://institute
forenergyresearch.org/analysis/oil-and-gas-production-on-federal
-lands-still-a-disappointment/.

13. Justin Worland, "President Trump Says He Wants 'Energy Dominance.' What Does He Mean?" *Time* magazine, June 30, 2017, http://
time.com/4839884/energy-dominance-energy-independence-donald
-trump/.

14. Brian Spegele, "China Doubles Down on Coal Despite Climate
Pledge," *The Wall Street Journal,* November 8, 2016, https://www.wsj
.com/articles/china-doubles-down-on-coal-despite-climate-pledge
-1478520063.

15. Ibid.

16. Brad Plumer, "Reality Check: Nearly 2,200 New Coal Power Plants in
Planning Worldwide," The Global Warming Policy Forum, July 11,
2015, https://www.thegwpf.com/reality-check-nearly-2200-new-coal
-power-plants-in-planning-worldwide/.

17. Jan Christoph Steckel, Ottmar Edenhofer, and Michael Jakob, "Drivers for the Renaissance of Coal," Proceedings of the National Academy
of Sciences of the United States of America, July 6, 2015, http://www
.pnas.org/content/early/2015/07/01/1422722112.

18. "Energy Market Impacts of Recent Federal Regulations on the Electric Power Sector," Energy Ventures Analysis, November 10, 2014,
http://evainc.com/wp-content/uploads/2014/10/Nov-2014.-EVA
-Energy-Market-Impacts-of-Recent-Federal-Regulations-on-the
-Electric-Power-Sector.pdf.

19. Annie Leonard, "Trump as President: Here's How We Get Through This," Greenpeace, November 9, 2016, https://www.greenpeace.org /usa/trump-president-heres-get/.

20. "Energy Industry Gets Sierra Clubbed," *Investor's Business Daily*, April 22, 2016, https://www.investors.com/politics/editorials/energy -industry-gets-sierra-clubbed/.

21. Michael E. Webber, "The Coal Industry Isn't Coming Back," *The New York Times*, November 15, 2016, https://www.nytimes.com/2016/11 /16/opinion/the-coal-industry-isnt-coming-back.html.

22. Matt Egan, "Why Coal Jobs Aren't Coming Back, Despite Trump's Actions," CNN Money, January 24, 2017, http://money.cnn.com /2017/01/24/investing/trump-coal-epa-regulation/index.html.

23. Sam Batkins, "EPA's Greenhouse Gas Regulation Expects Coal Generation to Decline 48 Percent," American Action Forum, August 4, 2015, https://www.americanactionforum.org/research/epas-green house-gas-regulation-expects-coal-generation-to-decline-48 -percen/.

24. Electric Power Monthly, "Table 1.1: Net Generation by Energy Source: Total (All Sectors), 2008–March 2018," U.S. Energy Information Administration, May 24, 2018, https://www.eia.gov/electricity/monthly /epm_table_grapher.php?t=epmt_1_01.

25. "EIA Forecasts Natural Gas to Remain Primary Energy Source for Electricity Generation," U.S. Energy Information Administration, January 22, 2018, https://www.eia.gov/todayinenergy/detail.php?id=3 4612.

26. "News Release: Gross Domestic Product by Industry: First Quarter 2017," Bureau of Economic Analysis, July 21, 2017, https://www.bea .gov/newsreleases/industry/gdpindustry/2017/gdpind117.htm.

27. Christopher Alessi and Alison Sider, "U.S. Oil Output Expected to Surpass Saudi Arabia, Rivaling Russia for Top Spot," *The Wall Street Journal*, January 19, 2018, https://www.wsj.com/articles/u-s -crude-production-expected-to-surpass-saudi-arabia-in-2018-15163 52405.

28. Olga Yagova and Libby George, "Trump's Revenge: U.S. Oil Floods Europe, Hurting OPEC and Russia," *Reuters*, April 23, 2018, https:// reut.rs/2HpYvG5.

CHAPTER 9: THE ART OF THE TRUMP TRADE DEAL

1. Donald Trump, "Remarks by President Trump Before Marine One Departure," The White House, May 23, 2018, https://www.whitehouse.gov/briefings-statements/remarks-president-trump-marine-one-departure-7/.
2. "Research Milestones: Drug Policy and Strategy Analyses to Inform R&D and Strategic Planning Decisions," Tufts Center for the Study of Drug Development, https://csdd.tufts.edu/research-milestones/.
3. Ronald Reagan, "Radio Address to the Nation on International Free Trade," November 20, 1982, online by Gerhard Peters and John T. Woolley, The American Presidency Project, http://www.presidency.ucsb.edu/ws/?pid=42022.
4. Christos Cabolis, "IMD World Competitiveness Yearbook: The 30th Edition," IMD World Competitiveness Center, May 2018, https://www.imd.org/wcc/world-competitiveness-center-publications/2018-com-may/.
5. "Economic Report of the President," The White House, February 2018, https://www.whitehouse.gov/wp-content/uploads/2018/02/ERP_2018_Final-FINAL.pdf.

POSTSCRIPT

1. Lucinda Shen, "Larry Summers Sees a Grim Future Under a Trump Presidency," *Fortune,* June 6, 2016, http://fortune.com/2016/06/06/larry-summers-trump-buffett/.
2. Daniel K. Williams, "Could Trump End Culture Wars?" *The New York Times,* November 9, 2016, https://www.nytimes.com/interactive/projects/cp/opinion/election-night-2016/could-trump-end-the-culture-wars.
3. Editorial Board, "A President Trump Could Destroy the World Economy," *The Washington Post,* October 5, 2016, https://www.washingtonpost.com/opinions/a-president-trump-could-destroy-the-world-economy/2016/10/05/f70019c0-84df-11e6-92c2-14b64f3d453f_story.html?noredirect=on&utm_term=.ce38f36c2152.

4. "Economy Lifts Trump to Best Score in 7 Months, Quinnipiac University National Poll Finds; Immigration, Foreign Policy Keep Approval Down," Quinnipiac University, February 7, 2018, https://poll.qu.edu/national/release-detail?ReleaseID=2518.

5. Jon Sindreu, Riva Gold, and Josh Mitchell, "Economic Growth in U.S. Leaves World Behind," *The Wall Street Journal,* June 14, 2017, https://www.wsj.com/articles/strong-spending-data-shows-u-s-economy-chugging-ahead-of-europe-and-asia-1528994914.

6. Joseph Epstein, "The Only Good Thing About Donald Trump Is All His Policies," *The Wall Street Journal,* February 26, 2018, https://www.wsj.com/articles/the-only-good-thing-about-donald-trump-is-all-his-policies-1519689494.

About the Authors

Laffer Associates; Heritage Foundation

STEPHEN MOORE and ARTHUR B. LAFFER, Ph.D., are the economists behind the job creation platform that brought Trump to victory. Stephen Moore is a former member of *The Wall Street Journal*'s editorial board and the Distinguished Visiting Fellow for The Heritage Foundation's Project for Economic Growth. Arthur B. Laffer, the father of supply-side economics, was a member of President Ronald Reagan's Economic Policy Advisory Board.